Inside
Blair House

Inside Blair House

Mary Edith Wilroy
and Lucie Prinz

Doubleday & Company, Inc., Garden City, New York, 1982

Library of Congress Cataloging in Publication Data

Wilroy, Mary Edith, 1910–
Inside blair house.

Includes index.
1. Blair House (Washington, D.C.)   2. Washington (D.C.)
—Social life and customs.   3. Wilroy, Mary Edith,
1910–   .   4. Washington (D.C.)—Biography.   5. Lovell,
Joseph.   6. Lee, Elizabeth Blair—Homes—Washington (D.C.)
7. Blair, Francis Preston, 1791–1876—Homes—Washington
(D.C.)   8. Washington (D.C.)—Dwellings.   I. Prinz,
Lucie, 1931–   .   II. Title.
F204.B5W54   975.3'04
AACR2
ISBN 0-385-15740-1
Library of Congress Catalog Card Number: 81–47870

For Jack, Dick, Ann, and Jenny

Foreword

WHEN I FIRST went to Blair House on March 2, 1961, as manager, the idea of writing a book never crossed my mind. True, I took notes, but they were often day-to-day reminders of what must be done the next day. Now that I have worked at writing about my experiences there, I wish I had written different notes, more about events, and had listed the names of people who touched my work there, perhaps only briefly, but helpfully. The event and the person I remember but names are sometimes lost in memory. I decided to write the book because so many people suggested that I should and encouraged me to do so. There has been so little written about Blair House, now the President's Guest House. It is not open to the public, so the vast majority of our citizens do not know what it looks like or what takes place inside. I hope this book will open the door a bit for a peek inside. It is a historic house of the past and living history every day. If any future historian could use bits of information from the book, then my efforts will have been worthwhile.

My number one priority was preparing for and following through on the visits of heads of state and heads of government who were here as guests of our President and our country. Providing a home away from home for them during their visit to Washington was a challenge, for their stay at Blair House might be their only opportunity to live in an American home atmosphere. It was also a privilege dreams are made of and an education in itself to meet them and to get to know so many from all over the world.

Then came the renovations each year. Reading the book may make one think that we were always renovating—and we were, but we had a schedule of visits and functions that must go on, and the renovations had to be sandwiched in between as the schedule permitted. Except for the one period when we moved out of the house altogether in 1963, the major work was accomplished during the month of August, when many officials were out of Washington and the house was closed. Renovations, planned in advance to cover what it was hoped could be accomplished during the month, went ahead, very often spilling over into September. This was routine every year except when a stray visit might interrupt. What was not completed was either done between scheduled events or left to the next August.

None of this could have been possible without the full cooperation, help, and advice of many people: all the chiefs of protocol under whom I served were most helpful and encouraging, as were their wives, all of whom were dedicated to making Blair House a beautiful and comfortable American home. The security agents from the Department of State assigned to the various visits for the first ten years of my tenure and the Secret Service agents who took over that job for the last five years were indispensable in many ways beyond the security they were providing. The officials of the General Services Administration responsible for our area and their carpenters, painters, plumbers, electricians, and contractors performed admirably, sometimes under emergency or very trying conditions. My own loyal conscientious staff—housekeepers, chef, butlers, maids, housemen, telephone operators—performed tirelessly, willingly, and courteously to please our guests. How many times one of them, noticing a strain showing on my face, would say, "Now, don't you worry, Mrs. Wilroy, we will have everything ready in time." I will be forever grateful to all of them.

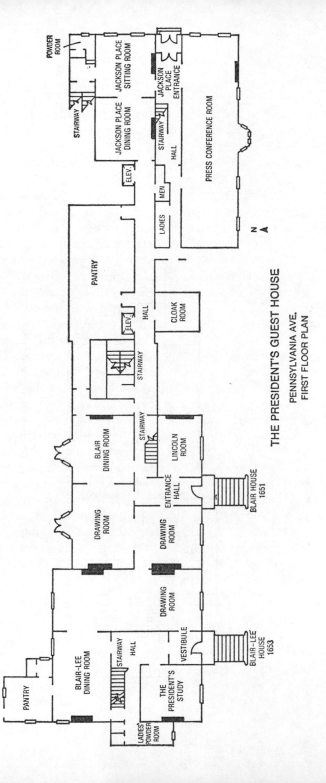

THE PRESIDENT'S GUEST HOUSE

PENNSYLVANIA AVE,
FIRST FLOOR PLAN

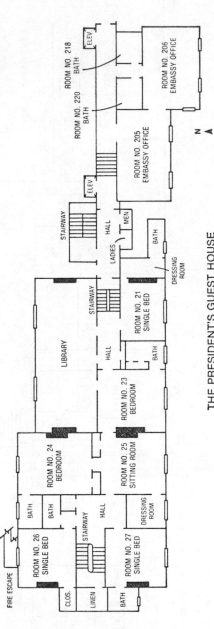

THE PRESIDENT'S GUEST HOUSE

PENNSYLVANIA AVE.
SECOND FLOOR PLAN

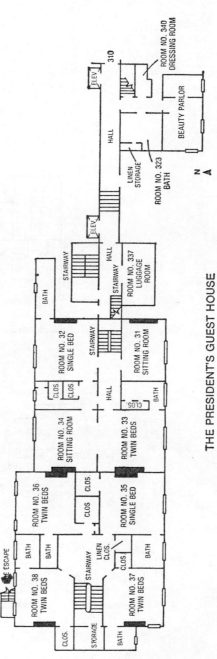

THE PRESIDENT'S GUEST HOUSE

PENNSYLVANIA AVE.
THIRD FLOOR PLAN

ROOM NO. 340
DRESSING ROOM

BEAUTY PARLOR

310

ELEV

HALL

LINEN
STORAGE

ROOM NO. 323
BATH

N

STAIRWAY

HALL

ELEV

ROOM NO. 337
LUGGAGE
ROOM

BATH

STAIRWAY

ROOM NO. 32
SINGLE BED

CLOS
CLOS

STAIRWAY

ROOM NO. 31
SITTING ROOM

HALL

CLOS.

BATH

ROOM NO. 34
SITTING ROOM

ROOM NO. 33
TWIN BEDS

ROOM NO. 36
TWIN BEDS

CLOS

CLOS

ROOM NO. 35
SINGLE BED

BATH

BATH

FIRE ESCAPE

LINEN
CLOS.

STAIRWAY

CLOS.

BATH

ROOM NO. 38
TWIN BEDS

CLOS.

STORAGE

ROOM NO. 37
TWIN BEDS

BATH

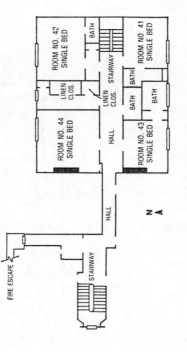

THE PRESIDENT'S GUEST HOUSE

PENNSYLVANIA AVE.
FOURTH FLOOR PLAN

Chapter One

ON A BEAUTIFUL morning in May 1961 I stood by the window of the Lincoln room in the mansion at 1651 Pennsylvania Avenue that is known as Blair House.

As I watched, a large black limousine, flags flying from both front fenders, pulled up to the curb and the President, John F. Kennedy, and President Habib Bourguiba of Tunisia emerged. Just behind the two men came the First Lady, Jacqueline Kennedy, and Mrs. Bourguiba. The four began to climb the steps, followed by an entourage of officials who had arrived in several other limousines a moment later. The two ladies had some trouble keeping up with the pace set by President Kennedy as with long strides he came toward the door of the house.

I had been anxiously planning for this day for more than a month. A great deal of work had gone into seeing that everything would go off perfectly, and although I had every confidence that it would, I admit that I was just a little nervous.

But then, as the presidential party reached the door, I realized that this was the young President's first visit from a head of state as well as mine. It hit me that the Kennedys might be just as apprehensive as I was, and that calmed me down.

I watched as Percy, the butler, swung open the door to admit the group just as they reached the top step, and a minute later I was in the entrance hall greeting the two Presidents, their wives, and the entourage that came in just behind them. It was my first meeting with the Kennedys.

I was to repeat this scene dozens of times, but I never forgot that first apprehensive moment, my official baptism as manager

of Blair House, a job I got by accident or default but one I kept
for fifteen exciting years.

Eventually I got to know five Presidents and their families,
but I never got over the awe I felt for the office. Nor was I ever
able to become entirely blasé about my encounters with Prime
Ministers, Kings, or Queens. To the very end, my time at Blair
House was more than a job. It was an adventure.

It all began with an innocuous phone call.

I was at home watching the evening news on a Saturday, in
mid-February when the phone rang. At the other end of the line
there was news of another kind, news that would change my life
and lead me into a uniquely fascinating career.

I was living in Takoma Park, Maryland, an old Washington
suburb. Only two of my four children, Ann (aged twenty) and
Jenny (seventeen), were still at home with me in the big house
surrounded by trees where we had lived for eight years. My job
as assistant administrative officer in the Office of the Chief of
Protocol at the Department of State was interesting and satisfying, and I looked forward to continuing it until I was eligible for
retirement.

But my "Hello" into that telephone was answered by the voice
of Joe Rosetti, security officer at the department. "Mary Edith, I
have some sad tidings," he said. "Victoria Geaney has just died."

Mrs. Geaney had been manager of Blair House ever since its
purchase in 1942 as the President's Guest House. I was the protocol officer assigned to help her with the administrative duties
of running the house, so I had gotten to know her well. She was
not a young woman, but still the suddenness of her death
shocked and saddened me. She had been my friend as well as
my co-worker.

During the hours that followed I tried to figure out how we
would make a smooth transition at Blair House. I called Katherine Laird, my immediate superior at the department, and we
made a date to go over to the house first thing Monday morning
to see what we needed to do right away. We spoke a bit about
finding a replacement for Victoria, but no names came immediately to mind. First things first, we agreed. We had to keep the
place going.

When Blair House is not in use as a residence for a visiting foreign head of state (such as a king) or head of government (a prime minister, for instance) it serves as the setting for luncheons, dinners, or receptions given by the Vice-President, members of the Cabinet, and other high-ranking people in the government. I knew that several such functions were on the schedule, and I could imagine that, with the Kennedy administration just settling into the White House, there would soon be a stream of visitors coming to stay at Blair House.

The next morning Katherine and I rang the doorbell at the house. James McHaney, the first houseman, opened the door for us. Behind him I could see the rest of the staff: William Dallas, the chef; Ingrid Carlson, a part-time housekeeper often hired by Mrs. Geaney; Cora Roache, a part-time chambermaid; and Bertha Emmerich, Mrs. Geaney's longtime companion and housekeeper. It was obvious that they were all very sad and distressed.

Katherine and I quickly went to the basement, where Victoria, who had lived at Blair House, had a small suite. She used the sitting room as her office. We wanted to take a look at her records and her calendar to see what was planned for the immediate future.

Mrs. Geaney operated Blair House with a revolving fund administered by the Department of State. Although I had helped her with the paper work that running the house entailed, I had no clear idea of how she managed things on a day-to-day basis. I suppose we hoped to find some kind of daily log or diary of Blair House activities that might guide us in the weeks to come. But all we found were the neat bundles of Mrs. Geaney's check stubs. A notebook with a few entries revealed that she had tried to begin a diary, but the hectic daily operation of the house had put an end to any regular record keeping of that sort. It was obvious that we would have to reconstruct the way the house was run and find out about any plans by talking to the staff.

When we called them in, Dallas was the first to speak. He had already ordered the food and was about to begin the preparations for a lunch planned for the next day, he said. We decided that, in deference to Mrs. Geaney, we would call it off. Dallas went to see about canceling what supplies he could. I called the host and explained the problem, and he said he'd arrange to inform the guests. That took care of the first priority.

The next few days we spent at Blair House talking to the staff. We made a complete list of the functions that had been scheduled, and soon we had a good idea of what was planned for the immediate future. At the end of the week we returned to the Protocol Office to report to Clement Conger, then deputy chief of protocol, serving under Chief of Protocol Angier Biddle Duke.

Clem listened carefully to what we had to say, and then he turned to me and said matter-of-factly, and with a smile, "Well, Mary Edith, looks like you'll just have to go over there and get that house running again."

I was floored. "I'm not really terribly interested," I managed to say. "What's more, I'm not qualified. First of all, I don't have any hotel experience, no training of that sort at all. How am I going to run Blair House?"

But Clem didn't want to hear about my reservations. "Look," he said after I'd finished, "you've run your own home. You've had guests. You know how to serve a meal and entertain. You know Blair House isn't a hotel. It's more like a private home, and if you manage it the way you do your own place I'm sure you'll do just fine."

I could see he wasn't going to take no for an answer. I had no choice. I agreed to try it under certain conditions: it would be a part-time job so that I could continue to perform my other duties at the department in my old office. Also, I had no intention of living at Blair House the way Mrs. Geaney had. I felt that my daughters needed me to be home as much as possible. And finally, I told Clem, I would take the job on a trial basis for six months. At the end of that time, if I thought I could do it to my own satisfaction, we would talk about my taking it on full-time.

Clem readily agreed to all of this, and the following Wednesday I began.

I spent that first week mainly on my feet. With Ingrid Carlson I walked through Blair House room by room by room. Ingrid had a good working knowledge of the house from her many days on duty there, and I sensed that she and I had similar standards, similar ways of looking at things. Both of us carried notebooks, and as we saw things that needed fixing or thought of items that were missing but necessary, we'd jot them down.

I'm a passionate list maker: I find it's the best way to keep organized. Over the years at Blair House I kept lists on steno pads like the ones Ingrid and I carried on those first tours. Fifteen years later, when I cleared out my office at my retirement, I found that I had several cardboard boxes filled with these notebooks. Some of the entries were routine ("Buy thermos bottles for bedrooms," or "Ask James to polish the brass on the fireplace in the library"), but others were my own way of expressing the frustration I often felt when things didn't go right ("If that painter doesn't stop smoking cigars in the bedroom I'll have to have him replaced"). In time the lists and notes became a kind of diary of my time there, and as I write these reminiscences I have referred to them to recall the details of those busy years.

We began on the first floor and worked our way through the house. There was not a corner of its thirty-five rooms that we did not explore, not a closet that escaped our scrutiny, not a bureau drawer that remained closed. We noted the dusty interiors, the missing drawer pulls, the cracked plaster.

It soon became obvious that many of the rooms were desperately in need of refurbishing. Quite a few floors needed sanding and varnishing. Some of the curtains were so tattered that they had to come down, and some windows were bare of curtains or drapes altogether. Fixtures were missing or broken in many of the bathrooms, and bedspreads and canopies on several of the beds reserved for the crowned and uncrowned heads of state had seen better days.

We meticulously counted linen and china. We took out the splendid collection of Blair House glass, admiring the beautiful crystal and cranberry glass and the many different kinds of goblets and vases the house owned. One dazzling afternoon I stood in the silver vault surrounded by its vast treasure of trays, bowls, tea services, and flatware—most of which could have used a thorough polishing. Not all the Blair House silver was stored in the vault as we began our inspection. One tea service was revealed, with its tray, as we rummaged in the dim interior of one of the upstairs closets. It was black with tarnish and had to be sent out for professional cleaning. When it came back it was clearly one of Blair House's oldest, most beautiful, and most precious tea sets.

The house was, in fact, filled with treasures. Many of the furnishings and nearly all of the paintings on the walls had been the property of the Blair family. Their beauty was enhanced by their having been witness to so much of America's history. Because it was owned for generations by the family of Francis Preston Blair, a man who was confidant to Presidents from Andrew Jackson to Ulysses S. Grant, and because of its location just across from the White House, Blair House had been the scene of many of the events of our past.

The house was built in 1824 by Dr. Joseph Lovell, the nation's first Surgeon General. Soon after the family moved in, the Lovell children were able to look out of the windows of their new home as the parade honoring the visit of General Lafayette passed by their door. The general was on his way to the Franklin Hotel, which at that time was host to the country's distinguished visitors.

In 1836 Dr. Lovell died suddenly and the family sold the house to Blair, who had come to Washington as editor of *The Globe*, a pro-Jackson newspaper. Blair had been looking for a house for some time, and he had nearly purchased the lovely Decatur House on nearby Lafayette Square for his family but thought it was too ostentatious. He was attracted to the Lovell House by an advertisement which promised an excellent well, a brick stable, and a carriage house on an alley, plus a "flower and fruit garden tastefully laid out and highly cultivated." On December 6, 1836, Blair bought the house for $6,500. He was delighted to find that there was even room for some livestock. He kept a horse and a cow, which was so productive that Blair was able to leave a pail of milk for his President on the White House steps every morning.

The Blair House that Ingrid and I were exploring consisted of the original Lovell House and the house next door, which had been built in 1859 by Admiral Phillips Lee as a home for himself and his wife, Elizabeth, the daughter of Francis Preston Blair.

Since their marriage Elizabeth, who was very attached to her family, had spent a great deal of time at her parents' country home in Silver Spring, Maryland, or visiting her oldest brother, Montgomery, who now lived full-time in Blair House. Elizabeth, apparently a strong-minded woman, was in frail health. Her physical condition caused her family great concern during her entire lifetime—all eighty-eight years of it. Admiral Lee, himself descended from the illustrious Lees of Virginia, decided he'd see more of his bride if he built a house nearer to her family. The so-called Blair-Lee House shares a wall with its neighbor. After the Lees moved in they often played host to Francis Preston Blair, who was not on good terms with his son's second wife. Francis Blair regularly came to Washington on business, since, to the end of his long life, he was active in the political affairs of the country.

Blair House is used today as if it were one large house, but for convenience its rooms are referred to as either Blair or Blair-Lee rooms. So, for example, the Blair-Lee dining room is the one reserved during visits for the head of state and his family and guests. Most public functions are held in the Blair or the Blair-Lee drawing rooms. But the two houses—and the additional space that was connected to the house during President Johnson's administration and furnished during President Nixon's—are officially known as Blair House.

Members of the Blair family continued to live at 1651 Pennsylvania Avenue until 1940, when the youngest son of Montgomery Blair, Gist Blair, died. He specified in his will that the house should not be dismantled, in order to preserve it as a kind of memorial to the place his family occupied in the history of the country.

In 1942, when air travel was beginning to bring an increasing number of visitors to Washington, the Blair portion of the house was purchased by President Franklin D. Roosevelt with $175,000 allocated for that purpose. He turned over the operation of the house to his Secretary of State, Cordell Hull, who, in turn, placed the responsibility in the hands of the chief of protocol, where it remains today.

According to an often repeated Washington story, the real impulse to buy a guest house for the President came from that powerful First Lady Eleanor Roosevelt. It is reliably reported that Mrs. Roosevelt, up early one morning striding through the White House living quarters on her way out on one of her many trips, encountered a corpulent figure, dressed in his nightgown, pacing the hall. In one hand he held a cigar, in the other a snifter of what might have been brandy. It was six-thirty.

"Winston, where are you going at this time of the morning?" she is said to have inquired.

"To see Franklin," he answered.

"Oh no you're not. You've kept him up half the night as it is," Eleanor Roosevelt replied firmly. "Now please just go back to your room and let him rest."

It seems quite plausible that the mighty leader of the British Empire, Prime Minister Winston Churchill, turned meekly around and padded back to his bedroom. It is even more believable that Eleanor Roosevelt convinced her husband that same evening that something had to be done about the visitors who were turning the White House into a hotel. Whatever the truth, within a few months FDR had signed the papers designating Blair House the official residence for guests of state.

One of the first guests was Russia's Commissar of Foreign Affairs Vyacheslav Molotov, under the *nom de guerre* of Mr. Brown. In the beginning, important visitors would stay at the White House for the first night and then move across the street for the rest of their visit. The lower-ranking members of the party were housed there from the start.

During the Eisenhower administration it was wisely decided that it would be simpler if the whole group just came directly from the airport or railroad station to Blair House, which then became the full-time residence of the country's guests. In acknowledgment of that fact the title "The President's Guest House" was added to its name and from then on appeared on Blair House stationery.

The Blair-Lee side of the house was bought by the government in 1943. The Lee family had sold it much earlier, and it contained offices and a commercial laundry. Until President Truman's stay in Blair House from 1949 to 1952, during the renovation of the White House, the two houses had remained quite separate. But then it was found that, for the convenience of the Trumans as well as to aid in the smooth running of the country, it would be more efficient if doors connected the two sides. So the entranceways that exist today were added.

Blair House has five floors, but if you enter at street level you will find yourself in the basement. All the Blair House services—laundry, kitchen, telephone switchboard, luggage room, and administrative offices—are found there. The real first floor, the one by which visitors enter, is reached from the street by two flights of steps leading to two front doors, which were the original entrances to the two then separate houses. This is especially convenient on days when, as so often happens, two functions are being held at the same time.

The first floor contains two double drawing rooms, two dining rooms, a small study known as the President's study (on the Blair-Lee side), and, on the Blair side, an exquisite little sitting room named for Abraham Lincoln. It was in this room that Mr. Lincoln signed the Emancipation Proclamation. The walls are hung with memorabilia of both Lincoln and Francis Preston Blair. Over the desk hangs a portrait of General Robert E. Lee, given to the house by the Daughters of the Confederacy to commemorate the fact that Lee had been offered the command of the Union Army in this room. Lincoln had asked Blair to suggest this to the general, since they were related by the marriage of Elizabeth Blair to Phillips Lee, but the general refused the commission, as we all know, saying that he could not turn his back on his beloved state of Virginia.

Over the mantel hangs a pen-and-ink drawing of President Lincoln. A member of the Daughters of the Confederacy was quite upset on a visit to Blair House that portraits of Lee and Lincoln were allowed to share the same room. When she complained to me about it, all I could think was that the Civil War was not yet over, at least for this lady.

The upstairs living area of the house includes a total of four suites and eleven bedrooms and dressing rooms. Many of the closets are the size of a small room.

The largest of the bedrooms on the second floor is reserved for the visiting head of state. It adjoins a spacious library, where guests often relax and receive visitors.

The other large suite is known as the Queen's Suite because in 1957, during the Eisenhower administration, it was refurbished in preparation for a visit from Queen Elizabeth of Britain. It didn't get finished in time for the visit, but it is called the Queen's Suite to this day. With its lovely four-poster canopy bed and scaled-down antiques, such as the lacquered sewing table originally owned by the Blair family, it is a perfect room for any woman.

President Eisenhower's chief of protocol, Wiley Buchanan, Jr., was the first person to try to modernize Blair House. He first concentrated on the bathrooms, which at that time were decidedly old-fashioned, featuring toilets with tanks mounted on the wall, with flush chains dangling from them. In addition to the Queen's Suite, Buchanan had also renovated the Head of State's Suite to some extent.

But in fact, up until 1961 very little had been done over the years to keep the house in good condition. Any place as old as Blair House needs constant care, since something is always cracking or breaking.

On the Blair side, the house was furnished with many lovely antiques, but the rooms on the upper floors of Blair-Lee contained the kind of furniture found in a modest hotel. It was clear to me that a great deal would have to be done about upkeep, repair, and refurnishing of the house if it was to function as guest house for the important visitors we were soon expecting.

Mrs. Kennedy had already begun to bring some long-stored treasures back into the White House, and I suppose I must have hoped, as I saw the problems at Blair House, that some of her enthusiasm would extend across the street. That first spring, however, I had no time to concentrate on such things. Long-range plans were put to one side as I was launched into Blair House routine. And that meant luncheon for twelve, followed a few hours later by cocktails for sixty or dinner for a dozen. Blair House was soon back in full swing.

I had decided that for a while, until I saw how things had been done under Victoria Geaney's direction, I would be an observer as well as general supervisor. There was no need to change what worked well, I thought.

In our wanderings through the house, however, Ingrid and I had discovered that many items essential to the comfort of our guests were simply not to be found. For instance, I was shocked to note that we didn't have a single breakfast set that could be used to serve guests in their rooms. We needed breakfast trays, too. It was necessary to get these things right away. In mid-April we were expecting Prime Minister and Mrs. Constantine Karamanlis of Greece.

Ambassador Duke suggested I just go out and get what I absolutely couldn't do without. There simply wasn't time to make out requisition forms or to do any comparison shopping. I bought some breakfast sets and some carafes for the nightstands. I also got several badly needed sets of bath and bed linens. Not only were our supplies of these small, but many of the sheets and towels showed signs of wear and long use.

Chef William Dallas—always called simply Dallas—and I began our long association that first week I was at Blair House. We had our first meeting to plan for a luncheon for sixteen guests invited by an assistant secretary of state. When we got to the choices for dessert, I was horrified to learn that it had been customary frequently to serve ready-made ice cream cups for dessert. They were just a step up from Dixie cups, but because they had elaborate decorations on top they were quite expensive. I didn't think they were a proper dessert for Blair House.

Dallas couldn't have agreed more. He volunteered that he knew several scrumptious desserts which he was eager to try out on our guests. On this particular occasion he made the little cream puffs with chocolate sauce for which he soon became famous. They eventually were the favorite and often requested desserts of such Blair House regulars as Secretary of State Dean Rusk, Vice-President Hubert Humphrey, Labor Secretary Arthur Goldberg, and many of our foreign visitors.

Dallas was a marvelous and naturally talented chef. A slender, unflappable black man who was in his thirties when I met him, Dallas hadn't gone to the Cordon Bleu or any other formal cooking school. He learned about food and how to prepare it in his mother's simple Georgia kitchen. Later he worked as a cook for a railroad, and during World War II he was a navy cook. Someone must have recognized his skill, because by war's end he was cooking for the Secretary of the Navy. When he left the service he was a cook in the Senate Dining Room at the Capitol and later worked for one of Washington's finest caterers. He had been hired by Mrs. Geaney about a month before her death and hadn't really begun to prepare all the fabulous dishes he whipped up for us over the years.

He was very good at cooking all kinds of meat, and his presentations of the carefully carved slices on a silver platter were works of art. His vegetables were perfectly cooked and his sauces divine. But I never could get him to make a soufflé or a mousse. "They're nothing but air," he'd say. He also refused to make that luncheon staple, quiche. "I'll try it next time," he said hundreds of times. "I've got this soup all ready for the first course today. Maybe we'll have quiche at Thursday's lunch." He didn't say why he didn't like to make quiche. He just never did it. The only suggestion he ever took from me was for a black cherry gelatin mold with black cherries in it. Otherwise he stuck to what was familiar and he cooked superbly.

I decided, from the day of that first luncheon, that we would never again serve food prepared outside of the house. If it couldn't be done in our kitchen we wouldn't have it.

We also planned, whenever possible, to serve the very best examples of American cuisine. Within the limits of our visitors' dietary restrictions or personal preferences, we were going to show off American cooking. We weren't going to serve Golda Meir pork chops, but we thought she'd love southern fried chicken. President Pompidou might enjoy a slice of real apple pie instead of *tarte aux pommes,* which he could get in Paris every day. We knew that Prime Minister Nehru liked lamb, but we felt it would be presumptuous for us to try to cook an Indian curry for him. On the other hand, how about roast leg of lamb with gravy and mint sauce?

For breakfast we offered kippered herring to the British or cheese to the Scandinavians or steaks to visitors who were about to leave on a long trip home and needed extra energy. In fact, we had about fifteen different choices for breakfast, which was the one meal we served to almost all our guests, since many of them were out for lunch and dinner. Among these choices were waffles and bacon or hot cakes with sausage and maple syrup. All these American specialties were relished by our guests, who often requested them when they came for a return visit.

While we were planning that first lunch the question of flowers naturally came up. The Protocol Office knew that I loved gardening because I often brought bouquets into the office during the summer. So when it was suggested that I could save quite a lot of money from my budget if I made my own flower arrangements, as often as possible from my own garden, I jumped at the chance. (Later, as I faced the flowers before a particularly hectic event, I sometimes regretted this decision, but most of the time I found arranging the bouquets for Blair House gave me a chance to stop and relax for a few minutes—and it did save us a bit of money.)

In the winter I had to buy flowers, of course. Since I obtained almost all my supplies from wholesalers, I thought I'd be able to get flowers that way, too. But I was told by Washington's biggest flower wholesaler that the local florists would be distressed at him if he permitted me to do business directly with him. So, after some study, I chose the nearby Nosegay Flower Shop, which had an excellent reputation and the extra advantage that it was close enough to the house for me to run over and select what I needed or, in an emergency, to arrange quick deliveries. During my entire time at Blair House I used the Nosegay and the expert help of its owner, Mr. Walter Charron, and the house was always graced with lovely flowers.

The first formal dinner I presided over was preceded by a cocktail reception. The guests gathered at around six-thirty. The house looked very festive. James, the houseman, had polished the place until it shone. James had been at Blair House for eight years and he took particular pride in keeping it in tiptop shape, polishing the brass accessories in the fireplaces before the first hint of dullness appeared and cleaning and waxing the floors before they showed the dust. He seemed to know everything about the house and had an uncanny memory for where everything was kept, including furnishings that had long ago been put into storage.

For the dinner the tables in the dining room were set with our heavy white linen damask cloths on which stood the beautiful Blair family Lowestoft plates with their blue grape and grape leaf design, a motif that was echoed in many of the Blair family possessions. On a long table in the drawing room from which hot hors d'oeuvres were served stood a silver epergne that was one of my favorite Blair House things. It was a delicate silver filagree footed bowl. Four small silver plates supported by curved silver standards extended from the ornate base. All of this was set on a mirrored tray edged with silver grapes and grape leaves. The epergne was filled with strawberries, grapes, peaches, and other fruits of the season, and more fruit rested on the tray on a bed of fresh green leaves. It made a most elegant centerpiece.

The guests had passed through a small receiving line, which included the hosts and the guest of honor, and they were now having drinks and hors d'oeuvres. I was mingling with them to make sure everyone was being served when I noticed Eva, one of the parlormaids, coming through the pantry door with a tray of canapés. It was not a particularly large tray, but it looked bigger than it was because it had on it only three very small, very lonely-looking crackers. Evidently Eva planned to serve these three canapés to a lucky few of the many guests.

In a split second I was at her side, gently moving her out of the room and back into the pantry, where she explained to me that Mrs. Geaney allotted five canapés to each guest. When they ran out, they ran out. We were, it seemed, down to the last three.

In something of a panic, I called Dallas on the pantry intercom, explaining our problem, and within a few minutes had some hastily created but delicious turkey, cheese, and toast concoctions for our guests.

That was the last time we ever came close to running out of food. We were always prepared for any eventualities, including extra guests or extraordinary appetites. No food ever went to waste. What wasn't consumed was served to the staff or frozen for future use. One of Dallas' improvisations (hastily thawed frozen shad roe on a cracker with a dab of tartar sauce, quickly broiled) became a cocktail favorite and a regular item in our repertoire.

After a few more meals I made another change in our serving habits. Traditionally, dinner at Blair House consisted of five courses: soup, seafood, entrée, a salad with cheese, and dessert. Since most people were becoming diet-conscious, we dropped the soup from our dinner menus. And because many of our luncheons were working sessions where busy people discussed important matters, we cut the number of courses to three by dropping the fish. We started with soup and served the salad with the entrée. Fewer courses eliminated much of the constant serving and taking away of plates, which interfered with the conversations being held around the table.

During that first March we had about twelve functions of various kinds, and although each had its moment of panic or a little surprise, we managed to get through them all without a major mishap.

By early April we were becoming a real team. I had made only one change in our staffing. I persuaded Mrs. Emmerich, then in her seventies, who had served for a long time as housekeeper-companion to Mrs. Geaney, that she was entitled to retire. She remained a Blair House regular, however, coming often to visit us in the last years of her life.

Ingrid had become my right hand, responsible on a full-time basis for supervising the chambermaids and housemen. She was the best housekeeper I ever had at Blair House. She was a source of excellent suggestions about how to make things run more efficiently and, in those early days, brought me lists of items she thought were needed. While I began to spend more and more time running the day-to-day activities of the house, she continued going through each room looking for cracks in the plaster and rips in the curtains. She was a marvel in every way, a small gray-haired woman with enormous energy and unflagging devotion to the house. I particularly admired her linen closets, which she set up to her high standards during times when we were not too busy. Woe to the chambermaid who got so much as a pillowcase out of place.

All through March we had been straining toward our first big test, the visit of Prime Minister Karamanlis, who would be arriving with a group of twelve on April 17 for a three-day visit. While we considered this first visit a kind of dress rehearsal for those to come, as far as the Prime Minister was concerned it was to be as professional and flawless a performance as we could muster.

I had no more guidelines for the visit of a foreign guest than I had for the general operation of the house, and it took quite a while to get the visits to measure up precisely to my high standards. I decided that the only way to learn how to run a visit was by running a visit.

Ingrid and I, both perfectionists, were agreed on one thing. By the day of the visit that house was going to sparkle.

I called Camilla Payne, a well-known Washington decorator who had done some work at Blair House for Ambassador Buchanan. By a miracle she managed to get curtains made for all the windows that needed them desperately.

We decided to put a bowl of fresh fruit in every occupied bedroom during a visit. In the library we had bowls of salted nuts, candy, and dried fruit—nibbles for the head of state and his guests. We also set up a small bar which might be stocked with nonalcoholic beverages if the guest wished.

Every room also had a supply of pads of paper printed with the words "Blair House: The President's Guest House," as well as matches, pencils, pens, and stationery similarly inscribed.

I was sure that our visitors would be taking these home with them, but Ingrid thought that they'd all be too sophisticated to be attracted to such things. She was wrong. Over the years these little mementos proved so popular that we were constantly reordering them in greater and greater quantities.

But our foreign guests were very polite and hesitant about taking anything out of the rooms, and I was often asked by a Prime Minister's secretary if it would be all right for him to take "one of those nice pens." Our distinguished visitors would ask permission before taking even a small pad of paper.

I wish I could say as much for the Americans. They simply helped themselves. I soon learned to wait until after the security check was completed before laying out the ball-point pens. They disappeared by the dozen before I discovered how much the security men liked them.

(On the other hand, I learned to order my food and have it safely put away *before* they were on duty in the house. I made this decision after watching a conscientious security man combing through a crate of fresh, tender strawberries—to make sure that they were not hiding an assassin's bomb, I suppose.)

Newspapers were delivered morning and afternoon to each room. The Washington *Post* and the New York *Times* were on each breakfast tray, and the Washington *Star* arrived at teatime. Current issues of all the news magazines were also on hand, and whenever possible we provided our guests with a newspaper from their own country or at least one printed in the language they spoke.

There were fresh flowers in the Head of State's Suite, the library, and all the ladies' bedrooms.

Before each state visit the embassy sent around a delegation, occasionally including the ambassador or his wife, to look over the accommodations and help make room selections. This practice was helpful because we had no way of knowing who the head of state would like to have close at hand. The guest list we were given in advance of each visit didn't provide this sort of information, but the embassy always knew. Only once or twice did it happen that the embassy staff had an unworkable suggestion —such as putting two ladies in a room with only one bed—and then we had to use our own brand of diplomatic persuasion to get the proper room assigned.

The day before the Karamanlis visit everything was in readiness. In each room we put a floor plan of the house indicating the various room assignments. Each room was equipped with a phone connecting the rooms and permitting calls to the pantry so that orders for breakfast or tea or whatever was needed could be received. The switchboard routed calls to the outside.

On the morning of the visit, Secretary of State and Mrs. Dean Rusk met the Karamanlises at the airport and escorted them to Blair House. Since the Prime Minister was the head of government, not head of state, he was being escorted not by our President, who served in this capacity for state visits only, but by Mr. Rusk, who was the Prime Minister's opposite number here.

I met the party in the Blair House entrance hall. After the introductions and a few minutes of cordial small talk, the Rusks left.

With the help of my staff, which now included three butlers and three parlormaids hired for the duration of the visit, the entire party was taken to their rooms. The butlers were to act as valets for the gentlemen in the party who had not brought their own, and our parlormaids assisted the ladies who needed help.

Mr. Karamanlis was a dignified-looking gentleman. Mrs. Karamanlis was a striking brunet beauty with a regal bearing and dark, shining eyes.

Since the Karamanlises were lunching at the White House

within an hour and a half of their arrival, Mrs. Karamanlis
wanted her luggage unpacked immediately so that she could
change. Getting the luggage to the correct rooms was always
one of the most important and often one of the trickiest aspects
of any visit.

While the Prime Minister and Mrs. Karamanlis were at the
White House, the rest of their party was served a buffet lunch at
Blair House. This became a regular part of our routine during
subsequent visits, since this was a convenient way of serving a
large and often unspecified number of people efficiently and informally.

Sometime during the first afternoon of the visit I learned that
Allen Dulles, head of the CIA, was coming with a small group
for breakfast the following morning, and so, on short notice,
Dallas prepared a sit-down meal for them as well as a breakfast
buffet for the staff and several trays to be served in various bedrooms.

From the prepared schedule we knew hour by hour what
official functions had been planned for the Prime Minister and
for his wife. This schedule was revised for several days before
the visit and there was no guarantee that it was absolutely accu-
rate. The department prepared a little booklet nicely printed
and bound in paper covers, bearing the seal of the United States
embossed in gold and decorated with a red, white, and blue
cord tied around the binding. This little booklet, which our
guests found in their rooms on arrival, was supposed to contain
the final and definite schedule, but even this was sometimes subject to revision either by the hosts or by the guests. Everyone
knew that the absence of an absolutely set schedule was routine.

Mr. Karamanlis had been Premier of Greece since 1955. In
1963 he was forced into exile. He returned to power in 1974, suc-
ceeding the military junta that had ruled the country since 1967.
A resilient fighter for his country's freedom, Premier Karamanlis
is, at this writing, the President of Greece at the age of seventy-
four.

The Karamanlis visit schedule was quite typical. There were
formal dinners at their embassy and lunches and meetings with
members of our government. Mrs. Karamanlis' days were every
bit as busy as her husband's and included a meeting with

members of the Washington Women's Press Corps and a luncheon at the National Gallery of Art. She heard the Prime Minister address a joint session of Congress on the day before they left.

By Thursday, April 20, the house was empty again and the staff had every reason to accept the many compliments the visitors had paid them before leaving. I realized we had passed our first test. President and Mrs. Bourguiba were due in just about two weeks. In the meantime we had at least six functions to prepare.

And often there were visitors who came to see the house. Such visits had to be cleared through the Office of the Chief of Protocol. One of our first guests was Mrs. Hugh Auchincloss, Mrs. Kennedy's mother, who came with Mrs. Elisabeth Draper, the decorator, one afternoon to admire our handsome antiques.

Another day Ambassador Duke called to say that Dr. Montgomery Blair was in town and wanted to stop by the house. As the executor of Major Gist Blair's estate, he had made all the arrangements when the house was sold to the government in 1942, and he had an understandable and abiding attachment to his family's ancestral home.

When he arrived at the house that morning in April, I was startled by how familiar he looked. I hadn't met Dr. Blair before but I was sure that I had seen him somewhere. As we went from room to room he pointed out which pieces had come down through the years from the Blair family and he entertained me with stories about his family.

In the Blair drawing room he stopped for a moment in front of the magnificent portrait of the earlier Montgomery Blair painted by Thomas Sully, and I suddenly knew where I had seen his face before. The resemblance between the two was uncanny.

The day of the Tunisian visit was fast approaching. We had been thinking about it as if we were heading for an opening on Broadway. We had every detail down pat.

Along with the usual itinerary the Tunisian Embassy had given us an idea of the President's taste in food, making special mention of an herb tea of which he was particularly fond.

I called every store I could think of, from the largest supermarket to my food wholesaler to the fancy Georgetown specialty shops, but none had any of the exotic tea. This was 1961, long before there were any health food shops. Today I'm sure I could pick up pounds of the stuff in even the smallest American town, but then it was impossible to find. We had orange pekoe tea, English breakfast tea, camomile tea, we even had linden tea, but we couldn't find the herb tea preferred by the President of Tunisia.

One of our butlers overheard me bemoaning my failure to Dallas. Rigoberto Rodriguez came from Cuba and knew all about this kind of tea. In fact, not only did he have some at home, he knew a little store that carried it for Washington's Spanish community. I could have hugged him. We literally bought every bit we could find, and what President Bourguiba didn't drink during his stay he took with him when he left.

The visit, which started out so promisingly with my first meeting with the Kennedys, continued to be a great success. The White House was beginning to earn a reputation under the new Administration as a marvelous place to go for an evening of elegant, original, and cultivated entertainment. The Kennedys knew how to have fun.

For President and Mrs. Bourguiba the highlight of the evening, after the state dinner, was to be a gala fireworks display. The sky between the White House South Lawn and the Washington Monument blazed with glorious bursts of color. The guests stood on the portico. It was an unexpectedly cool spring evening, so the ladies wore sweaters and shawls borrowed from Mrs. Kennedy over their ball gowns.

Habib Bourguiba was elected President of Tunisia when, having gained its independence from France in 1956, it became a republic in 1957. He has been reelected in every election since then. He is a lawyer, educated in France, who has brought many changes to his country. He was very concerned about the status of women and has outlawed polygamy, raised the marriage age of girls from fifteen to seventeen, and placed divorce under the jurisdiction of the courts, taking it away from the discretion of husbands who, in the past, could simply declare that they had divorced their wives.

President Bourguiba had seemed tired when he arrived on

what was actually the second leg of a long cross-country trip. He had already completed a state visit to Canada and was scheduled to see ten other American cities before leaving for home.

I supposed it was his fatigue that prompted him to ask one afternoon if we had a masseur on the premises. Of course we didn't, but I was able to get Mr. McGee, who ran the Metropolitan Club's Health Room, to come over twice during the visit. He arrived with all his tables and equipment and set them up in the somewhat formal library next to the head of state's bedroom, where they looked incongruous. I don't think that room ever resembled a gymnasium again.

However, massage didn't solve the President's problems. On the evening before the day of his scheduled departure he came back to the house after his last function and went straight to his room. Rigoberto, who had been helping him get ready for bed, came down to my office and announced that he thought our visitor was not feeling well at all.

I went upstairs and suggested that we call a doctor. Reluctantly President Bourguiba agreed. Dr. George Burkley came over from the White House within minutes. After examining him, he said that the President was not seriously ill but was completely exhausted and should really go to Walter Reed Army Medical Center for a few days of supervised rest. But it was clear that the patient didn't want to follow this recommendation. By this time President Bourguiba's son, who served as ambassador from his country, had arrived. I had known the younger Bourguiba for a long time, and so when he asked Ambassador Duke if his father could stay on with us until he felt stronger we were happy to be able to oblige him.

The doctor dropped off a special diet and we geared up for our first Blair House patient. The rest of the party, headed by Mrs. Bourguiba, were to leave the next morning as scheduled; they would stay in New York.

I was soon seated at a precious old desk in Montgomery Blair's old study doing what I like least, typing. Ambassador Duke, Clem Conger, and I spent the better part of the night devising telegrams to be sent to all the places around the country that were getting ready to welcome the President of Tunisia. By the next morning there were undoubtedly a lot of disappointed governors and mayors with keys to their cities that would not be presented and plans for lunches that would never be eaten.

President Bourguiba remained with us for eight more days. He seemed very happy with the accommodations and the care. He rested a great deal, watched a little television, drifted downstairs for some of his meals or for a cup of his special tea. His son came every day and told us each time how grateful he was for our devotion to his father.

The distinguished patient was no trouble. But I had wanted to get started on some of the most urgently needed repairs to the house and we couldn't very well have carpenters and painters running through rooms in which the President of Tunisia was taking his tea or having a nap, so those plans had to wait.

I was able to let most of the extra staff I had hired for the visit go home, but since it was an unbreakable law that a head of state had to have protection, several Department of State security men and some marines were with us during the extension of his stay.

Needless to say, the functions and the meetings also continued without pause. It all went to prove that there was no such thing as routine at Blair House. From the first my watchwords became "flexibility" and "adaptability." The staff and I learned to roll with the punches. It all went with the territory and added up to an interesting job, to say the least.

Chapter Two

✿ FROM THE START, I realized I had to arrange to stay in the house while we had overnight guests. Too often during a visit there were late-night emergencies. I liked being in the house when the visitors came home to make sure they all got to bed happily, and in the morning I wanted to be around at breakfast time. That added up to long hours followed by a long drive home and a sleepy trip back at dawn. I took one of the fourth-floor rooms for my own during visits.

Managing Blair House, however, was still considered part-time work, and I spent half my days at the Department of State doing what I had done before. There, in addition to administrative duties and paper work, budget preparations and other details for visits, with which I had assisted Katherine Laird, I had been in charge of arranging for the flags that were displayed at Blair House during visits. I also procured the little flags for the United States and the visitors' country that were given to the people who lined the street along the route the guests took from the airport or railroad station to the house. I designed a series of buttons, different for each visit, which authorized members of the party wore when they came to the house. The designs, often taken from the flag and enameled on a gilt background were really quite attractive, although they cost only seventy-five cents apiece. When I retired I had several of them made into charms for a bracelet, which I still wear.

Another part of my job was to attend to the gifts exchanged between visitors and hosts during a visit. I saw that everything was prepared for arrival ceremonies, including the carpeted

platforms on which the guests stood when they received and responded to welcoming speeches. I ordered office supplies and
did all sorts of other detail work. It had always been a full-time
job. Now I had to squeeze it in during "off hours" from Blair
House.

On the days I spent in the department office, I found it harder
and harder not to let my mind wander back to Blair House, but
I don't think I was ever there a whole day without a call from
Ingrid or Dallas with a question that just couldn't wait. I still
wasn't sure I wanted the Blair House position permanently, but
I knew something had to change.

One afternoon I met with Clem and Katherine. "This can't go
on," I said. "I've got to be either at Blair House full-time or here
full-time. I don't think that Blair House management is a part-
time job, not if you want it done right." I didn't think it was fair
to Katherine, since what I didn't get done fell on her shoulders.

They agreed, and after a moment's hesitation Clem said, "We'll
get someone over here to do your work in the office. You go on
and run Blair House. There's going to be a heavy schedule there
in the next few months."

It did seem that everyone was flying over to see President
Kennedy. You could almost imagine the Presidents and Prime
Ministers lined up at airports all over the world waiting to get
on the next plane to Washington. During the short administration of President Kennedy, forty-seven foreign guests came
to see him.

Our guests included several from newly independent African
countries. Their leaders had, on the whole, never visited here before.

On one such occasion, while the head of state was out on
official functions, we served meals buffet style to the rest of the
party, as had become our custom. At the first luncheon I noticed
that there seemed to be some sort of confusion in the room. The
thirteen gentlemen from Africa (there were no ladies in this
party) were not moving toward the buffet table. They stood in
small groups talking and looking out of the corners of their eyes
at the table, but no one took a single step toward it.

Two butlers and a parlormaid stood behind the table ready to
serve from steaming platters of meats and bowls of vegetables.

There was also a large selection of salads and cheeses and breads. But if they were tempted by this array of goodies, our guests did not show it.

I reasoned that they might not be familiar with buffet service or who was to start. I had often had the same thing happen at buffet dinners at home. No one seems to want to be first. For a moment I didn't know what to do. At home I would have just approached any guest and urged him to begin, but I decided that in this all-male group it would take a man to lead the guests to the table.

I went in search of one of the security men and explained the problem. With what I thought was great tact he simply approached one of the guests and suggested that he have lunch with him. He took his arm and led him gently to the buffet, where he was served. Then they both went to one of the smaller tables we had set up in the Blair dining room. The rest of the party had fallen silent and was watching all this with great interest. They soon followed the man's lead, and in a few minutes the awkward moment was over and the whole group were happily eating and drinking and obviously enjoying themselves.

Our plan of doing things the American way backfired one other time. Again it was a group from Africa, gathered, on this occasion, for breakfast and confronted with a stack of pancakes. They simply had never eaten pancakes before. This time our butler, realizing the problem, passed the melted butter and warm maple syrup and showed one of the party that you poured both on the pancakes. Soon the entire group was happily making its way through what became its favorite breakfast. Some even requested it again the next day.

When Prime Minister and Mrs. Hayato Ikeda of Japan came to visit, they seemed quite happy with our American food, but the Japanese Embassy sent over two young Japanese women in silk kimonos and obis to perform the traditional ceremony whenever the Ikedas wanted tea. The embassy also provided a special kind of tea and a lovely porcelain tea service on a lacquered tray for the ceremony. All day long the two ladies, dressed in their elaborate costumes, sat in the pantry waiting for the signal from the second floor at which they would spring into action to perform the complicated and graceful ceremony.

While tradition reigned on the upper floor we were serving tea to the other members of the party downstairs. Since it was quite warm outside we offered iced tea with every meal. It was the first time most of these Japanese had had their national beverage served that way, but they loved it and soon became addicted to drinking tea cold in a tall glass.

The Ikeda party was quite lively, particularly because it included three daughters and a son-in-law of the Prime Minister and the daughter of the Minister of Foreign Affairs. All were in their late teens and early twenties, and there was a great deal of giggling and gaiety, especially among the younger girls.

As an American woman I was fascinated to observe the way the women in the Ikeda party behaved toward their men. Outwardly they gave every indication of being completely subservient, not only to the Prime Minister but to every other man in the party. They were very demure, terribly ladylike in their demeanor, with many curtsies and bows and inclinations of the head. It was perfectly obvious to me, however, that they had the men completely wound around their little fingers. Each lady's slightest wish was every man's command, although the poor fellows didn't realize it. I have never seen men so beguiled—or so happy about it.

The Ikeda party was with us for three days, and when they left on the first day of summer, at ten in the morning, I began the usual job of getting the house back into shape. It looked as it always did right after a leave-taking—as if a small tornado had just passed through.

I was just getting the staff started on the cleaning up when the phone rang in my office. It was the Secret Service at the White House.

"Mrs. Kennedy wanted me to tell you that she'd like to come over to see Blair House in a little while, with a few people," he said.

"What do you mean by 'a little while'?" I asked, looking at the mess around me.

"Oh, about twenty minutes, I would think," he answered as I nearly fainted.

"Mrs. Kennedy doesn't want to see the whole house, does she?" I prayed.

"I'm pretty sure she does," he said, to my horror. "We'll see you in a few minutes."

"Right, in a few minutes," I sighed. I alerted the staff, and by some miracle and with quite a lot of quick hard work they got rid of the piles of newspapers and emptied the trash baskets in all the bedrooms, but I had decided that there was no way they could get all the beds made up. Half an hour later the house looked presentable. It was not as impeccable as we would have liked it to be for a visit from the First Lady, but it would have to do. I had an idea that Mrs. Kennedy would understand.

She seemed more like a friendly smiling neighbor than the wife of the President of the United States. She might have been coming over to borrow a cup of sugar. In her simple chemise dress and flat shoes and with no makeup she looked quite girlish. With her were William Walton, an artist and friend of the Kennedys who had been active in helping with the redecoration of the White House, and Janet Felton, who worked in the White House curator's office.

We began to walk through the house, room by room, and Mrs. Kennedy immediately showed that she was very knowledgeable and very interested in the furnishings.

In the Blair drawing room she stopped to admire the Queen Anne desk. I asked her if there was anything in particular she wanted to see, and she answered in that famous soft and whispery voice, "No, I simply want to see everything."

She appeared to be very pleased at the number of pieces that the Blair family had left in the house. At one point she said, "You have so much more than we have at the White House."

I was amazed at this because I was sure the White House was filled with beautiful antiques. But it turned out many had been in storage over the years.

Unlike Blair House, the White House reflects the taste of each current President and, more often, that of the First Lady. It also has to conform to the needs of a family, something that was called for at Blair House only once, during the Trumans' stay. The White House is redecorated every time a new administration takes over. Blair House remains constant no matter who is in the White House.

On the second floor, as we continued room by room, I was

impressed by Mrs. Kennedy's unerring eye for the very best pieces. She commented on a lovely lowboy in one bedroom and on an early American chest in another.

In one room she stopped and stood in the middle of the floor for a few moments, studying the furniture arrangement.

"Why don't we put these chairs over there," she suggested, and, "Don't you think this table would be shown off to much better effect if we had it here by the window?"

We naturally jumped in to move the pieces according to her ideas, but Mrs. Kennedy was too quick for us. Before we could help her she had moved the chairs and was lifting the little table. Rigoberto, who had come along to help, was stunned.

She suggested changes, gently and in her soft voice, in several rooms. "Can't we put this highboy downstairs, Mrs. Wilroy?" she said in one of the bedrooms. "It's too nice a piece to hide up here." I was afraid she was going to put it on her back then and there and start down the stairs with it, but she didn't. The next day the press reported that she had made this suggestion and that we had followed up on it. I don't know how they got the story, but they got it wrong. In fact, we needed that highboy where it was because we had nothing to replace it with. It was used as a bureau for the second-ranking member of the visiting party. We never were able to move it.

Mrs. Kennedy and Mr. Walton were naturally very interested in the many paintings that hung on the Blair House walls. She asked me if I knew who had painted this one and what that one was. I was able to answer some of her questions, but most of the paintings were a mystery to me. Almost all the family portraits were of various descendants of the Blairs, but there were many landscapes and still-lifes too.

As I told Mrs. Kennedy, we were in the process of getting the Smithsonian to help us identify and catalog these paintings.

Secretary Rusk had suggested this after he had been put on the spot once too often by some visitor wanting to know about the paintings. It was as embarrassing as not knowing about the art in your own house, he said. At his request, the Smithsonian had promised it would send for the paintings and have an expert make the identifications. A company specializing in making brass plaques stood ready to affix one to each painting as soon as we had the information gathered. But, although the Smithsonian had promised long before to get started on this project, nothing had been done.

Mrs. Kennedy moved through every floor of the house except the basement, with the little procession of Mr. Walton, Miss Felton, Rigoberto, and me following behind her. She was obviously enjoying herself and stopped to exclaim with enthusiasm whenever something caught her eye. Her excitement was infectious and I found myself having a wonderful time too.

She particularly liked a room on the fourth floor that was furnished with early New England pieces. It wasn't as elegant as some of the other rooms in the house, but it was one of my favorites also. As a matter of fact, this was the room that had become my bedroom during visits.

I must admit, however, that as we walked through the house I was a little worried that Mrs. Kennedy might be looking at the Blair House furnishings with an eye to taking some of them over to the White House. Of course, I later found out that she wanted only things that had originally been in the White House, but I was surprised at the proprietary attitude I had so quickly developed toward Blair House and its contents.

As we were coming down the narrow Blair House stairs, single file with Mrs. Kennedy in front, she turned to me and in a neighborly tone of voice said, "Isn't it too bad that Jack had a cold and couldn't be at the embassy last night for dinner with the Ikedas?"

"Yes, I heard about it and was sorry to hear he was ill," I responded before I realized that I was talking in this matter-of-fact way about "Jack" who just happened to be the President of the United States.

It took two hours for Mrs. Kennedy to see the whole house. "I envy you all these lovely pieces of furniture," she said as she was leaving. "I'm sure we'll soon be able to do some redecorating here and show them off in an even better setting," she promised.

Then she thanked us all and was gone.

Her suggestions had been excellent and set me to thinking about rearranging several of the rooms. And she had sparked one idea I decided to act on right away. When I got back to my office I ignored the usual stack of phone messages and put in a call to the Smithsonian.

"Mrs. Kennedy was just here," I told the man in charge. "She thinks it's just wonderful that you are going to identify our paintings for us."

It worked. The very next morning a truck pulled up in front of the house and the pictures went off to the Smithsonian for identification.

Chapter Three

ꙮ DURING MY first few months at Blair House our visitors arrived with a great deal of fanfare. Having been met at the
airport or at Union Station, they would proceed in a motorcade
beginning on Constitution Avenue, and ending on Pennsylvania
Avenue at our front door. Along the route, flags of both our
countries and of the District of Columbia hung from every light
pole and fluttered from the front of every vehicle in the motorcade. The people lining the streets carried flags of both countries, which they waved in greeting. On occasion the District's
schools would be let out for the parade, each child being given
flags to wave. The procession usually included a military band
or two and several units of marching soldiers or marines. Color
guards marched ahead of the bands, and across the street from
Blair House, at the old Executive Office Building, an enormous
United States flag was displayed. The visitors' flag flew from the
Blair House flagpole for the duration of the visit.

At the Blair House door, just inside the entrance hall, a welcoming ceremony took place. The president of the Board of
Commissioners of the District, Walter N. Trobiner, was in
charge of this ceremony until the government of the District of
Columbia was changed. Now this job falls to the mayor of the
city. After a few words of welcome, the head of state would receive the keys to the city. All of this took only a few minutes.

Today visitors land at airports or at Andrews Air Force Base
and are taken to the White House in a helicopter, landing in a
cloud of dust on the South Lawn landing pad. The ceremony of
welcome usually takes place there, after which the guests are
driven across the street to Blair House.

It was President Kennedy who broke with tradition. He thought the Andrews Air Force Base setting too cold compared to the lovely White House lawn. He also stopped the parades because he thought that blasé Washingtonians often gave the guests a lukewarm reception as they watched yet another motorcade go by.

But in the spring and early summer of 1961 we still had parades, and they came to our door three times. We welcomed President Mohammad Ayub Khan of Pakistan and his wife, the Begum, who were guests at a gala state dinner held not at the White House but at George Washington's home in Mount Vernon. The entire dinner party left from the Washington Navy Yard and sailed to Mount Vernon on the yacht *Sequoia* on a beautiful summer evening. President Ayub Khan and his wife returned to Blair House saying what a marvelous evening they had had.

Our next guest was the very tall Prime Minister of a new African nation, the Federation of Nigeria. Sir Abubakar Tafawa Balewa had been knighted by the Queen of Great Britain and was educated in Britain, but he was dressed in long flowing robes and always wore a colorful ceremonial cap on his head.

Our last visitor before the summer was over was the Premier of Nationalist China, Chen Cheng. Neither he nor Prime Minister Balewa brought along their wives. When there are no ladies in the party, the emphasis of a visit is usually more on business and the social occasions are often less elaborate. Consequently, stag visits are less hectic and, frankly, less fun.

In early August we closed the house for the rest of the summer, and that very day the General Services Administration moved in to begin to make some of the most needed repairs. The GSA is in charge of the general maintenance and care of the house. Presiding over a group of experts in electricity, plumbing, carpentry, and general house repairs was Mr. James Stanier. He was nicknamed "Slim," but during our long association we always remained "Mr. Stanier" and "Mrs. Wilroy." Mr. Stanier was buildings manager not only for Blair House, but also for the Executive Office Buildings (new and old) and the President's offices at the White House.

During my years at Blair House he literally bailed me out

dozens of times when the antiquated plumbing acted up, and I grew to rely on him completely in all sorts of emergencies. I could call him virtually any time of day or night and could count on someone from his office to appear to check on windows that refused to work and the thousands of other little and big things that went wrong. More than once the emergency came at an inopportune time, such as the middle of a dinner, and Mr. Stanier often had to muffle the sound of his men's hammers in order not to disturb a Prime Minister or King at his meal.

The GSA planned to do quite a lot of plastering and painting that summer, and we had prepared a long list of smaller repairs, which they promised to attend to.

Naturally I was most excited about the plans for an office that was to be set up for me on the ground-floor level just down the hall from the inconvenient room in which I had been trying to do all the paper work, telephoning, and other administrative activities. I was looking forward to a comfortable and roomy workplace.

I suppose that the plans for the office were the first indication that I now faced the big decision. The six-month trial period was just about up, and as I left for my vacation with my daughters I had just about made up my mind to take the job permanently.

My only worry was how such a demanding schedule would affect my girls. We talked it over, and both Jenny and Ann urged me to take the job. They were sure that they could take care of themselves even if I would have to be away quite often for several days at a time. I knew that they were certainly old enough for that, but I was pleased that they didn't seem to feel neglected because of my increasing involvement at Blair House.

My own feelings about the job had changed during just those months. When I first arrived at Blair House and saw what a huge responsibility it was and how much time and energy it would take I felt overwhelmed. But now, looking back at what we'd accomplished, I felt a good deal of satisfaction and, in fact, was anxious to get started on the many changes that were planned for the house. I wanted to be part of that process.

I realized I loved the job. I loved the excitement, the diversity, and most of all, the challenge.

When I got back from vacation, I called the office and announced to Clem and Katherine that, if they still wanted me, I was theirs.

"That's wonderful," Clem said. "We were so sure you'd take it we hadn't prepared for the other possibility at all. I don't know what we would have done if you'd said no."

I was elated that first day back to see that Mr. Stanier and his men had done a glorious job on my new office.

The floor was carpeted in government-issue broadloom, but it looked much nicer than the usual drab carpeting I was used to. My desk had been completely refinished, and I had a new desk chair that swiveled and had arms for extra comfort. The room was paneled in light wood; on one side the paneling was constructed to enclose my filing cabinets, and Mr. Stanier had added shelves for storage of office supplies. The paneling had sliding doors which, when closed, gave the appearance of a solid wall. There was plenty of room to move about the office, and it was light, cheerful, and comfortable.

Just before leaving on vacation I had found an old sofa in the basement. It had belonged to the Blair family, but it was not being used, so I cleaned it and had it re-covered with an inexpensive but pretty fabric. It now stood along the wall opposite the paneled closet. Draperies covered the window, and Ingrid had used leftover drapery material to cover an easy chair. All this provided an extra homey touch to the businesslike interior.

Within three months the sofa had received so many compliments that one day it was moved into an upstairs drawing room where "it could be seen by more people and get more use." It was replaced by another, less valuable couch.

There was nothing I could do about it. Off it went, and after a while someone knowledgeable about such things pronounced it "one of the best pieces of furniture in the house"! Today it remains in an upstairs room, re-covered now in a more expensive fabric. But whenever I walked by it, I thought of it as mine.

Chapter Four

IN SIX WEEKS Mr. Stanier's men had also done wonders in the rest of the house. Several rooms had been repainted after the cracks in the walls were repaired. One room had to be completely replastered before the paint could be applied. In spite of the fact that a lot still remained to be done, the house looked much better than it had.

We set to work immediately washing the windows and rehanging the draperies and glass curtains to get the house ready for the visit of the President of Peru, Don Manuel Prado y Ugarteche, and his wife, who were due in the middle of September.

By now we had established a set routine for each visit, and even though we were still revising it and adapting to the individual situations as we learned something from each group of guests, we stuck pretty much to the set plan we had hammered out over the first months of my tenure.

Each visit went something like this:

If we were lucky, about two weeks before the arrival date the embassy people came over to tour the house and make the room selections. (Often, in fact, they came much closer to the day of arrival.) At that time we tried to learn as much as possible about the personal habits and likes and dislikes of the guests. Eventually a written formula was devised for this information which also told us whether it was the visitor's custom to shake hands upon being greeted and included the proper form of address for the visitor and the members of his or her party. There's nothing worse than addressing His Royal Highness as "Your Excellency" by mistake, although I discovered that it was not as great a disgrace to promote a colonel to general in error. (I admit these honorifics did often come in handy when I forgot the name of a visitor.)

The embassy or the State Department would also send us reminders about any dietary restrictions imposed on our guests by their religion. And most important, we'd find out that President Prado, for example, liked fruit juices of all kinds and that both he and his wife enjoyed an occasional glass of port wine.

A surprisingly large number of our guests were teetotalers, and I found out over the years that even those who took a drink did so only in moderation—a small sherry before dinner, a glass of wine with the meal, and usually soft drinks during the cocktail hour.

For a while a few years later we were issued photographs of our expected guests, and that was a great help. For most of my time at Blair House, however, I had to rely on newspaper pictures of the heads of state and on my memory, after the arrival, for recognizing the other members of the party.

During each visit, marines in full dress uniform were stationed around the house. One was at the front door, another at the foot of the steps, and several more at other strategic posts. In addition to the protection they afforded our guests, they added a measure of color and pomp to the visits.

The week preceding the arrival was always a very busy time. Regardless of any other functions we had in the house, we were always focused on the impending visit. Every spare minute was spent ordering supplies, taking an inventory of our staple items and making sure we had enough stationery, matches, cigarettes, cigars, toiletries, toothbrushes, aspirin, and tissues. I'd also make a list of the newspapers we would need to buy. The lists, in fact, were endless.

A few days before the visit the Department of State sent over the guests' official schedule, which helped us figure out how many meals we would be serving and to how many guests. By this time Dallas and I would begin to think about the menus, keeping them flexible but making sure we had enough food on hand for any extra guests.

The Office of the Chief of Protocol, once informed about the room assignments, prepared the charts that would be given to our visitors and used by us. A copy of these charts and the visitors' schedules would be posted in the pantry for the information of the staff.

During my first weeks at Blair House, it became clear that we couldn't be constantly serving food in the rooms between meals, nor could we use our dining rooms for sit-down snacks. We were not a hotel, even though we had a form of room service available. So we set up a refreshment table in the Blair dining room.

In the morning, guests would find danish pastries and rolls along with butter and jam, and in the afternoon we'd have open-faced sandwiches of smoked salmon, turkey, and fish salad. Lettuce and tomato sandwiches with herbed mayonnaise seemed to be a favorite with many of the ladies. There was always a tray of cookies made by the talented woman who came in to help Dallas with the baking.

All during the day there would be orange juice and grape juice—the frozen, not the bottled, kind—which I saw that our visitors adored. We also had various kinds of soft drinks and, of course, pots filled with hot tea and coffee. In the summer, there was iced tea. In the afternoon, cut-glass decanters containing port and sherry stood at each end of the table.

Salted nuts and candy were also always available, but it was the dried fruit of all kinds that disappeared most quickly.

In all the public and private rooms we had china boxes and silver cups filled with cigarettes, and in the head of state's library, humidors containing the finest cigars.

For each visit one of the most important considerations was the number of extra people I'd need on staff. I had a list of self-employed butlers, chambermaids, housemaids, and parlormaids on whom I called on a regular basis. I added to this list from time to time as new people were recommended and tried out, and soon I had a group of people I could count on. Many of them put service at Blair House at the top of their list of jobs they liked doing.

The telephone system was vital to the smooth running of the house. We had installed phones that connected my office, the kitchen, and the pantries with the guest rooms. There was also a system of outside lines so that I didn't need a full-time phone operator on the staff, except during a visit, when we often had a telephone operator fluent in the visitors' language to handle calls. Several times at the head of state's request we set up a direct line to the guests' country for quick communication. Their embassies assumed the cost.

We found that we'd be serving only breakfast and one other meal—lunch—to President Prado, and so I decided we'd have filet mignon.

While the President and his official guests were served in the Blair-Lee dining room, the rest of the staff was served baked ham in the Blair dining room. Dallas had learned to juggle two entrées at the same time, although very often we served the same meal to both rooms.

On this occasion, after the President had gone upstairs for a post-lunch siesta, one of the members of his luncheon party wandered into the room where the buffet was still set up. Seeing a ham standing on the table, he asked whether he might have a slice. And a few of those vegetables, too, please. In the end he ate an entire ham lunch just as if he had not just dined on filet.

While the visitors were busy with their schedules outside the house, we were always busy making certain that the rooms were cleaned and that any emergency repairs were made. We attended to the laundry and cleaning that invariably had to be done.

The ladies' clothes and all the laundry were taken care of right in the house. We always kept a laundress on duty during a visit. Dry cleaning was sent out by eleven in the morning so that we could be sure it would be back in time for any evening activity.

It took some doing to devise a plan that would get the clothes back to the right people every time. Imagine having thirteen pairs of virtually identical men's black socks and a dozen white shirts, plus an assortment of men's undershorts to contend with. We worked out a system whereby every suit that went out had a little slip with the room number on it pinned to the inside pocket. The cleaner would put that room number on the outside of the garment bag when it was returned. Similar notes were pinned inside socks and underwear and all the other items we were washing or having cleaned. Both the butler and the housekeeper had a list against which they checked everything when it came back. Miraculously, during the time I was at Blair House we really never had a serious mixup, and only once or twice did the laundry shrink something or return anything torn.

During a visit I was on the go from early morning until late at night. I checked each room once a day to freshen the flowers and to remind the parlormaids to put fresh fruit in the bowls. I met with my staff to alert them to any changes in the schedule and to give general instructions for that day's services.

There were constant little crises and an occasional major emergency. I kept in touch with the members of the party who were in charge of the head of state's program in case they needed an additional place at the table or were planning a hastily called press conference.

And I was available to answer questions and to act on special requests. Often the women in the party wanted a hairdresser or a manicurist. Elizabeth Arden's Washington salon was accustomed to calls from Blair House and was always ready to send over someone even at very short notice.

Each party contained at least one avid shopper who wanted advice on how to get to the best stores, and several times we even sent escorts along to help with the shopping.

A number of our guests were interested in the house itself, so many times I'd give a guided tour. In general, I was around to help in whatever way I could or to stop for a chat, just as you would for a guest in your own home.

On occasion I'd have to call over to the White House to check on a detail about such important matters as "Will the First Lady be wearing gloves?" and "Does the Prime Minister's wife need to wear a hat to the Smithsonian?"

Usually, just before our guests left, I was summoned to the Head of State's Suite for formal thank-yous. Sometimes I was presented with a gift, an autographed picture, for instance, or some example of the handicrafts of the country, or a piece of jewelry. Most of our visitors also gave me an envelope containing gratuities for the staff, which I would divide among them according to the amount of time each had worked during the visit and the amount of responsibility they had been given.

We never accepted gifts for the house itself, although several of our guests made such offers. If we had, I'm sure we would now have a gallery of beautiful things from all over the world on display in the house. There would never have been room for them all, though, and besides, it would have turned Blair House into a museum instead of a carefully furnished house.

The visitors and our own President almost always exchanged gifts, however, and it became my job to see that anything, from a small jewel-encrusted box to a substantial piece of furniture, was sent over to the White House. At the same time I often had to have our country's gift to the visitors crated and shipped to their embassy and even, on occasion, out of the country.

We kept a supply of wrapping paper and ribbon on hand so that our guests could wrap things they had brought with them for friends or for our officials. I was forever running out of wrapping paper. The most requested was gold foil or blue, and most people wanted red, white, and blue ribbons.

When the door closed behind the departing visitors and the house was empty and quiet, we were still not ready to relax. We had to get everything back into shape, see that the silver was polished and replaced in the vault, and make sure that everything used only for visits was returned to its proper place. Beds had to be stripped and remade, rooms thoroughly cleaned, bathrooms scrubbed, and mountains of bath and bed linens brought to the laundry. Often just laundering all the linens used during a visit took several days.

Invariably after a visit something was left behind. Every closet and bureau drawer was searched for the stray glove or hat, which would be quickly dispatched to the embassy or to the next stop of the visitor's itinerary. Several times we found brief-cases containing important documents. Once a dresser drawer revealed a pile of men's underwear. Another time we got a call from the plane carrying our guests back home. The distraught minister on the line said he'd left all his money behind in a drawer. We searched but couldn't find it. We were relieved by a call a few hours later apologetically announcing that the money had been safely packed in the man's suitcase all the time.

My end-of-a-visit tasks were varied. First I would dismantle all the flower arrangements, saving any blossoms that could be reused. I would also try to return all the calls I'd had to put off during the visit, and look through my often unopened mail, forwarding anything meant for the visitors that had been received after their departure.

I would also prepare the paychecks for the staff, make out vouchers, and do the rest of the endless paper work that accompanied any visit.

When everything was done and the extra help had left, there was always a bit of a letdown. But it never lasted long. Before we could relax completely, the next function and often the next visit were upon us.

During the remainder of 1961 we were hosts to El Ferik Ibrahim Abboud, the Prime Minister of Sudan; President William V. S. Tubman of Liberia; President Léopold Sédar Senghor of Senegal; President Urho Kekkonen of Finland; and Prime Minister Jawaharlal Nehru of India, who brought along as his official hostess his daughter, Mrs. Indira Gandhi, who was later to become a familiar face at Blair House.

She was already an outspoken public figure, even though she did not yet hold office. On this visit she was invited to speak at the Women's National Press Club. There was a great deal in the news at the time about a nuclear test ban. She said that she was opposed to all nuclear testing. She also discussed India's controversial defense minister, Krishna Menon, who had come under fire for having communist friends. And she was asked about a proposed plebescite for the province of Kashmir and about her country's neutrality. "What is a neutral nation?" she asked. "There is no such thing as a neutral nation." It was clear that we were going to be hearing more from Mrs. Gandhi in the future.

Chapter Five

ONE DAY EARLY in the New Year of 1962, the phone rang in my office. I had been trying to get some paper work done during the relatively calm period we were just then enjoying. Our next visitor, Prime Minister Cyrille Adoula of the Congo (now Zaire) was not expected until the first week in February.

On the other end of the line was Attorney General Robert Kennedy's secretary.

"We've got a problem, Mrs. Wilroy," she said, "and I sure hope you can help us with it. The Protocol Office said you're a whiz at getting supplies and arranging things, and since this is a state visit—"

"Wait a minute," I interrupted. "What state visit?"

"The Attorney General is going on a goodwill tour to Asia and Europe next month and Mrs. Kennedy is going to go with him. Well, you know how they always take the ladies to visit schools and children's hospitals and orphanages. Mrs. Kennedy thought she'd like to bring the kids something from the U.S. We've decided it would be nice if we could have two thousand lollipops for her to take along."

"That shouldn't be hard," I said. "I'll call my candy supplier."

"Well, we'd like to have them in the shape of Uncle Sam," she said. "And we thought it would be nice if each lollipop had a red, white, and blue ribbon wrapped around the stick. Do you think you can get that done for us?"

I had no idea where to begin.

"Oh yes," she added, "we'd really like to get an old Boston firm Mrs. Kennedy mentioned to make the lollipops if possible."

So what could I do? I stopped working on my menu file, which I had established so that I would be less likely to serve any guest the same dinner two visits in a row. I got on the phone to Boston.

Of course, the people at the company were very eager to help Ethel Kennedy out, but after a series of calls back and forth they admitted that they weren't set up to make so many special-order items so quickly. "We'd only be able to make forty-five lollipops a day for you," the disappointed woman told me. "I'm afraid, at that rate, we'd never get them done by January the twenty-ninth."

I had been getting the candy for Blair House from the Fannie May candy store in Washington. So I called there and asked the manager whom to call in the corporate offices of the company. He put me in touch with a Mr. Robinson, who was cooperative and said he would get the project started right away.

As it happened, he discovered that they couldn't get an Uncle Sam mold made in such a short time, but when Mrs. Kennedy left, her luggage contained two thousand specially made lollipops tied with red, white, and blue ribbons.

The Fannie May Company was pleased to donate the candy and I was delighted to have been able to get it for Mrs. Kennedy, but at the same time I was afraid that from then on I would have a dangerous reputation for being THE person to call for just about any offbeat item.

In any case, I didn't have time to worry about eventualities. The realities of the coming year were upon us. During 1962 we had twenty or more official visits planned, and as it turned out, we gave more than one hundred functions of all sorts.

Prime Minister Cyrille Adoula of the Congo was only at Blair House overnight, and his visit was very uncomplicated, but our next guest was His Majesty Ibn Abd al-Aziz al-Saud, King of Saudi Arabia. He also stayed for only one night, but his was not a simple visit. As far as I know, simplicity is not a word that exists in the Saudi vocabulary.

His Majesty had undergone abdominal surgery and an operation for cataracts the previous month in Boston and had been recuperating in West Palm Beach. President Kennedy happened to be there at the same time visiting his ailing father. He met the

King and invited him to Washington for a brief stopover on his way back to what the Washington *Star* called "the land of camels and Cadillacs."

We received the following memo from the Protocol Office (a copy also went to Letitia Baldrige, Mrs. Kennedy's social secretary, at the White House):

> The following is a list of some major likes and dislikes of King Saud and Saudi Arabians generally.
>
> King Saud likes rack of lamb, fresh lamb chops, roast strip of sirloin (rare), creamed soups, rice cooked with chicken stock, sweet fruit juices with meals, mixed green salads with Russian or Roquefort dressing, spinach, mangoes, goat's milk, sweet desserts, soupy (not too hard) ice cream, and seedless green grapes.
>
> King Saud dislikes alcoholic beverages, fat meat, food cooked in fat, salty foods, shellfish, and ice in his drinking water.
>
> To Saudi Arabians, the serving of coffee indicates it is time for them to depart. Therefore, you may want to serve them coffee at an appropriate time following the dinner.

(We took the last note very seriously and found it to be perfectly true.)

I instructed the staff on how to set up the bedrooms:

1. *King's suite*
   No cigarettes
   No ice in carafes—use cold tap water
   Fruit, fruit juice, candy, and flowers (red roses)
   Kleenex in convenient places in King's suite
   Toothpicks on table by his bed and on dresser
   Two sets of bath linens, including two bath mats for King's use each time he bathes (three or four times a day)

2. *Other rooms*
   No cigarettes
   No ice in carafes—use cold tap water
   Fruit in all rooms

Flowers in all rooms in Blair-Lee House
Setup of Cokes, candy, cookies, fruit juice, and ice on landing third floor Blair-Lee House

Later I was asked to put a handbell by the King's bed so that
he could call his personal physician who traveled with him. He
also wanted Lavoris mouthwash in the bathroom, as well as a
large pitcher and an extra handbasin.

The King swept into Blair House in his white robes, surrounded by an entourage of fifteen men including four of his
older sons, Princes Fahd, Thamer, Mansour, and Khalid (who is
now the Saudi King). A large group of veiled ladies had arrived
just before the King appeared, and they had been dispersed into
several rooms in Blair-Lee, the ones in which we had put the
flowers. No men were allowed on that side of the house while
they were there, and several of the parlormaids were assigned to
serve them all their meals in their rooms. The extra food set up
on the landing was for them.

There was much speculation in the press about whether the
wife of the King, who had traveled with him in Florida, had accompanied him to Blair House. They had been told only that
"she will not be visible and will not be photographed while in
Washington." At one point in the afternoon all the ladies, now
dressed in lovely Western evening gowns and fabulous jewels,
came downstairs to meet briefly with the wife of the Saudi
Arabian ambassador. The Queen was among the group and I
was introduced to her, but I didn't tell the press about it. Pre-
serving our visitors' privacy was one of my primary jobs.

Armed guards in Arab robes were posted at the doors to all
the bedrooms on the Blair side of the house, and several men
slept on the floor in front of their ruler's door.

Before the arrival there had been all sorts of rumors about
what to expect. Visitors from the Arab countries were not often
seen here in 1962. People who swore they knew warned that you
had to be very careful about fire when the Saudis were in residence. They were known to roast whole lambs in the fireplaces,
these informants said. Since all the Blair House fireplaces were
blocked off, I never worried much about that. And the only

smoke I ever saw during King Saud's visit came from the braziers of incense they lit everywhere. But just to be safe, I had a fireman on duty around the clock. I never called on him, and dispensed with his services on subsequent visits.

It is true that there was an aura of intrigue hanging over their stay. The sweet smell of incense and the ladies in their veils added to an exotic atmosphere in the house, but the King's short visit was really quite uneventful.

The staff people assigned to the visit were dazzled by the many men in flowing robes and Arab headdresses moving through the house, and the next morning Domenic, one of the butlers, who had a flair for the dramatic, spent several minutes arguing with the guards in front of the Head of State's Suite before he was allowed to bring the King's breakfast tray in to him. (Thick Arab coffee had been brewed in our kitchen by the King's servants on their own brazier.) "If we get through this visit with our heads still on, we'll be lucky," he said when he came back downstairs.

The King was entertained at the White House with a stag dinner. He brought gifts for the Kennedy children, an Arab child's dress for Caroline, diminutive sheikh's robes for little John. In turn King Saud was given a detailed framed map of this country copied by a new method from a topographical globe made by Rand McNally.

King Saud left the next morning, Valentine's Day, and we were back in the real world again.

The visit of President Ahmadou Ahidjo of Cameroon got off to a hesitating sort of start. He was scheduled to arrive on Monday, March 12, but just before lunch on Sunday I was called at home and told he would be arriving that evening for dinner. The staff was quickly alerted, and dinner planned and cooked, and we were ready by three-fifteen with flowers on the table, chandelier gleaming, rooms made up, beds turned down. At six-fifteen the State Department visit officer called apologetically from New York to say they would be arriving on Monday after all.

Cameroon had just been established as a federal republic and so didn't have an embassy in Washington as yet. President Ahidjo, who was his country's first President (and is still in office), invited President Kennedy to lunch at Blair House. It was the first time our President had been invited to a function of any sort at the house.

We were particularly eager, therefore, to prepare a lunch the President would like. I called Ann Lincoln, the White House housekeeper, to ask her for any ideas.

"He loves fish chowder, clam chowder, anything like that," she said, "and he'll eat any dessert as long as it's chocolate."

When President Kennedy, bareheaded and without a coat in spite of the blustery March day, came sprinting up the Blair House steps, the President of Cameroon, wearing the traditional gold and white flowing robe called a gandoura and a matching, beautifully embroidered cap, met him at the door as if he were welcoming him to his residence in his own nation's capital.

They sat down to a lunch that began with Boston fish chowder. This was followed by prime roast sirloin of beef, fresh asparagus, cauliflower, rice, lettuce and tomato salad, cheese and crackers, and for dessert Dallas' cream puffs with maybe just an extra bit of chocolate sauce. Red wine and champagne were served with the meal.

Although I didn't see President Kennedy when he left Blair House around three o'clock, Percy and Domenic both reported that he had eaten, with gusto, everything that had been served. Miss Lincoln had confided to us that the President rarely got any dessert when he ate privately at the White House, since Mrs. Kennedy had him on a strict diet to keep his weight down. Under the circumstances, Dallas' cream puffs must have been a special treat.

At the beginning of April, President João Goulart of Brazil arrived for a two-day stay. He had the usual busy schedule of meetings, formal dinner, luncheons, and press conferences. Since South Americans are used to eating their evening meal late, we often served dinner at 11:00 P.M., which made for a long day for everyone. One afternoon around five I happened to be in the drawing room when President Goulart returned from his day of meetings. He'd been on the go since early that morning.

"Oh, Mrs. Wilroy," he sighed, as the butler helped him out of his coat, "it certainly is good to get home."

I was delighted that this important, busy, and obviously very tired man felt so comfortable at Blair House he called it "home."

By the second week of April an air of excitement and anticipation took hold of the house. We were about to have the first of many visits from the Shah of Iran and his wife; over the years I got to know them both quite well. As this was the first visit I would be supervising I was eager to see that everything was perfect.

His Imperial Majesty Mohammad Reza Shah Pahlavi, Shahanshah of Iran, and the Empress Farah arrived with a large entourage and piles of luggage. The Shah impressed me immediately with his pleasant and very straightforward manner. A luncheon was scheduled at the house a few hours after his arrival, and he invited several members of the welcoming party, including Ambassador and Mrs. Duke, to join him. Then he suddenly turned to me and very graciously extended the same invitation.

I hope I didn't stammer when I told him I was very grateful to have been asked, but I would have to decline. I simply had too many things to take care of at that time.

Just getting all the luggage to the right rooms was a job. The Empress traveled with an extraordinarily beautiful wardrobe. She had a different outfit for every occasion, and we all waited eagerly to see what she would be wearing the next time she came downstairs. I still remember one lovely light blue dress with a matching coat that she wore to visit a children's hospital on her second day with us.

But of course it was her evening clothes that were truly magnificent. The visit of the Shah coincided with a new elegance at the Kennedy White House. For that evening's white-tie state dinner the Shah's jacket was festooned with medals and the Empress wore a white satin off-the-shoulder gown. But her jewels were what caught everyone's attention. Huge emeralds formed the centerpiece of both her necklace and the diamond tiara. These crown jewels were on loan from the government of Iran, she told the press. They had just been reset by New York jeweler Harry Winston. The diamonds in the tiara ranged in size from five to twenty carats. She wore matching earrings. The pictures in the next day's papers of Mrs. Kennedy and the Empress show two breathtakingly beautiful women, elegantly dressed and smiling happily.

The Empress was very easy to talk to. Like her husband, she was straightforward and gracious. As I got to know her better, she told me a great deal about her life in Iran and about the role of Iranian women, which she was working hard to expand.

While the Shah and the Empress Farah stayed with us, every day was crammed full of activities for them both. The Shah was involved in meetings with the President, Secretary of State Rusk, and others and the Empress was shown the collection at the National Gallery of Art, visited the Islamic Center, and on the second day of the visit had lunch at the home of Mrs. Lyndon B. Johnson with a group of senators' wives. The Empress had a press conference at Blair House, and His Imperial Majesty taped an interview for television. That evening they gave a state dinner for the Kennedys at the Iranian Embassy. And so it went. The little booklet of their Washington schedules was fourteen pages long. Nearly every moment was planned. Every morning began with a breakfast meeting, every evening ended with a state dinner.

The Shah's activities were mainly concerned with military matters, and he inspected many of our installations, finally traveling to Patrick Air Force Base in Florida, where he spent Friday night. The Empress and her party were alone in the house that evening, and she left the following morning for New York. The Shah joined her there on Sunday.

Perhaps this would be a good place to pause to say that while I was at Blair House it was my job to make my guests welcome. I was a career officer in the Department of State and not a political appointee. It was not my role to make political judgments. The heads of state who came to stay at Blair House were of many political persuasions. Often I might not have agreed with their politics, but I was there to see that they were served their meals on time and to make certain that they were comfortable and had a restful, pleasant time during their visit with us. Their philosophies were none of my concern.

Terrible things have befallen many of the visitors we had. The King of Afghanistan who stayed with us was overthrown in a coup in 1973. In 1980 President William Tolbert of Liberia, whom I had come to know well, was brutally killed in the overthrow of his government. Others have also been deposed, imprisoned, exiled. Some of the men I met were considered dictators, others were great heroes to the world. But I remember them all as people I knew briefly and under very special conditions. I can't think of a single one I truly disliked.

When, like everyone else, I followed the story of the last months of the Shah of Iran's life, when I saw pictures of him ill, deposed, literally a man without a country, I could only remember the times he stayed at Blair House. I remembered the gracious, handsome, friendly man. Eventually, as I got to know the Shah and his wife better, I learned something about their family life. We discussed our children, and insofar as it was possible, we formed a kind of friendship.

In these reminiscences many so-called controversial people will be introduced. I was privileged to have been able to meet these people when they were guests of our government; and while they were with us politics took a backseat as we worked to provide comfort, privacy, and relaxation. Whether the visitors were from a new African nation or from a major European power, from a country that had close ties to the Eastern bloc or from a longtime ally, whether they were new friends or old, to us at Blair House they were always simply the guests of our nation, guests we welcomed and cared for.

Chapter Six

ANGIER BIDDLE DUKE was chief of protocol for the first four years of my time at Blair House. He had been my boss at the department when I was working there as an assistant administration officer and, of course, I got to know him very well. We must have been in touch at least several times a week during those four years, and he took an active interest in what was going on in the house.

He was very warm and encouraging to me as I began my full-time stay there and he always seemed to have the time to express his approval of what I was doing, to comment after a meal he particularly liked or to compliment me on a reception that had gone well. He and his charming Spanish wife Lulu were often at Blair House functions.

During the summer of 1961 Lulu Duke was tragically killed in an accident involving the small plane taking her to the Dukes' summer house in Southampton, Long Island. The Dukes had three young children, and all of Washington was shocked by this tragedy.

The wives of the chiefs of protocol often get quite interested in Blair House. They frequently serve as hostesses there, or they escort the wives of the visiting heads of state to their various functions, and they generally serve as their husbands' partners in supervising the running of the house. Lulu Duke was rather shy, and although I saw quite a lot of her, she was not as active in Blair House matters as some other protocol wives would be.

One day in the spring of 1962 Jay Rutherfurd, a special assistant to Ambassador Duke, called.

"About that list of things you say you need over at Blair House," he said, "or maybe I should say *lists* of things . . ." (I guess I *had* been bombarding the department with requests.) "Do you think you could hold off on them for now and maybe not push so hard? If you could wait, I think we're going to be getting a lot of those things very soon."

It all sounded very mysterious. I knew that Mrs. Kennedy was working very hard by then on the redecoration of the White House, and I guessed that maybe she was getting ready to work for Blair House, too, so I said, "Okay, Jay. Just as long as we don't have to wait too long. Some of those things are really vital. For instance—"

"Trust me," Jay interrupted. "I think you'll get just about everything you need. You'll see."

I was heartened and hopeful. A week later, Jay arrived at the house with two of the ambassador's children and a tall, blond, very attractive woman he introduced as Robin Lynn. I was told that she was a friend of Ambassador Duke's and, on her way to the movies with the children, she had dropped by "just to take a look at the house."

Mrs. Lynn walked around from room to room for about fifteen minutes. I could see that she was very interested in everything, but I didn't connect her little tour with my conversation with Jay about our plans for the house until she said, "I've been told there are quite a few things you need for this house." I described some of the things I thought were top-priority, such as upholstering some of the worn furniture and redoing the Blair-Lee drawing room completely. "The Blair drawing room has so many fine old pieces from the Blair family that there is a terrible contrast when you look from it into the Blair-Lee drawing room, which is almost stark by comparison. Look at that worn furniture and those plain walls," I said. She nodded her head in agreement.

She didn't say anything further about plans for the house, but she said she'd be back again soon.

She did come back several times, and soon we were "Robin" and "Mary Edith" and I looked forward to seeing her.

I suppose I wasn't surprised when I learned via the grapevine that Robin and the ambassador were going to be married that spring at the home of Mr. and Mrs. Walter Ridder. Mr. Ridder was Washington correspondent for the Ridder newspapers. I was invited to the reception, at the home of Senator and Mrs. Claiborne Pell. President and Mrs. Kennedy were among the guests.

Not long after her marriage, Robin Duke began to take an active role in making changes in Blair House. In fact, she made Blair House her special project, and what she accomplished set a standard for the renovation of the house that continued after her husband was no longer chief of protocol and other people took over her work. Little did I realize when Jay first promised me that I would get all the things I thought we needed at Blair House that I would be launched into a renovation program that would take many years.

Renovation seemed to be the most often heard word around Washington in those days. The buildings behind Blair House were being removed to make way for a new Executive Office Building. The plans also called for the two old brick carriage houses that Francis Preston Blair had found so useful to be torn down. We had been storing extra furniture and other rarely used things there. We found alternative storage space for these things next door to Blair House in the Carnegie House at the corner of Jackson Place and Pennsylvania Avenue. The carriage houses were also going to be missed because they had formed a very attractive background for the little Blair House garden. We would soon have to cope with a great many changes in back of the house.

I was quickly involved in nearly daily meetings with the General Services Administration and the State Department representatives who were in charge of the renovations. It was a very frustrating exercise in the intricacies and idiocies of bureaucracy. Every time I thought we had finally made a decision, someone found a reason why he had to change our minds.

Many of our consultations were concerned with the problem of running a quiet retreat for visiting dignitaries while the jackhammers and demolition balls were at their noisy work building the New Executive Office Building.

One morning, at the height of the destruction, I walked into the Blair-Lee dining room. The noise was deafening as usual, but suddenly I heard a new sound, the tinkling of glass. I looked up and was alarmed to see the enormous—not to mention priceless—chandelier swaying from side to side. I was sure it was going to come crashing down on my head.

I ran to the phone and called Mr. Stanier, who told me, in the calm voice men assume to reassure hysterical females, that the chandelier wouldn't fall. I was not convinced. "I think you ought to come over to see for yourself," I said, "and I think that the chandeliers all over the house should be checked now and then to make sure they aren't being loosened by these vibrations."

What I really wanted was for scaffolding to be put around the chandeliers, but since that couldn't be done, I depended on Mr. Stanier, who sent someone over every few days during the worst of the demolition to make sure the chandeliers were secure. We also managed, through magnificent cooperation from all, to work out a schedule so that the noise was curtailed during visits. Still, whenever I walked through that room and saw the chandelier swaying and heard that tinkling sound, I saw disaster around the corner.

In May the Prime Minister of Norway, Einar Gerhardsen, and his wife came for a two-day stay. Ingrid, who had been born in Norway, was terribly excited. We found out that the Prime Minister would be celebrating his birthday while he was with us, and Ingrid knew a Norwegian woman who would make a special Norwegian birthday cake for him.

We had the surprise birthday party at the end of a reception in honor of President and Mrs. Kennedy at Blair House on the night of May 10. (Mrs. Kennedy was ill and didn't attend.) The Gerhardsens were teetotalers, so the toasts were made in white grape juice, and they could not have been more enthusiastic if the glasses had been filled with champagne. Then the cake was brought in and everyone, including President Kennedy, sang "Happy Birthday." In spite of the presence of the President of the United States, the party was very informal and it looked as if everyone was having fun. The Gerhardsens were very down-to-earth people, not the sort to stand on ceremony.

Toward the end of May the President of the Ivory Coast, Félix Houphouët-Boigny, and his very beautiful wife came for three days. The President had been head of state a short time, since his country became independent in 1960; he is still President. Since I had heard that most of the members of the party spoke only French, I arranged for Mrs. Pavillard from the State Department to serve as interpreter during the visit.

The bit of French I had was very rusty since I hadn't had a chance to use it for many years. Besides, I knew I didn't have the vocabulary to speak French comfortably for three days.

Still, when the Houphouët-Boignys arrived I thought I'd greet them in their language. That was a very grave mistake and I never did it again. I barely got out my "Bonjour" and "Bienvenus à la Maison Blair" when a torrent of French was released from the entire party, happy to have found a French-speaking American. With the confusion that always accompanies the first few minutes of a visit (Where is my room? Have you seen my overnight bag? Did I leave my umbrella in the limousine?) it doesn't help to have everyone talking in a language you don't understand. I kept pushing Mrs. Pavillard forward and saying in my most polite manner, "Je ne comprend pas français," and so on.

And then a few days later I compounded the error. I was conversing with several members of the party through Mrs. Pavillard when one of them put a question to me in such simple French that I understood what was being said. Without thinking, I answered in English and everyone was sure, again, that I knew French but was pretending not to speak it. All during that visit I had to insist on using Mrs. Pavillard. But I think they never quite believed me.

Mme. Houphouët-Boigny was called the "Jacqueline Kennedy of Africa." She was slender and very beautiful, with Mrs. Kennedy's sense of style. Her clothes were all made in Paris and she had a series of lovely outfits, many of them with matching hats. These were the days of the Jacqueline Kennedy pillbox, and Mme. Houphouët-Boigny had her own version of it. She always looked perfectly dressed.

This visit was one of the first in which Robin Duke was involved as official hostess. She and the First Lady of the Ivory Coast seemed to get on very well. Late on the afternoon of the second day of the visit, Robin called me.

"I don't know what you can do about this," she said. "Mme.

Houphouët-Boigny is in a bit of a fix. She has this lovely bouffant gown to wear to the White House this evening, but someone forgot to pack the slip that goes under it and makes it bouffant. She won't be able to wear the dress without it. Do you think we could get her one somewhere?"

By then it was nearly closing time for most of the big downtown stores. I thought I might be able to find a slip among my daughters' things, but I knew I wouldn't have time to get it to Blair House. By sheer luck I managed to find a bridal shop still open. They said they had a good selection of bouffant slips in stock. I commandeered a car and driver and sent one of the maids over. She returned with several slips, size 6, from which the President's wife chose one. We made it just in time for her to leave for the White House, her white skirts standing out beautifully over the new slip.

After I'd been at Blair House for a few months and had lived through several emergencies of this sort, I gathered together a stock of the most frequently needed items. Our male visitors most often found that they had forgotten some important item of clothing, so that we had both black and white ties for formal occasions, cuff links, shirt studs, and other items. We also had a supply of ladies' stockings and gloves. Over the years we replenished our stock several times.

Our supplies of linens for the tables and liquors for the bar were replenished, from time to time, in quite a different way. Now and then we'd get a call from the Washington office of the United States Customs Bureau offering us items that had recently been confiscated. When people think of Customs confiscating things, they probably imagine great caches of illegal drugs or jewels. But the reality is more mundane. On the whole, Customs deals with items that have been stranded on the docks or at the airports because the duty on them has not been paid.

If the list sounded promising on the phone I'd ask to see it and then check off the items we needed. We often got the finest brandies and liqueurs that way, but I never trusted the wine that was offered. I preferred to deal with a reputable wine merchant.

The items we enjoyed getting the most were table linens. At various times we received lovely embroidered linen tablecloths with napkins to match or place mats and napkins. We never said no to napkins, since we needed so many of them. Some of the cloths turned out to be too small for our large tables, but Ingrid simply sewed two together. She also got quite good at turning small tablecloths into toast covers, bread tray doilies, and covers for the trays we sent to the guests' rooms. Whenever a linen shipment came in we spent a little time measuring everything and deciding what we needed most that could be made from the too-small items. Ingrid's patterns for these things were used for years after she left Blair House.

I still remember the time we got twelve hundred tea towels— bound for a hotel or store, I suppose. We didn't have to buy a tea towel for about six years.

Through the spring of 1962 the visits continued, and even while they were in progress I was becoming more deeply involved every day in additions to and changes in the house. Practically from my first day I had complained loudly about the inadequacies of the kitchen. How Dallas managed to prepare a series of beautiful meals and lavish receptions in a kitchen that didn't even have many of the simplest conveniences I could never imagine. We didn't even get a blender until we needed one for a guest who liked to drink daiquiris before his dinner. My complaints had been heard, it seemed, for now the GSA sent over a whole new design for the kitchen. It even included a new and much needed air-conditioning system, which I knew we'd never get until the rest of the house was also air-conditioned.

Dallas and I began to pore over books of kitchen equipment. Here was everything we'd ever dreamed about and some things I never had heard of, such as a bain-marie. This turned out to be a fancy steam table, which I realized would solve the problem of keeping food hot until it could be served.

The GSA sent over a woman engineer who specialized in heating and air conditioning for the contractor who had been selected to do that part of the work in the house. She was very sensitive to the fact that this was an old and precious place. We worked together to design a system that would be compatible with a nineteenth-century structure but would also fill the bill for twentieth-century guests from all over the world. We didn't want to install anything that would destroy the beautiful wood paneling in several of the rooms. Because many of our European visitors were not used to our overheated houses in winter and they thought we used too much cooling in the summer, we specified that the bedrooms had to have individually operated thermostats. She spent many days devising a system that would be unobtrusive and would do the job.

At the same time the National Park Service was trying to find some way of dealing with the garden, which now faced an unattractive pile of rubble created by the construction on Jackson Place.

They came up with a serviceable and perfectly awful fence of metal and plastic. It hid the rubble but was itself an even greater eyesore, I thought. I planted blue morning glories in front of the fence, and at least in the summer it was hidden by the lush quick-growing vines.

By late fall of 1962 Robin had begun setting up a committee to help in the redecoration of Blair House. The Blair House Fine Arts Committee was patterned after the one Mrs. Kennedy had formed when she began to redo the White House. Robin's group, like hers, was made up of people who wanted to contribute furnishings, those who wanted to give money, and several professionals active in the artistic world in Washington who acted as consultants to help ensure that the contributions would be of high quality. Among these experts was Mr. John Walker, director of the National Gallery of Art; Dr. Richard Howland, a curator at the Smithsonian; and Mr. William Walton, who was advising Mrs. Kennedy at the White House. Mrs. Kennedy was honorary chairman of the committee, and among its members was Dr. Montgomery Blair.

Robin was the committee's working chairman. She had come to Washington after several challenging careers. From 1958 until her marriage to Ambassador Duke she had been director of public relations for Pepsi-Cola International. Before that she had worked as a representative for a large brokerage firm. She had been a reporter on radio and television and had been the fashion editor of the New York *Journal-American*. She brought to this new undertaking a marvelous combination of administrative skills and the ability to communicate, as well as her own personal style, her innate tact, and her determination to make the plans for the house a reality. With so many people involved it took all her considerable talents, but she made it work.

At various times a generous gift was rejected because it simply did not fit into the scheme of things. This had to be done gently without hurting the donor's feelings, and Robin showed herself especially adept at saying no with such grace that often the prospective donor responded with another more suitable gift.

While the committee was still in its embryonic stages I was invited to participate, and as chiefs of protocol came and went the committee remained a constant in my busy life.

Of course, the visits and functions continued. Archbishop Makarios, President of Cyprus, and Prime Minister Robert Menzies of Australia each spent a couple of days with us. By now it had become quite routine for President Kennedy to walk over from the White House for lunch or dinner at Blair House during the visits, and many functions that might have been held at a visitor's embassy took place at the house instead, for the convenience of our President.

During the visit of President Roberto F. Chiari of Panama in June of 1962 the main topic of conversation was the Panama Canal. The Panamanians had let it be known that they thought we weren't giving them enough money to run the Canal and maintain the area and base around it. I was just coming into the Blair dining room during a reception for the Panamanians when I overheard Secretary of State Dean Rusk say, "Well, I think we're giving them enough money. What Panama really wants is the Canal itself." At this everyone burst out laughing. Everyone, except perhaps the Panamanians, could see this was an outlandish idea.

After the two-day visit of President Carlos Julio Arosemena Monroy of Ecuador at the end of July we began to strip the rooms that were going to be redone that summer of their furniture. At the same time a camera crew from Paramount Pictures was making a documentary about President Truman's life. So many of the events of his administration—including an assassination attempt—had taken place at Blair House that they had scheduled a full day of filming there. Mr. Truman was not well at that time, so he could not come to Washington, but his Secretary of State, Dean Acheson, spent one whole afternoon in the library while the cameras turned.

Jay's prophecy about our getting many of the things we needed for Blair House was already coming true. Robin's committee quickly had some success in securing donations from various American corporations. Coats & Clark had contributed sewing kits for all the second-floor bedrooms. These kits were perfect. They contained every possible color and kind of thread, needles, tape measure, thimbles, scissors—just about anything you'd need for a quick repair job.

Elizabeth Arden had been contributing all the toiletries we needed for both men and women. Soap, shaving cream, aftershave lotion, cologne for both sexes, perfume for the ladies, hair spray, shampoo: anything we wanted was provided in generous quantities, which were replenished whenever we ran out.

Just before the committee was formed, Martex had given us a large number of badly needed items for the bathrooms. All the towels were coordinated with the Blair House color scheme. But we still needed linens desperately.

Many other contributions were promised.

We were just about ready to leave the house for the summer so that the air conditioning could be installed when word came down there wasn't enough money in that year's budget to do the job. Although we were disappointed by the postponement of this essential work, it meant that we'd be able to have functions in the house even though there would be painting and plastering going on in the upstairs rooms.

All that summer, except for two weeks in August, we conducted business almost as usual.

Every day there were workmen inside the house and the exterior was also going to be attended to with new paint. I discovered that there were no plans to replace the windowsills, which I had noticed were rotted and damaged by exposure. The shutters were also badly in need of repair and paint. I convinced the GSA that these things had to be taken care of while the house was being painted, and it agreed.

Scaffolding went up along the front of the house, but the GSA managed to build it in such a way that our guests were able to come in the front entrance without bumping their heads.

Meanwhile the Smithsonian Institution had sent over experts to help us catalog the furniture, silver, glass, and other valuable items we had from the Blair family. Robin wanted an exact count of how much and what we actually had before she started to solicit people for donations for such items.

Every day these knowledgeable people were in our silver vault, in the glass room, in all the rooms, inspecting and cataloging everything. We found quite a few treasures still stashed away in drawers and closets. Little by little we began to realize what a marvelous repository of American furnishings Blair House really was.

Our silver collection was one of the finest the Smithsonian's silver curator had ever seen. I had always loved good silver, and I spent a great deal of time with him. At first he spent days simply separating the American from the European silver.

One day while we were sitting in the vault he said, "If you could pick one piece out of all these, which would you like to have?" I hardly had to think a minute. I had always loved a little teapot that we used whenever our guests wanted to serve tea to a small group in their rooms. It turned out that the little teapot had been made by an American silversmith in Massachusetts for one of the crown-appointed governors of the state long before the Revolution. It was one of the best pieces we had.

He also unearthed an original Paul Revere tankard among our many other fine pieces. One little Sheffield basket with a blue glass liner was featured in a book on early American antiques in the Blair House library. It was clear that the Blair family had been very selective and knowledgeable in what they collected.

Now it was time for my vacation. The summer was almost over and several visits were scheduled for early fall. I said farewell to Blair House and went off for two solid weeks with my daughters.

"If you need me, I'll be at home, puttering around," I said gaily as I left. I had been looking forward to doing a little redecorating at my own house, to sleeping late, and to having some time to be with my children. But the telephone didn't stop ringing the whole time. I decided I'd never again take an in-town vacation.

Anyway, before I knew it, the two weeks were up and I was back in the thick of things at 1651 Pennsylvania Avenue.

Chapter Seven

ONE OF OUR first visitors that fall was Prime Minister Ahmed Ben Bella of Algeria. I was interested in seeing what sort of person he was. I knew he was friendly to the iron curtain countries and I thought, naïvely, as it turned out, that I might get some ideas of his thinking about the world by talking to him or his party.

Some time back I had followed on television the New York visit of Fidel Castro, and I knew that Ben Bella was going to Cuba after his visit with us. During their visit to New York it had been rumored that Castro's people roasted chickens in the hallways of their hotel, and I had seen the rowdy demonstrations in the streets of New York protesting or supporting him.

When the Ben Bella party arrived I expected to engage in many interesting political discussions. The world seemed to be changing so quickly that I was eager to talk to someone who might be able to give me some insight into what was happening in what we were beginning to call the Third World.

But it was not to be. Even the most accessible members of the Ben Bella party refused to discuss politics. They were very adamant about this.

Ben Bella himself was the very opposite of the Castro we had seen on television. He was a perfect gentleman, soft-spoken, elegantly dressed, meticulous in every aspect of his appearance and behavior. He spoke English and was easy to talk to—on any subject but politics. He was particularly interested in the house and its history.

When Ben Bella left and accounts of his Cuban visit began to appear in the press I was fascinated. There was Castro enveloping his guest in a huge bear hug, there were the two men smiling at each other, making speeches, emerging from secret meetings. I couldn't imagine two such different personalities getting along. Ben Bella came to us after spending several years in prison. His rule of Algeria came to an end in 1965, when he was deposed by Colonel Houari Boumedienne, who had him imprisoned again. Later he was released to house arrest, from which he did not emerge until the late 1970s. When I saw his picture in the paper the day he was freed, he didn't seem much different from the way I remembered him, just a bit older.

After brief visits from the Crown Prince of Libya and the Prime Minister of Uganda, our next scheduled guests were the Maharaja and Maharani of Jaipur. (They were personal friends of the Kennedys and were staying at the house as their guests, not as official visitors to the country. The cost of this visit was paid by President and Mrs. Kennedy.)

I coordinated our plans for this special visit with J. B. West, the chief usher at the White House. The Maharaja and Maharani had entertained Mrs. Kennedy and her sister, Princess Lee Radziwill, when they visited India, and the First Lady wanted everything to be as gala and as comfortable as possible.

The visit was scheduled for the week of October 22. There was to be a dinner dance at the White House on Tuesday the twenty-third, when the guests would be arriving from the Virginia estate of Mrs. Winston Guest. Mrs. Guest, who is called "C.Z.," and her husband raised racehorses, one of the Maharaja's passions, and a highlight of their visit was to be the National Horse Show.

Over the weekend an air of tension arose. We couldn't quite put our finger on it, but something serious was happening.

Then on Monday morning it was announced that President Kennedy was going to address the nation that evening on a very urgent matter. Like everyone else, we sat glued to the television set that night and heard the President say:

"Good evening, my fellow citizens.

"This government, as promised, has maintained the closest surveillance of the Soviet military buildup on the island of

Cuba. Within the past week, unmistakable evidence has established the fact that a series of offensive missile sites is now in preparation on that imprisoned island. The purpose of these bases can be none other than to provide a nuclear strike capability against the Western Hemisphere. . . ."

Earlier that Monday Mr. West had called to say that the dinner dance had been canceled and that the President and Mrs. Kennedy were planning to entertain the Jaipurs (as we called them) informally at a small White House supper the next evening instead. J.B. had been very cryptic about this change in plans, but now I understood it. The Cuban missile crisis had begun.

The next morning, with the crisis on everyone's mind, I tried to get the house in order, the flowers arranged, and everything ready for the guests' arrival. The Jaipurs were sending over the Maharaja's valet to get his things laid out and his bedroom set up. Mrs. Kennedy was providing a lady's maid for the Maharani.

The valet came earlier than we had expected and was given someplace to wait until the room where he was to stay was ready.

At 3:30 P.M. Mrs. Kennedy arrived to wait for her guests. We walked through the house together so that she could be sure everything was ready and to her liking.

Fresh flowers were everywhere. The maid she had sent over was already at work making sure that everything was in order in the Queen's Suite for the Maharani, and there was really nothing for us to do but wait.

Mrs. Kennedy showed the strain of the past few days. She was paler than usual and seemed quite agitated. Ingrid got us some tea and we sat in the Lincoln sitting room making small talk and smoking.

At one point, fidgety from sitting too long, she said, "Let's just take another look in the pantry, Mrs. Wilroy." So off we went to make sure that Ingrid had ordered enough orange juice and the Jaipurs' favorite brand of tea and some of the thick honey they liked for breakfast.

I had put my cigarette, just lit, down in the ashtray when we went off to the pantry. When we came back minutes later, Mrs. Kennedy absentmindedly picked it up and finished it.

After a long forty-five minutes the Maharani and Maharaja arrived and Mrs. Kennedy took them to their rooms, saw them settled in, and left to see about the dinner arrangements across the street.

It was a trying time for the country and for the Kennedys, but luckily the schedule for their guests had been carefully arranged in advance with a great many activities that did not involve the White House.

The Maharani's first stop the next morning after breakfast was Elizabeth Arden's for a massage, and just after 1:00 P.M. we served lunch to a small group of their friends.

In the evening the Jaipurs were guests at the home of the Joseph Alsops. He was one of Washington's most respected journalists and his wife, Susan Mary, was considered one of the city's most interesting and charming women.

Princess Radziwill came by at seven that evening to take them to dinner, and I made sure they had their horse show tickets, which had been sent over from the White House earlier in the day.

The Maharani was a tiny, very pretty woman. Her husband was a tall, slender, and quite regal man. They had both served in the Indian Parliament as representatives from the district of Jaipur. She was born near the foot of the Himalayas at a place not far from the Chinese border. While we were in the midst of the dangerous Cuban missile crisis, the Chinese Communists were invading India not far from the Maharani's birthplace. Because of this they were cutting short their trip and would be leaving for home after two days instead of spending a week, as planned.

Just before they left the Maharani called me to her room. She thanked me for "everything" and gave me a very pretty cigarette box designed and made in Jaipur.

The visit that was to have been such a happy whirl had turned out to be rather subdued. The shadow of the two crises hovered over us, and to this day whenever I hear the Cuban missile crisis mentioned I remember the aura of strain and tension that pervaded the house and the entire city during that time.

We had almost a month before our next visitor. Chancellor

Konrad Adenauer was coming on November 13 for three days, and I was looking forward to meeting this great statesman.

On our usual round of the house with the embassy officials, someone had remarked that the house was too warm. "The Chancellor is quite unused to so much heat in the bedroom," I was told.

"No problem," I said, throwing open the window to the roar of Pennsylvania Avenue traffic.

"It's a little noisy, I think," said the attaché in charge of arrangements. "The Chancellor will be taking a nap during the day and he'll never be able to sleep with this going on outside his window."

"Easily solved," I said. "We'll just move his bed into the library, where it is much quieter."

Then it turned out that the bathroom adjoining the bedroom would really be quite chilly with the heat turned off and the windows open next door. So I ordered several space heaters for the bathroom. The embassy people finally gave us their okay and we were ready for the Chancellor.

The day of the visit, shortly before the guest's arrival, we always unfurled the flag of the visitors' country and raised it at the front of the house to signify that during their stay Blair House is their official home. The State Department has a collection of flags of every country. They are sent where they are needed in long cardboard boxes.

When the German flag arrived I opened it; somehow it didn't look quite right. Luckily I had tacked a chart of the flags of all nations, clipped from the *National Geographic*, to my wall and I could see that what I had was not the flag of the Federal Republic of Germany but that of Belgium. I quickly called the Protocol Office to get the right flag and avoided embarrassment.

The Chancellor's visit was very pleasant. He traveled with his daughter, Mrs. Wertheim, with whom I became quite friendly. During this visit I also saw a great deal of Secretary of State and Mrs. Dean Rusk. From the very first I had found them to be very easygoing people, and I was beginning to build a very good working relationship with them. Mrs. Rusk was a rather modest, unassuming woman, not interested in fashion and formality. Instead she wanted to know what she could do to help make our guests more comfortable and somehow seemed to be there whenever I needed her. She often came to the house to change her clothes before a reception or a dinner. Her friendship and support were very important to me. I always knew I could depend on her.

While Chancellor Adenauer had been quite elderly and therefore on a reduced schedule designed not to tax his strength, our next guest, Prime Minister Abdirashid Ali Shermarke of Somalia, who came with a group of male aides, had a crowded itinerary of social and business events. The Prime Minister spoke Italian, Arabic, and excellent English, so we had no language problems for this visit.

At a Blair House reception he and our President exchanged gifts. The Somalis had come with several boxes of charming handicrafts from their country. One of these was a wooden carving about a foot high which, we were told, was called a "devil" doll. It was balanced in a way that made it impossible to push over. I suppose that children were told that a devil or some sort of magic caused this miracle. It was hard not to push the brightly painted toy in an attempt to make it fall over. It teetered tantalizingly on the brink of toppling but never did.

When the formal reception was over and we were about to pack the gifts up to have them sent over to the White House, President Kennedy appeared in the doorway.

"Say, Mrs. Wilroy," he said, "do you have that little wooden devil doll, by any chance? I'd like to take it home with me to give to the children before they go to bed tonight."

That evening there was to be a white-tie dinner at the State Department, and we had arranged for rental suits for the Prime Minister and his aides. I sent the butler up to see if they needed any help with studs or cuff links or ties.

He came back rather quickly. "I think we need some more people to help," he announced. "I found the Prime Minister having some trouble putting on his shirt. I don't think they're used to wearing white tie in Somalia."

I hurriedly rounded up every man in the house and they rushed upstairs to help in any way they could to get the group dressed. I remembered that there had been quite a bit of grumbling when the Prime Minister had announced that the din-

ner would be white-tie. But when the men came downstairs
looking very dashing, one of them asked if there would be a
photographer at the dinner so he could show the people back
home how he looked in his formal clothes.

I called the Protocol Office and got an assurance that every
member of the party would have his picture taken by the photographer who was, as usual, assigned to the dinner.

In spite of the success of this dinner, all in all, the Somalis
didn't have the best of times with us. Before their short visit was
over, Dr. Burkley had to be called several times, once for an
upset stomach and again for a mild flu. Another member of the
group, who suffered from asthma, had forgotten to bring along
his medicine. We had an arrangement with the local pharmacy
to honor the prescriptions of our guests, and Dr. Burkley often
had to be consulted so that we could determine the correct
American equivalent for whatever medication was needed.

Over the years we had surprisingly little trouble with this arrangement. Once, however, we were completely stumped. A military man traveling with the Shah of Iran on one of his many
visits asked me to get him something at the drugstore. He wrote
the name of whatever it was on a piece of paper and I called Dr.
Mishtowt at the Department of State and read it to him over the
phone. He was completely baffled. He had never heard of the
drug, he said. But he'd check further. When he called back he
was still mystified. None of his reference books listed the medication and no one he had asked had ever heard of it.

I went back to the Iranian general and confessed that we were
stymied. "Perhaps if our doctor knew what your problem was,
we could suggest an American equivalent for this medicine," I
told him. He burst out laughing.

"Medicine," he said. "That's not medicine. That's a hair dye."

In fact, I had no more luck finding the dye in our drugstore. I
had to call a professional beauty supply house and they finally
came up with the right thing.

Early in December His Excellency Don Jorge Alessandri
Rodríguez, the President of Chile, arrived with a party of thirteen gentlemen. President Alessandri was a bachelor and a reluctant traveler. We knew that he particularly disliked cold
weather, but still he chose to come to Washington at the coldest

time of the year. It was his bad luck to leave Chile in the middle of a heat wave and arrive at our front door just as a light snow was beginning to fall.

President Kennedy brought him over at about eleven-thirty. It was noon before he was settled into his room. His first appointment of the day was a lunch at the White House, and as he left he asked that the dress suits the gentlemen were going to wear to that evening's formal dinner at the State Department be sent out to be pressed.

Domenic collected the suits and gave them to the dry-cleaning man who had been summoned and was waiting at the side door. His shop was in the suburbs, but he assured us that he'd have the cleaning finished and back to us by five-thirty, in plenty of time for everyone to get ready for dinner.

As the afternoon progressed, the snow began to fall in earnest. I looked out of the window at about three-thirty and thought, "We'll never get those suits back in time if this keeps up." But when I called the shop the owner assured me that there would be no problem.

"Don't you worry about a thing," he said. "We'll have those suits back to you in plenty of time."

Those two words "Don't worry" always make me nervous. I worried. By five o'clock, when I called again, I was told, "The truck is on its way."

Outside our window the traffic had slowed to a crawl. You could hardly see out by this time, there was so much snow. Upstairs the Chileans were beginning to fret about their suits. Domenic was using his best Spanish to reassure them that I was doing everything I could to get them there in time.

But I had no idea what to do.

At about six the phone rang. It was the driver of the cleaning truck. He was stuck in snow and traffic and there was no chance that he would get going soon.

"Where are you?" I asked, and when he told me I said, "Don't move. Just stay there. We'll come get the suits."

"Don't worry, lady. I'm not going anywhere." He laughed. I didn't. I still had no idea how I was going to get those suits out of that truck short of getting on skis and going there myself.

The radio said traffic conditions were bad and getting worse.

In desperation I called the chief of police.

"I know you've got your hands full," I said, "but we're on the verge of an international incident here and I hope you can help us out."

I must say, considering the state of the traffic jam he was contending with and the really rather frivolous nature of the mission I had in mind, he was very kind and understanding. "I'll do what I can. Keep your fingers crossed."

I not only kept my fingers crossed. I prayed. Dinner was at eight o'clock.

At seven-twenty I heard a siren. I looked out and saw a Black Maria pulling up at the side entrance. Two officers got out carrying the suits in their plastic wraps.

I quickly got everyone available in the house to distribute the suits to the various rooms.

By 7:50 P.M. fourteen formally dressed men came down the stairs ready for an evening out. President Alessandri was really quite jolly when he saw me in the hall and kidded me about what he might have worn if the suits had not arrived on time.

When the Chileans came back, completely covered with snow, they reported that the dinner had been splendid. Many of the guests had been late, they said, and some had called to say that the snow made it impossible for them to get there. Those that managed to arrive enjoyed the feeling of having won out over the natural elements. For a man who didn't like the cold, President Alessandri was a very good sport about it all, and I suspect that when he got home he dined out on his experience at Blair House in the snow for several weeks.

The Chileans were the last scheduled guests in 1962, so we began to work on some of the projects that had been put aside during the past few hectic weeks.

The Library of Congress had lent the house a series of early-nineteenth-century paintings of eastern seaboard cities. They were hanging on a stairwell on the Blair-Lee side of the house. The Library wanted to make an inventory of these pictures, which were quite valuable, before it stored them for us while the house was under renovation during the latter part of the coming year.

In the meantime the National Gallery wanted to inventory the pictures it had lent Blair House shortly after it was purchased by the government. Over the phone it gave me a list of all the pictures we had so that I could check to see if they were all on display. Any that were not being displayed would go back to the Gallery. I was soon launched on a sort of scavenger hunt through the house looking for missing pictures. When several of those on my list were not discovered on the walls, I began to look in closets and out-of-the-way corridors, and finally, to my relief, I found them all.

The Chilean visit had made it clear that we needed an awning for the house to protect our visitors from the weather. We had been talking about this for quite a while, but after the spectacle of the snow-covered visitors from the south it seemed a matter of some urgency.

By late December a design for the awning had been submitted and approved. I don't know, to this day, who chose white as the best color for the awning. I knew that it wouldn't remain white long with all the dirt and pollution from Pennsylvania Avenue to which it would be subjected, but the awning that was put up was white—at least at first.

Putting up the awning meant tearing up the sidewalk to install a frame. When it was finally installed, a process that took about three days, the supports nearest to the street were found to have been placed in such a way that a car pulling up in front of the house could not discharge its passengers because the doors couldn't open. The supports had to be moved back, which meant more sidewalk demolition, more delays.

Finally the awning was in place. After four months the canvas had turned a dark gray. The next awning was green, a much more suitable, more serviceable color.

Christmas was approaching and we began to think about decorating the house for the season. During my years at Blair House we collected a wonderful supply of Christmas ornaments, but in 1962 we didn't have much in the way of artificial decorations, colored balls, or angels. We did have lots of wonderful silver and brass, though, and I discovered a pair of brass candlesticks almost eighteen inches tall that held fat candles, two inches in diameter and two feet tall.

We filled silver bowls with holly and greenery and turned one of our big brass bowls upside down and put another on top of it. Inside the second we put pine boughs. The two tall candlesticks stood on either side, and thus we had a stately arrangement for the table in the front hall. We found out the first day that we couldn't keep the candles lit. The first time the front door opened the candles blew out and wax flew in all directions. I didn't mind. It appealed to my frugal nature, and we used that arrangement for several years without having to replace the candles.

The front doors of the house were decorated with fresh green wreaths tied with red ribbons, and ropes of greenery and ribbons were entwined around the staircases and on the mantelpieces.

As the year ended, it was decided that Ingrid, who had been living in the house, should move out, and a permanent professional guard took over. It was a little strange after a dinner was over to be handing the keys of the house to a guard instead of just saying good night to Ingrid. For the first weeks there were a few problems having to do with the complicated electrical system that had been installed in Blair House bit by bit over the years. Certain light switches were connected to the refrigerator, for some reason, and it took some time for the guard to sort all of this out. Several times we came back in the morning to find the freezer defrosting and the milk beginning to turn. The electrical circuits were on the "revamp" list. And in a year or so, guarding the house would also be less complex since we were planning to install a burglar alarm system.

We looked forward to the new year, which promised so many major renovations both functional and decorative in Blair House. But 1963 would also be one of the most tragic years that Blair House ever witnessed.

Chapter Eight

"WE'RE GOING to get started on our renovation plans this year in earnest," Robin Duke told me as 1963 began. "Prepare yourself, Mary Edith. There are going to be lots of changes, lots of meetings, and plenty to do."

I was as eager for the renovations to get under way as anyone was. I knew I would have to become adept at juggling our everyday Blair House functions and visits during this unsettled period, but I didn't mind. I knew it would be worth it.

Behind the house, the New Executive Office Building was taking shape. The windows of this tall building looked down on our garden, but they were fitted with one-way glass so that the privacy of our guests was assured. They also provided an extra lookout station for the security men guarding our visitors. The old carriage houses had long been torn down, as part of the Lafayette Square project, along with a great many smaller buildings on Jackson Place. Many of these were almost as old as Blair House, and we hated to see them demolished, but in the name of progress they had to be sacrificed. Those that were saved, I am happy to report, were gutted and beautifully restored.

The Lafayette Square project created noise, dust, and the ugly temporary fence that now bounded our garden. But the worst was yet to come. In February we began to notice that new unwelcome tenants had declared squatter's rights in Blair House. We were overrun by rats. Their old nests had been destroyed by the construction and they had moved into our walls. It took many months and no end of trouble to get rid of them.

On February 19 President Rómulo Betancourt of Venezuela

was our guest, along with his wife and their daughter and a large group of government people.

They had hardly been installed in their rooms when the President called me to his suite.

"I'm in desperate need of some shirts," he announced. "In fact, I don't really have one good enough to wear to the White House for lunch today." He gave me his shirt size and said he hoped I'd be able to help him.

By then it was eleven-thirty and lunch was at one o'clock. Luckily, because I had had such requests before, I was able to call Garfinckel's Men's Shop, which was not far from Blair House, and send a houseman over in a car to pick up half a dozen shirts, including one or two dress shirts, just in case the President needed one for that evening. They seemed to fit the bill, and President Betancourt selected enough to last him for the visit. I can't imagine why he didn't pack any.

The Venezuelans made themselves thoroughly at home at Blair House and there was always someone going out or coming in. It was a lively, happy visit.

On their last evening we were prepared to serve the Betancourts a simple supper when they came back to the house after a reception at their embassy. We had planned a buffet for the rest of the party, and that was just getting under way when the presidential party arrived at the front door. I told Mrs. Betancourt that we would be serving them dinner in their suite in about fifteen minutes.

"No, we don't want any special arrangements," said Mrs. Betancourt, getting into line with the rest of the group. "We'll have what everyone else is having. It looks marvelous."

It was a relief not having another sit-down meal with all the extra attention that would have required, no matter how simple the menu.

I joined the line, too, at Mrs. Betancourt's insistence, and we had a beautiful evening, charmed particularly by the infectious gaiety the First Lady brought to every occasion. We laughed and enjoyed ourselves for more than a hour.

But our next guests were not so easily pleased. King Savang Vatthana of Laos, his Minister of Foreign Affairs, his son, and several other male ministers arrived the next Monday.

They spoke no English but seemed very cheerful, smiling all the time and speaking in a soft musical language to each other. But the smiles soon faded.

For once we couldn't find any American food that our guests ate with gusto. Dallas went to a great deal of effort to prepare highly spiced dishes, and we served hot sauce with everything that was bland. Only the morning eggs were spared. But nothing was quite right. Even the rice we served was so different from what they were used to having that they had trouble eating it.

At the end of the visit most of the Laotians had stomach problems of some sort. I suspect that they had come down with flu. They didn't seem to trust our Western doctors either, and their embassy sent over a Laotian physician who sensibly prescribed a diet of toast and tea and broth for everyone. After a day of this and a little rest, everyone perked up, the smiles reappeared, and by the time they said good-bye everyone was back in good shape. Dallas was very upset, however. He hated to see people dissatisfied with the food.

A few days later, Robin invited me to her house. The time had come to get going with the Blair House Fine Arts Committee. Jim Bowers, assistant chief of protocol, and I were the only guests.

Robin had prepared a list of the people she wanted for her committee. It was a long and distinguished list, carefully thought out to include not only professionals such as the directors of the National Gallery and the Smithsonian, but such civic-minded, knowledgeable people as Mr. and Mrs. C. Douglas Dillon, who had expressed an interest in donating something essential to the house. Others had been suggested as people whose connections would serve to solicit contributions from either private citizens or corporations.

Robin planned to write to everyone on the list and she thought we would soon be getting answers. "When we see what the committee looks like, we can really get started," she said. She was pretty certain that most of the people she had listed would be willing, even eager, to serve.

We tried to think of specific things we would be needing and talked about finding donors for some of these items.

We also decided to meet again on March 11 to discuss in more detail what items we would be asking for outright. Since we hadn't decided on an official decorator, we planned to ask Camilla Payne to join us for the next meeting, which would be held at Blair House.

It had become clear to me that the redecoration of Blair House was becoming a necessity. After almost every visit I found some piece of furniture broken or damaged because so much of what we had was old and not suited to the heavy use it received.

Robin had a master plan for the house. The first and second floors, including fifteen rooms and nine baths, were going to be done in the coming year. Then, if there were enough donations or enough time, we could make a start on the third floor. It was a very ambitious plan, but I had seen what Robin's determination and her organizational abilities could accomplish. I knew that if she said it would be done, it could be done.

Our first furniture donation came from Mrs. Kennedy, who planned to give us anything donated to the White House for which she didn't have room. The day after our meeting on the eleventh, during which we mainly toured the house, Mr. Elder, from the White House storage facility, came by with some photographs of the furniture Mrs. Kennedy thought we could use.

It was his first visit to Blair House and he was especially intrigued with the Blair House side.

"You've got to have an architect on your committee," he said. "If you let amateurs tamper with the structure of this house you're going to lose much of its charm."

I assured him that neither Blair nor Blair-Lee House was going to be changed structurally at all. The only thing of that nature that we were planning was to open some of the bricked-up fireplaces upstairs.

Within a few weeks of our first meeting I began getting calls at Blair House from the people on Robin's list. She had been right about the response.

But now I had to turn my attention to the next visit. His Majesty King Hassan II of Morocco was arriving in New York on March 26 aboard the U.S.S. *Constitution*. The plan was for the King and some members of his party to stay overnight in Philadelphia while other members of his group and most of the luggage would be coming to Blair House directly. I had been juggling room assignments because the list of those staying with us changed almost daily.

The house was filled with tiger lilies and orange gladiolus, since we had been told the King loved orange flowers. He smoked L&M's, drank goat's milk and raisin juice, loved dates, and adored mint tea. Of course, there would be no shellfish, pork, or alcoholic beverages for this visit of a Moslem monarch, but we had plenty of orange juice, and white grape juice was to be used for toasts at official meals.

Change was the key word for this visit.

On the twenty-sixth, when we were all ready for the luggage and the advance party to arrive, we were told that no one (and nothing) would be coming until the following day. We had been warned to expect about one hundred pieces of luggage. The King was traveling with an entourage of eighty, many more than the house could handle, of course, and many of them would be staying at a hotel.

But we knew that the King would have a large contingent of servants, and in anticipation of that we put as many extra beds as we could on the third and fourth floors. When we were finished we had sleeping space for about twenty-five.

At noon on the twenty-seventh the King arrived at Union Station and was met by President Kennedy. The motorcade stopped at our door, the keys to the city were presented, I was introduced to His Majesty and to his sister, Princess Laila; his younger brother, Prince Aly; the royal physician, and several military aides.

We never did know how many servants came along with the group. But my staff was appalled at the sight of the large group settling in on the fourth floor. They knew immediately that they would be serving the servants as well as the masters.

There was the usual getting-settled confusion and then His Majesty went off to lunch at the State Department. I took a tour upstairs just to see that everything was in good order. It was not.

I quickly got on the phone to the embassy. "It looks like His Majesty has changed everything we planned," I said in what I hoped was a proper diplomatic tone. "All the names on all the rooms have been switched around. Only his room has remained the same. I think this will cause a lot of confusion."

I tried to explain that I had given the telephone operator a list of who was in what room and it was all obsolete now, one hour after the visit began. The prince and princess were on the second floor, but the doctor was on the third. I was sure that we'd never get the luggage sorted out correctly. I knew the phone calls would get mixed up.

"Oh, there won't be any problems," said the embassy attaché. "Just deliver all the luggage to the servants. They'll see that it gets to the right person. As for the telephone, the only ones using it will be the King and the prince and princess. So don't worry, everything will be just fine."

There was nothing I could say. It was impossible to communicate with the servants, since they spoke only French or Arabic. So I crossed my fingers and sent the luggage up to them. As promised, there was an enormous amount of luggage. His Majesty had brought along eighty pairs of shoes. The closet in the Queen's Suite, one of the chambermaids reported, was lined with his shoes. In fact, the servants managed to get all the luggage to the right person and I never heard any complaints.

That was, however, all the servants did. Four or five of them were assigned to the royal family and they hung around their rooms, but I never saw them do anything. The rest of the crew holed up in their rooms. They ate and drank prodigiously and slept between meals. They were a thoroughly lazy, whiny lot. We stopped serving trays to the fourth floor the very first day.

We gave the servants their meals downstairs in the basement and they all appeared promptly at mealtime, if not ten minutes before. The rest of the time they were out of sight. Our chambermaids complained they couldn't make the beds; there were always people asleep in them. So finally we ignored the servants' quarters and concentrated on the royal family.

After the first day we had established a sort of routine. The occupants of the fourth floor got used to our schedule and we almost got used to them. Two servants always slept in front of the King's door, but they never appeared in his presence. By the time he arose in the morning, the vigilant sleepers were gone.

The King had also brought along a cook, ostensibly to prepare his meals the way he liked them. He went everywhere with the King, even to dinner at the White House and the State Department. But he never cooked anything, as far as I knew. He explained to Dallas what His Majesty would like, Dallas would cook it, he would pick it up and serve the King either in the house or at the various functions. I suspect he was there to make certain that no one poisoned King Hassan. The King ate our food with obvious pleasure. He was used to having a great many things prepared for him from which he could make a selection. So we always had two kinds of meat, half a dozen vegetables, several desserts. For dessert he often chose strawberries in heavy cream.

Unlike most visits, this one had an air of uncertainty to it. We knew what activities were planned, such as dinner at the White House or His Majesty's appearance on "Meet the Press" at NBC. But in between we never knew where the meals would be served, or when, or who was invited. The decisions were made by His Majesty, and even his family was not informed about what was going to take place.

Princess Laila and her lady-in-waiting had dinner one evening with Mrs. Duke, and there were several other activities planned for her, but I thought she seemed lonely and bored at Blair House.

One night, apparently unable to sleep, the princess called the night butler, Rigoberto, to her suite. It was one-thirty in the morning.

"Please would you call the wife of the minister at the Moroccan Embassy for me," Princess Laila requested.

A few minutes later, in response to the princess's call, a taxi pulled up to the front door and the minister's wife emerged. The taxi waited while she went upstairs to the Queen's Suite and Rigoberto brought the ladies tea.

After about an hour the visitor came downstairs.

"I'm a bit embarrassed about this," she said to Rigoberto as he helped her on with her coat. "In my rush to get here I seem to have forgotten to take any money. Could you lend me enough to pay this taxi?"

Rigoberto, always prepared for anything, graciously gave her enough to pay the cab and off she went.

Like the Saudis, the Moroccans used a great deal of incense, and when they left for their next stop, New York's Plaza Hotel, the house retained the definite but not unpleasant perfume in every room.

Nina Lytle, who was in charge of international visitors at the Plaza, was one of my many telephone friends. We had often talked in the past, sharing information about our mutual guests, since many of our visitors either stayed at the Plaza before coming to Blair House or stopped there on their way back through New York on the way home. In preparation for the New York visit of King Hassan and company, I made many more calls than usual to her. I thought she would benefit from what we had learned during this fascinating, strenuous, and challenging visit.

Chapter Nine

Now THAT QUITE a few people had expressed an interest in helping Robin Duke refurbish Blair House, she came often to show such prospective committee members through the house, or she sent them over and I conducted the tour.

One day she brought two men whom she introduced as decorators. The official decorators for the committee had not yet been designated, and I gathered these two fellows were auditioning for the job. They were going to rearrange the furniture in the Blair drawing room so that the committee could get an idea of their style.

Robin gave them carte blanche. They were to take furniture from any room they liked and, I heard her say, "just do what you want to do."

They changed everything around. Some of the furniture from the fourth floor found its way downstairs, and when they announced one afternoon that they were done I could see they had left nothing the way it had been.

I was appalled. I couldn't believe my eyes. From my point of view it looked just awful, just a jumble of furniture with no sense of proportion or taste.

In addition, their changes created havoc with the work of the Smithsonian's experts, who had just begun to label and list everything, room by room. Now they couldn't be sure where anything belonged.

The scene upstairs was equally alarming. There were blank squares on the walls where pictures had been removed; many really vital pieces—such as useful small tables and chairs—had

been removed from more than one room. In preparation for the
next visit we decided there was nothing we could do but put
some of the more important pieces back where they belonged.

I could hardly wait for Robin to see what the two decorators
had accomplished. The gentlemen were the special pets of two
ladies on the committee who thought everything they did was
just perfect.

When Robin came over with the two sponsors of these decorators I could see that she was as displeased as I. But there was no
way of tactfully telling the ladies how she felt.

"Why don't we show the entire committee what they have
done?" she suggested.

"Oh, this is not a good enough test," one of the ladies said.
"Let's get them to do another room or two and then show the
whole committee."

So back the decorators came, moving more things and cover-
ing a larger area with their awful ideas.

When Robin arrived for the meeting of the entire committee a
few days later she whispered to me, "I hate to have anyone see
the house looking like this." Then, out loud, she complimented
Ingrid on her tea table and admired the flower arrangements.

By this time most of the committee members were quite familiar with the house and I could see that several of them were astonished at what the decorators had done.

Mrs. Duke gathered them all in the library and began the
meeting by reiterating the purpose of the committee and giving
a brief outline of her plans for the house.

The range of the list reflected the care she had taken to select
the kind of people who would try to preserve the authenticity of
the house while increasing the comfort to our guests.

Mrs. Lyndon B. Johnson was now serving as honorary chairman, Mrs. Dean Rusk was honorary vice-chairman, Robin was
the chairman, and Mr. Ronald Tree was vice-chairman. Mrs.
Kennedy, who had been honorary chairman, found that she was
going to be too involved in her own White House project to do
any more.

While it was an impressive group, it was also unwieldy.
Smaller subcommittees were formed. Each had a specific area of
the house or a special project to work on. Mrs. Dillon concen-

trated on furnishings for the Blair-Lee drawing room. Mrs. Averell Harriman agreed to take over the redecoration of the library. Mrs. Stewart Udall was in charge of securing books for the library, and she contacted Mrs. Donald Klopfer, whose husband was executive vice-president of Random House. Mrs. Klopfer agreed to donate the complete Modern Library. Both the Book-of-the-Month Club and the Literary Guild contributed books at Mrs. Udall's request.

Every possible need was covered. Only when there was a controversial decision to be made—such as whether to paint the pine paneling in the Blair-Lee dining room or what color to use on the walls of the library—did the entire group get together to vote. Splitting up the large group worked very well and kept dissension to a minimum. It also permitted people to get really involved in things that interested them instead of spending endless hours in meetings about other matters.

After the group left that day Robin said to me, "Just put the house back the way it was. I think we're all agreed those two fellows are not thinking along our lines. Just put everything back where it belongs and we'll try to forget the whole thing." And shaking her head, she left.

On April 30 Her Royal Highness Charlotte, Grand Duchess of Luxembourg, came to stay at Blair House with her oldest son, His Royal Highness Prince Jean, Hereditary Grand Duke. The Duchess was the first woman head of state to stay at Blair House during my tenure there. In consultation with the embassy people, we had chosen the Queen's Suite for her and the head of state's more masculine accommodations for her son.

We filled the prettiest vases with pink roses, her Royal Highness's favorite flowers, and they looked lovely blending right in with the pink, cream, and blue of the suite.

Their Royal Highnesses were bringing both a valet and a lady's maid, but I made arrangements with Elizabeth Arden for a hairdresser. She was there when the party arrived so that she could do the Duchess's hair before she began her round of official functions with a luncheon given by Undersecretary of State George Ball and Mrs. Ball.

Mrs. Kennedy was vacationing at the Kennedy family compound at Hyannis on Cape Cod, so Mrs. Sargent Shriver acted

as her brother's hostess, greeting the royal couple when they
landed on the helicopter pad on the South Lawn. The Duchess's
daughter had gone to school with Mrs. Shriver, and so they were
old acquaintances.

It was a happy visit. The Duchess was quite approachable
and easygoing. She and her son had drinks—sherry for her and
daiquiris made with our hastily purchased blender for him—in
the library of his suite before dinner. Whenever they came
downstairs they were pleasant and smiling, and the visit was
relaxed even though there were fourteen people staying in the
house.

We were even made to feel like honorary members of the
royal family when they shared with us one morning the news
that during the night the Duchess had become a grandmother
for the twenty-third time.

Our last visit that spring was from Dr. Sarvepalli Radhakrishnan, the President of India, who was due on June 3. After that, I
told Ambassador Duke, we'd really have to close the house for
the summer to let the renovations begin.

Much of my time was already being taken up with committee
meetings or preparations. On the first of May—a typical day—I
got to work at about nine-thirty. Ingrid met me in the hall to tell
me that Miss Connie Callenberg, staff assistant in Mr. Duke's
office, had already arrived for that day's meeting. She had been
assigned to spend part of her time on Mrs. Duke's project. We
were all going to meet at ten-fifteen with Mrs. Francis Henry
Lenygon and Mr. Stephen Jussel, who were decorators from
New York. Mrs. Lenygon was chairman of the committee on historic preservation of the American Institute of Interior Designers. (I suspected that things would be different from my last
encounter with members of their profession.) Mrs. Duke would
be bringing Mrs. John Sherman Cooper, another committee
member, and they would all be staying for lunch.

I saw that I would have a little time before the meeting began
to get some work done. I called "Hello" to Connie, suggested she
get herself a cup of coffee, and dashed off to my office to make a
few necessary phone calls.

Before I could lift the receiver the phone rang. Sam King, assistant chief for visits in the Office of the Chief of Protocol,

called to ask if I could accompany him and a security officer to see a house in Georgetown that might be suitable for temporary quarters during the months Blair House would be closed. We would need a house during September, when the King of Afghanistan was expected, and for three subsequent visitors, Emperor Haile Selassie of Ethiopia, the Prime Minister of Ireland, and the President of Bolivia.

Mr. King and I set a time for meeting the next day. We'd already seen several houses but none fit the bill. Our needs were very special and I was beginning to despair of finding the right place.

As I hung up, Dallas appeared in the doorway to discuss the luncheon menu. We had a lot of food in the freezer left over from various visits and functions, and since we were about to close the house we were eager to use it up.

Then I ran upstairs with the houseman to show him how the furniture should be placed in the Blair dining room for that evening's reception. I checked our supply of liquor and made a list of what we needed from the cellar, so that the bar could be set up in the Blair-Lee drawing room. Back in my office, I discussed flower arrangements with Ingrid so that she could set the tables up, and then, leaving a reception menu on my desk where Dallas would find it, I went upstairs with Ingrid to choose the setting for the luncheon.

We decided on the Blair House blue and white Lowestoft china and white linen cloths embroidered in blue. I thought that these lovely things would not be lost on that day's luncheon guests. For most meals we used the blue and gold china with the State Department seal embossed on it, since we had that in larger quantities. Last night's flowers—irises, tulips, and baby's breath—were still fresh and made a lovely spring centerpiece. I had just pulled off one or two dead blossoms when the phone and doorbell rang simultaneously.

Ingrid went to the door. On the telephone, the wife of the ambassador who had been to dinner the night before asked if we had found a pair of eyeglasses while we were cleaning up. I learned that one of the parlormaids had found them under the lady's chair. Later in the day the ambassador dropped by to pick them up.

Ingrid announced that Mrs. Lenygon and Mr. Jussel were here. I went in to introduce myself, and just as Ingrid was serving everyone coffee, Robin arrived but without Mrs. Cooper, who would be late. We sat drinking coffee and making conversation for a little while and then took the New York visitors on their first tour of the house. My phone just wouldn't stop ringing, so Robin was tour director.

Undersecretary Ball's secretary called to discuss a luncheon he was giving for Mr. James Callaghan of the British Labour Party in a couple of days. Mrs. Laird called from the State Department to ask how much a small dinner for sixteen would cost if I shaved it down to three courses and two wines. She hoped I could manage to get the figures for her by the next morning. "You can bring them when you come to the office meeting then," she added.

By this time Mrs. Cooper had arrived and she and I joined the others on the second floor.

Mrs. Lenygon had already decided that, for her part of the project, she'd like to redo the Blair drawing room. She thought she could find donors for most of the items she needed, including materials for draperies and upholstery. For some time the discussion concerned such things as colors and fabrics.

We continued talking over lunch. The discussion was very lively and extremely useful. Mrs. Lenygon had a great deal of respect for the house and its furnishings. It was clear that she wanted to save as much of the original drawing room as she could. She planned to make a sketch of what she had in mind and she wanted to have the committee pass on her design before she began her work.

One of the things I had wanted to talk to the committee about was the entrance hall to the Blair-Lee House. The wooden floor was very old and in very bad condition. The Blair entrance hall still had its lovely original black and white marble floor and it would have been nice to have something similar.

Mr. Jussel suggested some tile that closely resembled marble although it was a man-made material. He said he was certain he could get it donated from the manufacturer.

Just as lunch was over, a group from the Indian Embassy came by to be taken through the house to select the rooms for the impending visit of their President. As I left, the committee was exploring the idea of making the telephone room at the rear of the Lincoln room into a place for hanging coats during a reception.

Mrs. Duke and her committee left while I was making the last-minute check on that evening's reception. I saw that I was not going to be able to make do with leftover flowers and so called the Nosegay for a couple of bunches of chrysanthemums to fill in where needed. I made five arrangements, and by the time they were done the butlers and parlormaids had arrived and Domenic went down to the cellar with me to get the liquor for the bar.

As I was on my way to my room to change for the evening I realized that the guest list had not arrived. Without this list it is very hard to announce the guests or control who is to be admitted. I quickly called the office and they assured me it would be over by six. I usually liked to take a look at the list before the reception began so that I could help introduce people. Since the guests were expected at six-thirty I wouldn't have much time to study it before the first person rang the doorbell.

Washington receptions start promptly. I have seen limousines circle the block several times in order to arrive not a minute too early, and it is rare for people to be more than fifteen minutes late. Both the guests and the hosts are often invited to another function later in the evening, and so Blair House parties had to be geared to their schedules and ended promptly.

When the messenger arrived with the list he was followed almost immediately by that evening's host and hostess.

After taking them into the drawing room and showing them how everything had been set up, I stationed myself in the hall to direct the guests to the cloakroom and the drawing room.

The butler at the door had an automatic counter, and when about 70 percent of the expected guests had passed through the door I began to circulate through the crowd to make sure that everyone was being served, that all the guests were comfortable, and that things were going smoothly in general.

This had been an especially crowded day, so when I was certain all was going smoothly, I slipped out and went to work on my daily record keeping.

I came back just in time to see the last guests off. Usually the bar, with the host's approval, is shut down by eight-thirty. By nine the house was empty again.

It took the reception staff about an hour to put everything away and then they were ready to go home. The first floor would be closed up, the lights turned out, and I would only have to check that everything was secure before going home myself.

By the middle of 1962 I had begun to stay in the house not only during visits but often after dinners, too, when they ran late. But I always went home on the weekend, no matter how late a Friday night banquet had lasted, unless there was a visit in progress.

With variations, every day consisted of just the kind of meetings, luncheons, receptions, and emergencies I have just described, and I was busy almost always from early morning until late at night.

The next day I set out to look at yet another possible interim Blair House. We had seen half a dozen private houses, had even inspected several hotels, and had considered Decatur House. None of them were suitable for our purposes.

Private houses rarely have enough bedrooms, and those that did had inadequate baths or kitchens that were too small. As for Decatur House, Francis Blair may have thought it was too ostentatious for him, but I found it quite the opposite. For one thing, it had no kitchen to speak of and we needed a very good, very large, and well-equipped kitchen.

I knew I was hard to please, but I also knew what we had to have for a state visit and so far I hadn't found it in any of the houses we had seen.

The Georgetown house we went to look at that day was lovely, perfect for a family, but it wouldn't do for us. We were quite discouraged when we parted that afternoon.

More encouraging was the fact that the donations were fairly pouring in to Blair House. We had received a dozen small black and white portable television sets from the Admiral Corporation, which also gave us a dozen clock radios. Miss Kay Halle of Washington and her brother Walter, who owned Halle's Department Store in Cleveland, had given us six breakfast trays and six breakfast sets of beautiful Lenox china. The same number of breakfast trays and china to match came from Mrs. Arthur Gardner, who owned the Pineapple Shop in Georgetown. The Singer Company had promised a sewing machine, and there were many more donations on the way from all over the country. All of this was evidence that the committee was hard at work.

We got a great deal of publicity about the committee after Robin gave a tea and tour of the house for members of the Women's National Press Corps. Stories appeared in papers all over the country through wire services and syndicates, and soon telephone calls and letters offering help were pouring in faster than we could handle them. Most of the callers thought Robin had an office in Blair House, and I often wished that she did. During President Radhakrishnan's visit the operator handled as many calls from people wanting to know what they could do for the house as she did for members of the visiting party.

The Radhakrishnan visit passed very quickly and the staff, under Ingrid's able supervision, was able to handle some of the routine by then, permitting me a little extra time for renovation and committee business.

I spent one full day just deciding where the outlets for the television sets and the telephones would go in the rooms that were slated for refurbishing, and since I knew that the decorators would be moving furniture about, most of what I was deciding was based on what I hoped were educated and not haphazard guesses. I made a chart of where every outlet was to go and hoped the electricians would follow it to the letter.

The staff and I were going to move part of our operation to the eighth floor of the Department of State. We would be giving luncheons, teas, dinners, and receptions there until a house could be found for us. For the moment we were feeling like displaced persons.

We had to decide what equipment would go with us and what we would be storing with Security Storage Company. We did a thorough appraisal of the eighth floor to see what they had on hand and found, by our standards, they didn't have much.

The job of storing what we didn't need was gigantic. Every item had to be labeled and listed. Forty rooms and closets and baths had to be packed up, ticketed, and stored. The General Services Administration was taking our lawn furniture; the Library of Congress was storing the beautiful collection of prints it had loaned to Blair House; the storage company was going to crate and store the remainder of the pictures, as well as our huge mirrors; the awning company would take down the awning, give it a much needed cleaning, and store it.

The inventory alone, never mind the logistics of getting everything out, was staggering.

During June there were always crowds of people in the house. Robin's committee members came in and out. Mrs. Lenygon and several other decorators visited us on more than one occasion and, in the midst of it all, we had tea for the wives of the Cabinet officers. As their project, under the chairmanship of Mrs. Willard Wirtz, wife of the Secretary of Labor, they were making needlepoint chair covers for the Blair-Lee dining room. An artist was designing the seats, using the Blair Lowestoft grape and grape leaf design. The seats were to be off-white and the grape leaves and grapes a blue to match the Lowestoft.

GSA contractors came in to see the areas that concerned them, and I often had to accompany them on their tours to make sure they didn't miss anything. They were in charge of plastering, painting, replacing floors, electrical wiring, and, most important, the new heating and cooling system.

My days began before nine every morning and I was lucky to get away by eight any evening. I tried to reserve the last two hours of every day for listing the things we had accomplished and planning for the next day's activities. Coordinating the whole operation was like organizing a runaway river. Little things kept slipping and sliding over the dams and sandbags of planning I had tried so hard to put into place.

It was organized chaos at best but slowly, very slowly, it was getting done. We still didn't know, however, where we would be housing our next guests. On October 7 we were expecting our next visitor, the King of Afghanistan, or so I thought then.

I was wrong again.

On June 21 Ambassador Duke asked me to come over to his home on Foxhall Road, which is in Northwest Washington, beyond Georgetown University. When I arrived he told me that

President Julius Nyerere of Tanganyika (now Tanzania) was unexpectedly and informally calling on President Kennedy on July 15. Although it was not officially a state visit, we had to have some place to put the President and his party.

"How about right here?" Angie Duke said, looking around his large living room. "Robin and I will move out and you can have the house. We'll try it for this one visit and we'll see how it works."

It was clear that we would need a much larger house for the other visits, but when I walked around the place with Angie, I could see that this house had distinct possibilities.

We made a date for a day the following week when I would come back and make a list of what was needed from Blair House and which of the Dukes' things would go into storage.

We quickly improvised a new game plan. Some of the things we'd earmarked for the eighth floor of the State Department would go to Foxhall Road. Some things taken to Foxhall Road would probably have to be stored later, but we'd worry about that then. We'd have to rescue some items that had already been packed and tagged for storage.

It was very painstaking and complicated work. Every item had to be tagged as to its location; every box had to be marked, inventoried, numbered, and cross-indexed so that we could retrieve it quickly.

The moving vans were scheduled to come July 1. We didn't have much time.

Dallas was packing in the kitchen, Ingrid and Cora were packing in all the other rooms. Movers were crating paintings, china, crystal. There were boxes, crates, lists, and people everywhere. At least a hundred times a day I would be asked where this would go, how that should be tagged, was this to be packed.

It took six days to get everything moved out. Fourteen of the biggest moving vans I've ever seen pulled up to the front of the house one by one and carried everything off.

Now came the job of moving over to the Duke house.

"We're taking most of our personal belongings out of your way," Robin said. "You can store whatever you don't want to use in the attic. Just move in what you want and push our things out of the way. The house is yours to use any way you want. You just make any changes you think are needed."

But in order to really make 2400 Foxhall Road into a house that could be used by the President of Tanganyika and his aides in about two weeks we had to do a great deal of work, both inside and outside.

To the ordinary person, the Duke house looked perfectly splendid. It was a stone house with a two-car attached garage. It had a circular drive. The entrance was framed by a small portico. In the back the Dukes had let the underbrush take over a bit for the sake of privacy. The tall grass and bushes shielded the house from the eyes of anyone passing by.

"The underbrush will have to be cut down," was the first thing the man from the State Department Security Division said. "And we need lights both in back and in front of the house so that we can see anyone who might be prowling around at night."

It took five days, including a Saturday, to get these relatively minor changes made.

Robin came by and went through the house with me several times. She simply removed the things she thought we ought to pack up, fragile decorative items or just personal things we wouldn't be needing.

The air-conditioners for three of the upstairs bedrooms were not working well, Robin told me, but she knew a good repair service. (In fact, during our stay at 2400 Foxhall Road the air-conditioners never could keep up with our needs, and as luck would have it, the visit coincided with one of Washington's humid summers.)

We had to set up a phone system for the visit and I spent hours with the phone company people getting it installed.

We had brought over bed, bath, and table linens, china and glassware, and our silverware. No private home has enough of these things to accommodate a state visit.

Our big event in the house during President Nyerere's visit was to be a reception he was giving for President Kennedy. We decided to get a caterer to handle this. As it was, Dallas was going to have to do some of the cooking for the visit in the much larger kitchen of the department, but he simply couldn't handle everything.

My days, already crowded with the details of the move, began to be fragmented because of the number of stops I had to make.

Foxhall Road, unlike Blair House, was not close to the shopping areas. My florist, candy shop, and bank were in town, so every day I went first to Blair House to answer any questions the workmen might have and usually to pick up what we had forgotten. Then I stopped at the Nosegay to see about the flowers. I would do whatever other in-town errands I had and then go to the State Department to check with Dallas about menus and so on. Before I went to Foxhall Road I often stopped by the Protocol Office to see if it had any more information on the visit.

At the end of the day I would stop by Blair House again on my way home to pick up messages. My car got a lot of use and my days grew longer as the details piled up and the visit drew closer.

On Friday we got in the supplies for the visit, which was to start on Monday morning.

Six members of the party were to stay in the house. That would fill up the six bedrooms with adjoining baths. On the first floor there were two large and beautiful drawing rooms, a dining room, and a pleasant little stone porch where we planned to serve breakfast. There was also a large entrance hall and a first-floor bathroom.

Downstairs, in the basement, a large recreation room opened onto a patio and a swimming pool. A small decorative pool was built into the garden at the side of the house.

We decided to use the recreation room for the reception because it was the largest room in the house and, weather permitting, people could go outside around the pool, which was a pretty setting and was certain to be cooler than the house.

Two hundred and fifty people had been invited to the reception, creating some problems for our security people. They had taken over the garage as a command post and had stationed a man at each entrance to the house and, during the reception, at the entrance to the house to direct people and traffic. They may have been worried about gate-crashers. As it turned out, we didn't have any uninvited guests.

Finally the phones were in, the beds set up and made, the food ordered, the floors waxed, flowers in all the rooms.

We were ready.

As usual, there were a few unexpected changes. We were told that everyone except President Nyerere was going to arrive at twelve-thirty and we had planned a lovely buffet for them. Mr. Nyerere was going to the National Press Club for lunch right after his arrival at the White House. At twelve-thirty sharp the luggage arrived, but no guests. They were coming at two-thirty with the President. Mrs. Kennedy had greeted him, but since this was not a state visit and it included no ladies, she did not come with the party.

So we distributed the luggage to the rooms and served the buffet to the security men and the rest of the staff assigned to the house.

Angie also accompanied President Nyerere to the house. We took one look at the President and it was clear to all of us that he wasn't feeling very well. He had seen a doctor while visiting Boston just before his trip to Washington and President Kennedy had offered him the services of Dr. Burkley, but President Nyerere seemed to want to avoid medical treatment, made light of his illness, and was determined to go on with his schedule.

In addition to our concern about our guest we were worried about the air-conditioners. In the bedrooms they were working, but the one downstairs could not keep up with the flow of people. Thank goodness, I thought, that these people are from a warm climate. A group from Norway, for example, would have found the heat very oppressive.

The telephones didn't work either. For some reason known only to the phone company, calls meant for the Prime Minister's room upstairs were inexplicably received in the pantry and there was no way for us to transfer them upstairs.

Just to make things worse, we found that the house's wiring simply couldn't handle the demands we made on it and the lights dimmed or went out completely with appalling regularity.

We spent the first evening of the visit trying to iron out these annoying problems.

Our wonderfully efficient ice-making machine was over at the

State Department because we had been assured by an ice company that they could deliver all we needed at a moment's notice. We rented several large containers and were ready to accept the ice, which, believe me, we needed. It never did come when they said it would. I must have called fifty times during that visit just for ice. It became a joke whenever anyone asked, "Has the ice come?"

The next morning President Nyerere really looked ill. He was running a fever and Dr. Burkley came over from the White House. But the President just shrugged it off as a minor flu and wouldn't let the doctor prescribe any medicine.

After breakfast the entire party left for the day's activities. I was looking forward to a relaxed afternoon since there would be no one in the house for lunch except the staff. Then the phone rang. It was Robin.

"I know you're busy," she said. "I'm at Blair House with a representative from the Fieldcrest company. We're coming over to talk to you about the gift of linens they're making." (Mrs. Luther Hodges, wife of the Secretary of Commerce, had secured this gift from Mr. Harold Whitcomb, the president of Fieldcrest Mills.) Robin and the Fieldcrest representative came at about ten forty-five and stayed through lunch while we decided exactly what we wanted. The Fieldcrest gift was extremely generous and we looked forward to having all the towels, blankets, and sheets we needed at Blair House. Our meeting that afternoon concerned colors, sizes, and quantities. Everything was to be coordinated with the plans for refurbishing the rooms. We made our choices and anticipated the great luxury of never again having to make do with linens during a visit. It was a dream of a present.

When the meeting was over, the caterers arrived to set up the reception. The phones were ringing all the time, the visitors were arriving and leaving for various appointments. It was all rather hectic but festive, too.

At four-thirty I quickly changed for the reception, which was to start at six. A half hour later I heard someone say, "Where do you want this organ?"

It was the first any of us had heard that there was going to be music. In addition to the organ, there was a group of six musicians from the Marine Band milling around in the front hall with their instruments.

Forced to be resourceful once again, we pushed some of the furniture to one side of the recreation room and set the organ in a corner with the little band around it.

In another part of the room protocol officers were trying to picture what the receiving line would look like. I could see, and so could they, that where we had it planned, people would be bumping into each other. So we changed that with the help of Angie, who had just arrived. I can imagine how he felt when he saw what we had done to his home. But he looked as calm and composed as ever.

The ice had not arrived and the time for the first guests to appear was drawing close. I was wearing a light summer dress, but I could feel the heat engulfing the room. The air-conditioner was working, but as people came in and out, opening and closing the door, it gulped and gasped, trying to cool the room. Our only hope was that, as the sun sank, the temperature and the humidity would, too.

The ice arrived just when I had completely given up on it, and just as the first guest arrived.

The room filled up quickly with members of the diplomatic corps and the entire Cabinet. Many senators and congressmen were there, as well as a large number of editors and top writers from the various newspapers and wire services and syndicates. There was a large contingent of business leaders and the heads of some of the country's leading foundations, as well as several presidents of universities. Dr. Martin Luther King, Jr., was there and so were several less well known clergymen. Also invited and now standing shyly in corners of the room were some Tanganyikan students who were enrolled in schools in the Washington area.

President Kennedy came early and left after chatting with President Nyerere for about a quarter of an hour.

President Nyerere circulated among the guests and the party looked as if it was going well. No one seemed to be making any move to leave even after President Kennedy and most of the members of the diplomatic corps had said their good-byes.

The outside patio saved the evening. It was much cooler out there and the extra space around the swimming pool made it possible for us to accommodate this large number of guests comfortably. When it started to rain at eight o'clock or so, the sizable group still remaining came inside and the party continued. President Nyerere had long since gone off to dinner, but still they stayed.

I looked around the room and saw a good party in progress. Perhaps the fact that this was a private home made people feel comfortable about violating the usually airtight Washington rule that you came on time and left on time. Or maybe it was that it was just too nice a party to leave.

In one corner Dr. Martin Luther King sat on a couch deep in conversation with Attorney General Robert Kennedy. In another part of the room members of President Nyerere's party were talking with congressmen, members of the press, and others. Some people had wandered up to the first floor now that the rain had helped lower the temperature. Throughout the house there was the satisfying hum of good conversation.

President Nyerere returned from dinner to find a large group of his guests still there. We never did have our usual buffet. Instead, we simply added the buffet food to the reception table or passed it to our guests.

By midnight the last guest finally went home and our visitors got ready for bed.

I was utterly exhausted but also pleased. Even if the party hadn't gone at all as I had planned it, it was a great success. And, in spite of the many snafus, the unexpected organ arrival and changes in the supper plans, there had been no serious mishaps. No one had fallen into the pool. Everyone had had a good time. I was a bit numb as I crawled into bed but happy that it had all gone so splendidly.

Chapter Ten

❧ IT WAS LIKE striking a stage set.

The Tanganyikans left the following morning right after breakfast, which we served on the little stone porch. Then we began to put the Dukes' house back the way it had been.

We removed the outside lights, and the security officers stripped the garage of the desk and chairs and paraphernalia they had used to guard our visitors.

The florist took back the containers we had used for flower arrangements and the caterer came by for his things. We removed the extra beds we had installed and restored the Duke children's play equipment to the side yard.

It would take a while for the plantings to grow back to provide the privacy the Dukes had had, but in every other way we left the house in the same condition we had found it.

When Robin came back to put her personal belongings back in place, the clothes in the closets, the family photographs back on the grand piano, she found her house clean and shining.

She was delighted with the way it looked.

"I've never had such a clean house," she told me. "Your staff is really marvelous. You don't suppose I could use one of your chambermaids one or two days a week so that I can keep it this way, do you?"

I said I would check with Lillian Johnson, one of the parlor-maids, and as it happened, she did have some extra time and from then on went to the Duke house several days a week when we were not busy with a visit.

For the time being we operated as if we were going to use the

Foxhall Road house for the Afghanistan visit. A delegation from the Afghan Embassy came to look at it, just in case.

From the last week in July we were extremely busy with functions on the eighth floor of the State Department. We had from one to three luncheons, dinners, receptions, or teas a day.

There were several large, beautiful rooms at State and a fairly adequate kitchen. My office, however, was right across from the passageway leading not only to the kitchen but also to the main hallway and elevator. Everyone who had any business on the eighth floor—and many who didn't—came through that hall. It was often hard to concentrate since I had an open-door policy in my office to make it easier for the staff to contact me when they needed to.

The eighth floor, which was a showcase for beautiful furniture and paintings collected by Clem Conger for the department, was in really bad shape. James said he didn't see how we could serve food in the dining room as long as the floors were so dirty. He washed, polished, and waxed them until they shone.

Some of the beautiful tables were also in need of cleaning before we could polish them. The dining room rug, which had been designed especially for the room, was so spotted you could hardly see the design, and I confess that I nagged and nagged poor Charlie Shinkwin, who was in charge of government services to the State Department, until he got the rug cleaned.

We took out all the silver and china that had been donated to the eighth floor and cleaned it. Ingrid spent much of her spare time cleaning the stained damask dining room chair covers. There were one hundred chairs, but by the time we left the eighth floor they had all been cleaned.

One day, after we had been operating out of these quarters for about a week, I looked up from my desk, attracted by something passing through the hall. There, adjusting her rubber gloves, was a State Department cleaning lady. She was pushing a large cart laden with all sorts of cleaning equipment: mops, brooms, a large trash can, and polishes and waxes of all kinds.

She passed by and I went back to what I was doing. A few minutes later Ingrid came in. She was trying to suppress her laughter.

"You've got to come and see this," she said, almost pulling me out of my chair.

We walked the length of the huge dining room, then through a slightly smaller reception room to the door of the Thomas Jefferson room, a large, beautifully furnished reception area.

We opened the door a crack and peeped through. There was the cleaning woman, walking very slowly around the furniture, flicking a feather duster here and there with one hand, while pushing the cart in front of her with the other. She was moving very gracefully, I can say that for her, with a rhythmic wave of the duster and then a little push of the cart in a kind of accompaniment to her slow dance. But if cleaning was what she was aiming at doing, she wasn't getting very much done.

"I've watched her go through three rooms just like that," Ingrid said. "No wonder the place is so dirty."

She was laughing as she said this, but I know it offended her sense of order and her pride in her work. As a person who hated to waste time, Ingrid was shocked by what she had just witnessed.

It was such a silly picture: this marvelously equipped cleaning woman and her ridiculous feather duster. I had to laugh along with Ingrid but when I got back to my office I called Charlie and told him I thought we could manage the cleaning without any help from GSA while we were there.

A few years ago I read that Mrs. Jimmy Carter had thought up a clever way of checking on whether the White House living quarters were being taken care of as well as they should have been. She put a cracker on a coffee table, and if it was still there after the cleaning person had left the room, she knew the table hadn't been touched. I never had to resort to that sort of trick in all my time at Blair House. Our staff took such pride in their work they didn't have to be reminded to do the dusting.

While the eighth floor served nicely for functions, we still needed a place for visits. So I continued to be busy looking at possible houses. Once again Decatur House was mentioned, but after a large delegation went over to look at it, it was definitely decided that it would not do.

In August I had a meeting with Robin and a representative from Lord & Taylor, the New York department store, which had volunteered to redo the Queen's Suite. After our meeting, Angie joined us and, together with Pamela Turnure, Mrs. Kennedy's social secretary, we went over to a house on Twenty-second Street, just off Connecticut Avenue, which everyone thought might fill the bill. I had my fingers crossed as we drove over.

The house belonged to Mrs. George Willmot Renchard and her husband, our consul general in Bermuda. The house was vacant and available if we wanted it.

Number 1743 Twenty-second Street, N.W., was no larger than most of the houses we had seen, but for our purposes it was more suitably planned than any of the others. The kitchen and pantry were large, and my spirits lifted considerably when I saw that there would even be space for our own ice maker and an extra refrigerator and freezer. The stove was bigger than those found in most private homes. It had six burners and two ovens and even a warming oven. I knew Dallas would approve.

On the second floor there was a master bedroom with a dressing room and a private bath. Another bath served the other bedrooms. On the third floor there were more bedrooms and two additional baths. Although we would need to furnish some of the bedrooms and have several of them painted, the sleeping quarters seemed adequate. All in all, the house met with our approval.

Looking around at the two large drawing rooms and the nicely proportioned dining room, I thought, yes, this will do. On the first floor there was even a small powder room, and the large walled patio at the rear of the house contained a pool.

We were told that we could move in by August 28. I made a date to come back in a day or so to study each room and make a list of the furnishings we would need so I could let Security Storage know how to release them to us. I also needed to decide which of the Renchards' things should be stored.

The decision to take the house relieved me of a great worry. I had been apprehensive about trying to manage the two upcoming visits in the Duke house since, nice as it was, it was not quite what we needed. The King of Afghanistan was now due on September 5.

On August 21 Angie and I went to the Renchard house with a representative of the Ethiopian Embassy so that we could select rooms for the visit of His Imperial Majesty Emperor Haile Selassie.

Once again the security people settled themselves into a garage. Telephone installers arrived to put in the switchboard and the extra phones that would be needed for the visits we had planned. I was busy every day setting in motion the various components of our move.

Begg's, Inc., the realtors, who managed the house for the Renchards, had prepared an inventory of its contents with Mrs. Renchard before they moved out. The inventory filled fifty-six pages in a green folder, which Mrs. Murphy, the realty agency representative, handed to me when I met her at the house. Next to each item was Mrs. Renchard's meticulous description of the condition of each piece. Unfortunately, as I compared these entries with the pieces of furniture, I found some important discrepancies. Mrs. Murphy and I spent about eight hours on two different days going over the inventory item by item. She changed the descriptions to coincide with the actual facts, and I noted which pieces we were going to remove from the house into storage. The revised inventory was seventy pages long.

The house had a lovely curving staircase made of highly polished wood, but the stairs were uncarpeted and my first thought on seeing them was, "Someone is liable to trip on that staircase." Another place just waiting for an accident to happen was the Aubusson rug in the drawing room, called the music room because it contained a piano. The rug was pretty but small and not anchored down. Without a pad to hold it, I was certain it was going to cause someone to fall.

Mr. Holman from Begg's, the real estate agent, was just as certain that Mrs. Renchard didn't want her stairs carpeted. Several other people said I was being too fussy about that little rug, and so I gave in and did nothing. But whenever I looked at those stairs I foresaw trouble.

I had two of the upstairs rooms painted in a hurry. In the master bedroom the furniture consisted of some unusual and extremely beautiful Spanish antiques. The wood was heavily carved, and the huge bed stood so high off the floor you needed to climb a flight of carved steps to get into it.

Downstairs we added furniture and lamps, and we brought

over some decorative items to put on bureaus, chests, and tables. The Renchards had taken most of their more personal possessions with them. Those they had left were displayed in locked cabinets.

Many rooms needed curtains and several of the window seats had to be recovered. The ever valuable and willing Camilla Payne was once again pressed into service, and in record time new curtains and seat covers were in place.

By August 28 we had everything in pretty good order. I went to Blair House and picked up a carful of items we would need, including almost the entire contents of the silver vault. When I got over to the Renchards', Security Storage was there unloading the furniture I had requested. The telephones were being installed and electricians were putting in additional wall outlets and repairing several light fixtures.

A landscaper had been hired to put some plants around the pool. The pots of flowering trees made the pool area look much brighter and less bare.

Just as I thought everything had been taken care of, I noticed there was no flagpole. I had asked someone to see to that, but nothing had been heard from him and in the busy days that month I simply hadn't thought again about it.

I called the flagpole man and he said there was no way to install a pole, so he had just dropped the project.

I knew there had to be some way to install that pole. I called our awning man, and when he came over to look at the proposed site he agreed that there were problems but he thought he could find a way to get a flagpole in by the day of the visitors' arrival. And he did.

The day before the visit I had a call from a woman named Suzanne Clarke. She had been the Renchards' houseguest in Bermuda the week before and had just returned. She brought with her a box of passion flowers that had been given to the Renchards by the government of Bermuda. These flowers were meant to be used in the house during the Afghan visit. Mrs. Renchard had sent a note with the flowers explaining this. It was all very complicated. I sent a car to Miss Clarke's house and had the flowers taken over to the Nosegay, where they were refrigerated until we needed them. When they arrived it turned out there were not nearly enough for a centerpiece, as we had planned. So I had to order a suitable centerpiece from the Nosegay at the last moment.

The first day of the Afghan visit it poured. Everyone in the welcoming party was soaked except for Their Majesties, who had been protected by enormous umbrellas.

Queen Homira was dressed in a white outfit with a matching white turban and she looked very lovely and unruffled in spite of the terrible weather.

But the rain fitted our mood. On August 7 Mrs. Kennedy had given birth to Patrick Bouvier Kennedy, who died shortly after his birth. She was still resting in Hyannis, and Mrs. Shriver was filling in for her as hostess.

We had an abbreviated ceremony in the entrance hall and the President, looking pale and tired, left almost immediately.

Their Majesties went directly to their rooms to change for lunch. The Queen was accompanied by her lady-in-waiting. I went up with the ladies, and Ambassador Duke escorted the King, Mohammed Zahir Shah, to his bedroom.

I had come downstairs and was talking to some of the members of the party when I heard a sickening thud on the stairs. Ambassador Duke had slipped and fallen down several steps. By the time I ran over he was already picking himself up, a bit sheepishly, but saying that he wasn't the least bit hurt. I decided that Mrs. Renchard or no Mrs. Renchard, those stairs were going to be carpeted.

A little later, while the members of the party were gathering downstairs to go off to lunch, one of the assistant secretaries of state got his feet tangled in the little Aubusson and fell down. He wasn't hurt either, but I called James in and told him to put the rug in the attic.

Lunch had been planned aboard the presidential yacht, the *Sequoia,* but because of the rain all the windows on the deck would have to be closed, and with the combination of the spray from the Potomac and the storm the guests would miss seeing the sights along the way. But the Queen said that the rain was a sign of good luck.

"We get so little rain in our country," she said graciously. "It's refreshing to see so much in just a single day."

Queen Homira, a tall, regal-looking woman, had been instrumental in removing the veil from the women of her country.

King Zahir was deposed in a coup ten years later, after which the country came under the domination of its neighbor the Soviet Union.

The minute the guests left, I had one of the butlers measure the music room; I called Mr. Hintlian, my oriental-rug man, and asked him if he could deliver a rug large enough to fit the room that afternoon.

I also told him to send someone over to measure the stairs and to find a carpet that could be laid that evening while the guests were out to dinner at the White House.

It was a tall order, but he came through. By three o'clock the music room had a beautiful new oriental rug safely anchored by a pad. From the group of samples I selected a deep red carpeting that would go well with the dark wood on the stairs. That evening, while Their Majesties were dressing for dinner, the truck with the carpet and a little army of installers was parked outside. The minute the limousines pulled away from the curb the men came in to do their work. The rest of the Afghan party was being served a buffet dinner in the dining room to the accompaniment of the sounds of hammers on the stairs. But it couldn't be helped. I was determined that when the King and Queen climbed those stairs that night the rug would be in place.

The Queen, saddened as we all were by the death of the Kennedy baby, wanted to express her sorrow by giving special presents to John and Caroline Kennedy, who were on Cape Cod with their mother. She asked Mrs. Kennedy's mother, Mrs. Hugh Auchincloss, at dinner at the White House, to find out their sizes for her. Mrs. Auchincloss called the Cape, leaving a message for Miss Shaw, the children's governess. Later in the visit Miss Shaw called me and I was able to give the children's sizes to Queen Homira.

Meanwhile, President Kennedy's gift to the Afghanistan visitors was a very handsome desk with a marble top. It was my responsibility to have the huge piece of furniture crated and shipped to the United Nations in New York, where the Afghanistan ambassador would see to its delivery overseas.

The visit proceeded quite smoothly. The Renchard house

functioned well, the guests appeared to be having a pleasant time, and I thought they were quite comfortable. They left on a Saturday morning right after a somewhat hastily eaten breakfast in the usual whirlwind of farewells.

I was very busy seeing that Her Majesty and her lady-in-waiting, Mrs. Suliaman, got off on time, and when I finally closed the door on the silent house I breathed a sigh of relief that the leave-taking had been so uneventful.

As usual, I walked from room to room looking for the inevitable left-behind bag or suitcase or scarf. But everything seemed to be in good order. Then I opened the door to one of the third-floor bedrooms. There sat three of Their Majesties' servants with their hand luggage, waiting for the signal to leave. They were quite distressed when I informed them that everyone had already gone.

I knew that Lou Deaner, the security man assigned to the visit, was still downstairs at his post. Until the visitors' airplane is off the ground, or their train has left the station, the security people remain on duty. Lou radioed the royal motorcade and asked our security men to send a car back for the hapless servants.

Instead, in a matter of minutes, the whole motorcade pulled up in front of the house, the servants got into one of the cars, and everyone started off again. The servants were smiling and waving good-bye as I turned to go back into the house.

We held several luncheons and functions at the Renchard house before October 1, the date of the visit of Emperor Haile Selassie of Ethiopia. We had stretched our accommodations to make room for nine people. The Emperor was traveling with his granddaughter, who would act as his hostess. She had brought her own attendant. The second floor was used for the royal family and several high-ranking officials. The rest of the group was on the third floor.

Mrs. Kennedy came back from Hyannis just to greet His Imperial Majesty at Union Station, but then she and her sister, Princess Radziwill, went off for a short vacation. The President thought a change of scene would do her good. They had been invited to spend two weeks sailing in the Greek islands with Aristotle Onassis.

The Emperor wore a military uniform and held himself very straight. This gave the impression he was always standing at attention. He was extremely formal and there was an aura of respect and ceremony surrounding him. At first glance it was not immediately obvious that the Lion of Judah was a very short man. Not until I stood next to him did I see that he couldn't have been much more than five feet tall. His erect bearing made him seem more imposing than he really was.

Of course we put him into the master bedroom, the one with the lovely Spanish furniture including the massive bed with the flight of steps. As usual, I saw to it that he was settled in his room. A little later he left for the first of his official functions.

He had only been gone a short time when Jay Rutherfurd, the protocol officer assigned to the visit, called me aside.

"Mary Edith, we've got a problem," he said, sounding a little embarrassed. "I've just spoken to the Ethiopian ambassador and he wonders if there isn't something we could do about the Emperor's bed. It's just too big for him. The Emperor doesn't feel comfortable in it."

I said I'd try to get another bed, but I knew it was not going to be easy. We had plenty of Blair House beds we could use. The problem was taking the Renchard bed apart and getting it out of the room. It was Mrs. Renchard's pride and joy, so I knew any damage would not be lightly dismissed.

I called Security Storage, which by now was used to handling our emergencies, and within an hour two strong men arrived with one of Blair House's double beds.

James and Domenic and several other men had to be pressed into service. They spent the rest of the afternoon taking the Renchard bed apart. It was so heavy it took two men to lift the various parts while two others unscrewed the legs and the headboard. Everyone helped carry the pieces into the attic for storage.

By the time he returned to the house the Emperor had a new, smaller bed.

When he came down that evening with all his medals gleaming on his jacket, he thanked me, very formally, and then went off to dinner at the White House.

In dealing with His Imperial Majesty there were more than

the usual number of rules. The most important was that one did not address the Emperor until he spoke. He was surrounded by his staff and by a kind of deferential quiet that I had never experienced during any of our other visits. His privacy and peace were precious to him and sacred to his staff.

I often wished that we were back at Blair House, where it would have been much easier to comply with his wishes. For instance, at the Renchard house it was almost impossible to serve a formal uninterrupted meal in the dining room, which had two entrances, one from the hall, the other from the music room, in addition to the one leading to the pantry.

Someone was always opening one of the doors to see what was on the other side, and I could see that the Emperor was not pleased at these intrusions. So we locked the one door that had a key and stationed someone at each of the others.

The Emperor used the drawing room for receiving guests, and the members of his party did not enter unless invited. That left only the much smaller music room for them to stretch out in.

I spent much of my time trying to shush the brash American visitors to the house. The normal American exuberance often threatened to shatter the serenity that pervaded the house during His Imperial Majesty's stay.

On the day of his departure I was summoned to come to the drawing room. One of the Emperor's ministers, in full uniform, came to get me. Another minister stood at attention at the entrance. When I entered, Haile Selassie, his military aide standing at his side, rose to receive me.

I remembered to let him speak first, but I must say I had an almost uncontrollable urge to curtsy. He thanked me for the visit; I thanked him for the honor of having him stay with us and for his courtesy.

Then I was escorted out. It was all done so perfectly I thought, "This must be what it is like being knighted."

For about half an hour I floated along, under the spell of the hushed regal splendor that accompanied the visit. Then, in the usual bustle of luggage, limousines, and farewells, they were gone. I was back to being myself.

Two days later I was at Blair House with Robin taking a look at how the renovations were coming along when the phone rang. It was the real estate representative.

"I just thought you'd like to know that Mrs. Renchard is in town for a day or two," he said.

I thanked him for the information, but I didn't really understand why he was telling me about it. But when I got back to 1743 Twenty-second Street I found out. Fifteen minutes after I arrived, who should sail through the front door unannounced but Mrs. Renchard herself.

She was very pleasant, but during the hour she stayed, she did a very thorough tour of the house and checked on each little detail. We had by then restored the bed, thank goodness. You could see that she was searching for nicks and cracks in the furniture, stains on the carpets, broken teacup handles, everything. When she saw the carpeted steps she said, "I see you've added a little something here," and she asked at once what had happened to the rug in the music room.

I could see that we would have trouble with this lady when it came time to leave the house. I didn't look forward to checking her inventory with her.

When she left at four that afternoon Ingrid and I heaved a sigh of relief, almost in unison. We were both longing to be back in our own Blair House.

Chapter Eleven

WE HAD TWO more pleasant and uneventful visits during our Renchard house sojourn. The Prime Minister of Ireland, Sean F. Lemass, and the President of Bolivia, Señor Victor Paz Estenssoro, each spent three days with us.

I learned that our Irish visitors preferred scotch or bourbon to the Irish whiskey I had specially ordered for them. And although President Paz and his party came on rather short notice —we had only two days to prepare—that visit went quite well except for a short period of anger on the part of the President. He was upset with someone on his staff. We never did find out what he was miffed about, but his displeasure could be distinctly felt one evening. However, he was soon restored to a good mood and left us with the usual thank-yous on October 24.

As soon as the Bolivians had departed we began packing. Our lease was up on October 31.

Once again the huge vans came and picked up all the Blair House furniture and items we had brought over with us. These things went back to Blair House, where they were simply set down anywhere we could find room for them in a house that was still in the throes of renovation. Wherever the varnish was dry on the floor or the painters finished with the walls, we would put the furniture. Nothing was where it really belonged.

Then came the day I had been dreading. Mrs. Renchard arrived with her notebook for the inventory. It was Friday, November 1.

Mrs. Murphy came too, of course, and with the ladies were two men whose only job, as far as I could see, was to check each piece of furniture for even the tiniest scratch. They also examined the woodwork all over the house for any signs of wear that might have appeared during our two months in residence.

One of the men was in the business of making repairs. As we went along he quoted prices for fixing this or that minor damage. I suggested that our GSA people could do the work for much less, which didn't seem to please him at all; he became downright nasty, I thought.

While we were having our little discussion Mrs. Renchard broke in to say that all repairs had to be made that very day, since she was going to go back to Bermuda almost immediately and wanted to check that everything was perfect.

"I also want everything out of here that you people have put in," she added. "It was my understanding that the house would be returned to me in the exact condition in which you found it. That rug on the staircase and everything else will have to go."

"I don't think we can get it all done that quickly or without the approval of the Protocol Office," I said as calmly as possible and as firmly as I could. Mrs. Renchard was a formidable lady.

In the end she gave in a little and agreed to meet with me and Mr. Bowers on Monday morning to see to the details of any repairs.

In fact the house was in much better shape than it had been on August 28 and I think that under all that bluster Mrs. Renchard knew it.

I checked with Jim Bowers after I left the Renchard house that day, and he agreed with me completely. We set our meeting time for nine on Monday.

To my astonishment, on Monday Mrs. Renchard couldn't have been more cooperative. She never mentioned any of the items under discussion the previous Friday. I had made a complete list of every piece she had claimed was damaged, but I never brought it out. She even agreed that the carpeting on the stairs could stay. Her Aubusson was by then back in the music room.

She said she'd make the few repairs that were most necessary and would send us the bill. I suppose she recognized that it would be impossible to take the paint off the walls in the bedrooms and silly to strip the attractive perfectly new covers off the window seats.

We all signed releases and I returned the keys to her house and that was that. In retrospect, I decided that she'd been egged on by all those specialists she had brought over to the house. Left to her own decisions, she could be a reasonable if somewhat meticulous woman. Being a perfectionist myself, I had some sympathy for her. We parted with mutual thanks.

Coming back to Blair House was like coming home.

But it was one grand mess. Rugs and draperies were being installed in the few rooms that had been finished on the third floor, but no rooms on the first or second floors on either side of the house were anywhere near ready for the furniture to be moved back in.

On the Blair-Lee side several fireplaces were being installed and dirt, plaster, and pieces of marble were everywhere. It was noisy as well as dusty, and there was constant turmoil, with workmen coming and going everywhere carrying ladders and tracking plaster dust into every room.

Into this chaos, on our first day back, Robin brought the members of the Fine Arts Committee. We met in the President's study, and after the business meeting was over tea was served in the Blair-Lee dining room.

Ingrid had set a lovely table and Dallas and his assistant had managed to prepare a delicious spread in the not-quite-complete kitchen.

In order to get to the table, however, the guests had to pick their way over the two-by-fours scattered on the floor. Sawdust and wood shavings completed the decorations for that particular tea. Balancing their teacups, the ladies tried to find a level place to stand.

It was a ridiculously incongruous picture, but we made some vital decisions that day. The committee had come specifically to look at the paneling in the dining room. It was dark wood, which made the room look rather dim and murky. It was decided to paint the paneling white. The committee members must have been pleased, since the destruction they were seeing all around them simply meant that their efforts were beginning to bear fruit.

By the middle of November the furniture that had been in storage began to arrive back at the house. We had scheduled it to arrive one truckload at a time so that, with James overseeing things, we could put everything back in approximately the right rooms even if they weren't completely done. Everything went smoothly until the mattresses began to arrive. They had been boxed, but someone had forgotten to mark the boxes with the appropriate room numbers. So we had the terrible job of unpacking the mattresses and then matching them with the proper beds.

While the furniture was being moved back there was the constant noise of the machines that were finishing the floors, and Ingrid and I were adding to the general din with shouted instructions. The dust rose in clouds from the fireplaces where new mantels were being installed. Workmen were coming in and out all day long. It was bedlam.

But in the midst of it all there was one island of complete calm. In the first-floor powder room Mary Ponsart, an artist who had donated her talents, was sitting peacefully on a small chair or standing quietly on a stepladder painting the flowers of the fifty states on the walls, which had been covered with canvas. Later, whenever I saw those painstakingly done, charming pastel-colored flowers, I recalled the chaotic conditions under which they had been painted and I smiled.

Mrs. Lenygon was also at the house nearly every day making her way over the drop cloths and bricks to plan where to hang pictures and to place furniture. Whenever I had time or room, I served these valiant ladies lunch.

As if we didn't have enough problems, our old enemies the rats were back in force. The GSA extermination squads were doing battle with them, but it was a hard fight. Every night we covered the tables with drop cloths to protect them from the rats.

There were no towel racks or soap dishes or toilet paper holders in any of the upstairs bathrooms, and in the Queen's bathroom the little sconces on the walls had been put in upside down. If I had been that sort of woman, I would have wept when I saw them, but it was only one more thing in a series of daily problems.

Ingrid was busy supervising the replacement of the china, crystal, and other items in both the pantry and the glass room.

The silver would have to wait until the vault was lined with the special dark blue cloth that would keep the tarnish at a minimum.

Whenever a wall was plastered and painted and the paint had dried, Security Storage would come and hang the pictures that belonged in that room. Little by little we were restoring order to the house.

We could all see that progress was being made, but when, on November 21, Robin brought Angie by, we could see he was simply horrified by what he saw. Robin showed him some of the upstairs rooms, which were more nearly finished, and he seemed a bit more hopeful when he came back down.

One thing was fortunate. The kitchen had been one of the first rooms to be finished. Within a week after we got back, Dallas was able to prepare lunch and sometimes even a dinner in his newly refurbished kitchen.

On Friday, November 22, shortly after lunch, I was in my office with Ingrid going over a long list of things that we needed to do when the phone rang. It was my younger daughter calling me from St. Francis College in Pennsylvania.

"I can't believe it, Mom," she was saying, and I could tell she was crying. "I can't believe the President is dead."

I had no idea what she was talking about. We had been too busy to hook up any television sets and we hadn't thought of turning on the radio. Consequently we hadn't heard the terrible news from Dallas.

I immediately called the department and the news was confirmed. Someone got a radio and plugged it in, and in a while someone hooked up one of our portable television sets. So, like everyone else in the country, we sat stunned while the terrible events were replayed in front of our eyes.

I was numb. But suddenly it dawned on me.

"They're going to need this house," I said to Ingrid.

I left the TV set on and went to my office, already making plans in my head. I decided to concentrate on the Blair House side because Blair-Lee was still too torn up to be usable. I called in Ingrid and Dallas and gave them instructions on how to proceed and to get going at once.

I called the GSA for as many laborers and extra staff as they could spare. I made a list of what was essential. I spent hours mobilizing people for the gigantic task we had ahead of us.

Everyone I called was pleased to help, and most of them were grateful that they had something to do during this terrible time. I have never gotten such superb cooperation or such prompt service from so many busy and good people.

Several times in the late afternoon I spoke to Robin. "If you need the house," I told her, "it will be ready for you."

That evening when I got home she called me and said, "I took you at your word. Several of the Kennedys' close friends would like to come over tomorrow at about eleven-thirty before going to the White House. You're sure you can accommodate them?"

I assured her that I would be ready and we decided to serve some light refreshments to anyone who wanted them.

I had heard from Mr. West at the White House that President Johnson had invited former President Truman and his family to stay at Blair House during the days of the funeral. They were coming at about three the next afternoon. Because Mrs. Truman was not well she could not be along. Margaret Truman Daniel and her husband would be accompanying her father.

Everyone was on the job at seven the next morning. I had ordered flowers and Dallas had ordered food. He was hard at work in the kitchen when I came in.

Robin came by at nine-thirty on her way to the White House. She looked pale and shaken. The Kennedys were among her closest friends. She took one look at the disorder that was Blair House and shook her head as if to say, "You'll never manage this, Mary Edith." Then she left.

By eleven-thirty the little army of people we had assembled had managed to get the first floor completely set up. There was a table of refreshments, and parlormaids and butlers in their black and white uniforms were on hand to serve. The Nosegay had prepared several especially beautiful flower arrangements. The floors were clean, if not sparkling, and the rugs and furniture were in place.

The workmen who had accomplished this miracle were now hard at work on the second floor, where, under Ingrid's supervision, they were getting the bedrooms ready for the Truman party's arrival.

At eleven-thirty Robin and her guests appeared. She couldn't believe her eyes.

After about an hour we all went over to the White House. President Kennedy's flag-draped casket rested on a catafalque covered in black velvet and standing in the center of the room. Two lighted candles were placed at the head of the closed coffin. The honor guard stood at rigid attention at the four corners of the catafalque. With a large crowd of other visitors I walked past the coffin and said a prayer. Then I had to go back to Blair House, where there was work to be done.

As I walked back across the street I saw literally hundreds of people outside the White House fence and clustered in Lafayette Park. It was pouring, but they stood there as if somehow just being near the White House would ease their pain and grief.

A short time after I returned to Blair House a car pulled up to the front entrance and President Truman, with his two military aides and his friend Frank Gavin, got out. They were escorted by Secret Service men. After greeting them, I had their few pieces of luggage taken to their rooms.

Almost immediately visitors began to arrive to see the former President, so I put one butler in charge of Mr. Truman and his guests. Margaret Truman Daniel was expected by train at around four-thirty that same afternoon. However, there was an accident on the tracks and the train was held up. She and her husband didn't get to Blair House until seven forty-five that evening.

Late in the afternoon Robin called.

"I need some carnations," she said.

"Of course. No problem," I replied, thinking of the Nosegay's quick and reliable service.

"I don't mean just a few bouquets," Robin said. "I mean probably thousands of carnations. And they have to be red. We'll be needing them to be made into a floral arch through which the funeral procession will pass on the way to the grave site at Arlington Cemetery. I'll let you know where to have them sent."

I didn't know exactly where I would be able to get thousands of red carnations, but I knew that if anyone could help me it would be Mr. Charron of the Nosegay. He'd been president of the National Florist Telegraph Delivery Association and so knew just about everyone in the business.

I called him at home.

"Most of our carnations come from Denver," he informed me. "I'll give the wholesaler there a call."

Naturally, the minute they heard why we needed the flowers the Denver wholesalers cooperated fully. They promised to hold all the carnations they had until they heard from us.

Anyone wanting to buy a red carnation on November 23 or 24 was out of luck. Every carnation in this country was on hold in Denver. Mr. Charron was standing by in Washington ready to work all night dispatching the flowers to the people who were going to fashion them into the arch he had designed.

It was not until Sunday afternoon that word came from the White House that Mrs. Kennedy had vetoed the idea of a floral arch. She wanted to keep the ceremony simple and thought an arch of red carnations would be too showy.

So I called Mr. Charron and released the carnations. For twenty-four hours we had cornered the red carnation market.

Beginning on Saturday morning right after breakfast and for much of the day the visitors continued to pay their respects to Mr. Truman. In the afternoon, after returning from a visit to the White House, Margaret Truman Daniel asked me to get Dr. Burkley to come and check her father. She was concerned that he was overdoing it.

Dr. Burkley agreed with her, and it was decided that Mr. Truman should spend the rest of the day and the evening in bed. The former President was not a man easily kept down, but he obediently went to bed and we served him his supper there that night.

The funeral procession passed by Blair House. We stood on the steps, tears running down our cheeks. The sight of Mrs. Kennedy walking firmly, flanked by her husband's two brothers, her head held high amid all those foreign dignitaries, was heartbreaking, but I felt enormously proud of her dignity and strength.

I can still hear the mournful wail of the bagpipes that seemed to echo what all of us were feeling.

Amid all the sadness there was only one moment when I smiled. Who, I wondered, was in charge of placing the heads of state in the procession? Who had had the brilliant idea of having the more-than-six-foot-tall President de Gaulle marching alongside Emperor Haile Selassie, who came up to his belt buckle? It certainly took every inch of the straight-backed military bearing the Lion of Judah had to maintain his regal hauteur next to the tallest leader of all.

As I stood on those steps I couldn't help remembering the day —it seemed only a few months ago—when I had watched our young, handsome President running up the steps toward me, bareheaded and so very much alive, while his young, girlish-looking wife tried to keep up with him. It was hard to imagine that anything would ever be the same again.

Chapter Twelve

THE NEXT DAY, at the top of my list of things to do was the one word "rats."

General Vaughan, one of President Truman's aides, reported that the former President had seen a rat in his room during his stay with us. Of course, President Truman hadn't mentioned this to me when he left the afternoon of President Kennedy's funeral. He had returned from the graveside with Margaret and her husband, Clifton Daniel, and with former President and Mrs. Dwight D. Eisenhower. We had prepared refreshments for Mr. Truman's return, knowing that he would have someone with him. The two former Presidents visited for about an hour. Then the Eisenhowers returned to Gettysburg and Mr. Truman flew back to Independence.

Before the Daniels left to stay with friends in Washington, Margaret made a point of saying how much she had enjoyed being back in her "old room" again. But in all my years at Blair House there was never a period that was sadder than the days just following the Kennedy assassination.

Two days later it was Thanksgiving. It didn't seem that there was anything to be thankful for. I gave the staff the long weekend off. Lord knows they deserved it. But the workmen were there even on Saturday and Sunday, putting the house back into shape.

The next scheduled visit, that of Chancellor Ludwig Erhard of West Germany, had been canceled (although the Chancellor attended the funeral), but we did have a few functions planned for December.

And I simply had to solve the rat problem before then.

I met with Mr. Stanier, and we decided to mount a concerted effort, an out-and-out offensive against the invasion. The GSA put out massive amounts of poison all through the house. This seemed to get rid of the animals but created an additional problem. The rats often died in the walls, causing an awful odor that lingered for weeks.

We were preparing for the visit of President Antonio Segni of Italy in January when the smell suddenly became very prevalent. We searched everywhere but couldn't find the rat. With a heavy hand we sprayed everything with deodorant and room freshener, and by the day of the visit the odor was pretty nearly gone. But I knew this was not the way to solve our problem.

Finally I appealed to Mr. Stanier. I knew that we had to do more than just kill the rats inside the house. We had to find out where they were entering and block their route. By emphasizing the seriousness of the problem, Mr. Stanier was finally able to secure the funds with which to hire a commercial company to get rid of the rats once and for all.

Their first day on the job, the experts found the rats' entryway, and plugged it, and that was the end of that. Mr. Stanier was so pleased with our success that he hired them to check both Blair House and the White House on a monthly basis. They came regularly and their periodic inspections prevented any further trouble. Just before I left Blair House, in an economy move, their services were dispensed with. I could never understand this cut in the budget and I hope that it has by now been restored.

In turn, throughout the house many of the major things were being taken care of, but most of the small details remained to be attended to.

None of the bedroom doors had retained the little brass frames into which we placed the card with the name of the guest assigned to that room. On the third and fourth floors several light fixtures needed replacing, locks were missing on more than one or two doors, soap holders were needed in some of the bathrooms. Many of the brass door numbers, put on the doors several years before, had not been replaced. The list of things was endless.

Mrs. Lyndon Johnson, now the First Lady, came for lunch

with Robin and several other members of the Fine Arts Committee for a formal tour of the house so that she could see the progress that had been made.

Although she was an enthusiastic honorary chairman of the Fine Arts Committee, she now had so many duties as First Lady that she was unable to do much of the actual work on the committee. She will probably always be better known for what she did to help make America's landscape more beautiful. She encouraged people all over the country to plant flowers and clean up neighborhoods. To set an example for such projects elsewhere, she was responsible for many of the lovely plantings of spring flowers that bloom in Washington's parks.

As we took Mrs. Johnson on that tour of the house I was suddenly struck by the progress we had already made. Slowly the house was beginning to look like the showplace it would soon be. But I was also aware of what still remained undone. I was not prepared for Robin's idea of giving a party and tour of the house for members of the press in January. I thought she was rushing things. Only three rooms would be completely finished by then, and I didn't think the press would be able to imagine what the house would look like when finished without an idea of the overall plan.

In addition, on the same day, the Dukes were to play host at the house for the many people who had contributed to it. Not only members of the committee but the carpenters, painters, plasterers, and electricians were invited.

In spite of my misgivings the discussions and plans for these parties, which would be given back-to-back on one afternoon, continued.

And we learned that the Carnegie House would eventually be joined to Blair House to give us some much needed space. As the renovations progressed we had continued to use Carnegie House to store some of the things formerly kept in the by now demolished carriage houses.

Robin came over every day during December to take care of such chores as choosing paint and making decisions about staining the floors or colors of woodwork. In addition, she was working with *Look* magazine on an article about the house.

As Christmas approached we were very busy with all these

things, but the pervading atmosphere was still one of mourning. The shock of the assassination had not worn off. Every day we would recall happy memories from the Kennedy years. We didn't look forward to Christmas the way we had in other years, and our decorations were modest. We hung wreaths at the doors, but inside the house there were only a few bowls of holly. That Christmas was a subdued, halfhearted holiday.

Only one really bright moment stands out in my memories of that bleak time.

Fieldcrest had delivered our new bed and bath linens a few days before Christmas. There were about a dozen huge packing boxes stored in an unused bedroom on the fourth floor.

One morning I said to Ingrid, "Let's open those boxes." She knew immediately which ones I meant. We had both been dreaming about getting our hands on those linens and had often mentioned it, but there just hadn't been time.

Because I stopped to talk to someone, Ingrid got to the room first and started tearing off the wrappings. She had everything laid out on the bed when I arrived a little bit later.

I have never seen such a glorious array of linens.

There were three different sizes of towels, and bath mats, washcloths, and bath mitts in all colors that matched the bathrooms. Other boxes were filled with sheets, blanket covers, pillowcases, and both winter and summer blankets. Each piece was monogrammed with the letters *BH*.

For the Head of State's Suite there were two dozen sheets, two dozen pillowcases, six blanket covers, and three summer and three winter blankets. For the bath there were one dozen generously sized bath towels and one dozen each of fingertip towels, hand towels, and washcloths. In addition, there were six bath mitts, six bath mats, and six scatter rugs.

The same number of both bath and bed linens was meant for the Queen's Suite, again in colors matching the room. Each of the other bedrooms was also provided with as many sheets and towels as we needed.

Ingrid and I felt as if we had been let loose in a department store and told to choose the most beautiful linens they had. It was an extraordinarily generous gift.

Several months after we got the linens, King Hussein of Jordan was our guest. He inquired about the possibility of getting the same kind of towels and sheets for his palace in Amman. I understand that he subsequently had a large supply shipped to him from Fieldcrest.

By December the Blair-Lee drawing room was nearly finished. Robin and Mrs. Dillon spent a great deal of time with Mrs. Archibald M. Brown of McMillen, Inc., the New York decorators, putting furniture into place and making notes of what still needed to be found. Nearly each time they came they brought with them another lovely piece to add to the room, which was obviously going to be one of the finest in the house.

I was meeting some of the new people at the White House. Toward the end of the year Robin brought over Bess Abell, Mrs. Johnson's social secretary, and Liz Carpenter, her press secretary. We had a quiet lunch together to talk about the renovation project and gave them a tour of the house. They brought with them a large manila envelope in which I found a framed portrait of President and Mrs. Johnson. The photo was meant for the table in the Blair drawing room from which we had taken a similar portrait of President and Mrs. Kennedy on November 25.

For me the arrival of the Johnson photo marked the beginning of Lyndon Baines Johnson's administration . . . and the end of the Kennedy era.

Chapter Thirteen

As 1964 BEGAN WE were in a mad scramble to have at least the second floor of Blair House finished in time for the press reception and party for the workmen and the committee members. The event was scheduled for January 9. Everyone worked nearly around the clock to get things into shape.

Lord & Taylor was in charge of redoing the Queen's Suite. Mr. Raymond Waldron, the store's decorator, had selected the furnishings and was ready to bring them in just as soon as the painting was done, the wallpaper was hung, and the scraping and refinishing of the floors was completed. We worked very hard to meet the January 9 deadline, but it seemed that there was always one more thing to do.

Every day contributions poured in. The Singer sewing machine arrived. It was the very latest model, and we were promised that an instructor would soon appear to help Ingrid master its intricacies. A new freezer was due on January 6.

Workmen were unpacking mirrors and glass table tops, which we had put into storage until we could restore them to their proper places. The Library of Congress returned the framed prints of early Washington that it had been keeping for us until the walls along the Blair-Lee staircase were repainted. Hanging the prints in an ascending row from the first to the fourth floor was tricky. It took hours of painstaking work and much trial and error before it was done.

Mrs. Edgar W. Garbisch, the former Bernice Chrysler, whose father had founded the automotive company bearing his name, donated ninety pieces of Lowestoft. Since they bore her initial—

B for Beatrice—and were decorated in a blue that matched the Blair House Lowestoft, they were perfect for the Blair-Lee dining room. We wanted to display part of the collection on open shelves in niches on either side of the fireplace, but we didn't have enough stands. I tried everyplace I could think of but just couldn't get enough holders of any one sort.

Finally Mr. McDonald at Galt & Bro., Inc., Washington's oldest jewelry store and one of its finest, offered to lend us thirty-six of the holders he used for window and store displays. A few weeks later he called to say he had replaced the holders and we could keep the ones he had lent us. They still hold Mrs. Garbisch's plates in the dining room, standing in the niches just the way they were placed there by Mrs. C. Douglas Dillon and Mrs. Harcourt Amory of the Fine Arts Committee in the early days of 1964.

The day of the reception everything appeared to be in order. Though the new table in the Blair-Lee dining room was set up just minutes before the guests arrived, it looked very festive.

People were just coming through the front door when I decided to take a quick peek at the Queen's Suite, where Mr. Waldron was working on the last little details.

I found the poor man nearly buried in a sea of packing boxes, paper, and string that flowed out of the room and onto the landing.

I quickly called James and stationed him on the backstairs. Then I stood at the top of the landing and began throwing boxes and tissue paper and string down to him. Several times he had to duck but he managed to avoid getting hit and to hide his obvious shock at the sight of this madwoman hurling paper. In turn he took the boxes and threw them farther down into the basement. We simply had to get the debris out of sight.

By now the press had assembled in the drawing room; after a briefing from Robin they began to tour the house. We confined them to the first and second floors, but there was plenty to see and so many questions that some of the press people were still drinking tea when the committee-workmen reception began.

Mrs. Johnson, Robin, and Mrs. Dean Rusk formed the receiving line greeting the guests. It was especially nice to see so many of the people who had done the hard work on the house go through that line with their wives to receive thanks for all they had accomplished.

The Blair-Lee dining room caused quite a lot of comment. It had been transformed into a Georgian paneled room through the generosity of three brothers, George, Harry, and Congressman Peter Frelinghuysen. The paneling came from the Frelinghuysen family home in Morristown, New Jersey, and had been carefully refitted into the dining room. The funds to transport the lovely old wood from New Jersey had been donated by the Honorable William Clayton, former undersecretary of state.

The press party was followed in one week by the arrival of President Antonio Segni of Italy and Mrs. Segni, President Johnson's first state visitors. This was also our first visit since the redecoration of the second floor.

Look magazine was still in the process of taking photos for its article. The *Look* photographer, Fred Maroon, received permission to take pictures during the visit of President Segni, the very first time such permission had been granted to any photographer. Mr. Maroon had been thoroughly briefed about our procedures during a visit and had promised to use tact and discretion in order not to interfere with our visitors' privacy or the smooth running of the visit.

Two days before President Segni was to arrive, it snowed hard enough to cover the ground completely, providing a beautiful setting for the exterior photographs.

The snow was so deep by Monday, the day before the visit, that both Ingrid and I stayed overnight for fear that we might not be able to make it in from our homes the next morning. We spent the evening doing all sorts of little necessary things we usually saved for the morning of a visit, such as inserting name cards into the card holders on the bedroom doors and distributing invitations and room assignments to each room. I made and posted menus and other information in the pantry for the staff.

James was mopping the entrance hall every half hour because the embassy officials, who arrived all morning long, before President Segni appeared, tracked in so much snow. But inside the house fourteen flower arrangements helped to dispel some of the winter gloom.

Mr. Trobiner of the District of Columbia was waiting inside to present the keys to the city to our guest, and marines in long coats over dress uniforms waited outside in the snow.

When the guests finally arrived, they spent some time milling about in the entrance hall, and after President and Mrs. Johnson departed for the White House we had a small reception to warm up the thoroughly chilled group.

After President and Mrs. Segni had been shown to their rooms, I stopped on the first floor to chat with some of the U.S. officials reluctant to go out in the snow. A few minutes later the butler assigned to distribute the more than sixty pieces of luggage the Italians had brought with them came in very upset and angry.

"I don't see how we're going to manage," he said; "the Italian security men seem to be very jittery about extra people in the house and they've sent away all those luggage handlers that had been sent over to help. They're planning to distribute the luggage themselves and they don't even know where the rooms are, much less who gets what."

With two butlers and two housemen (by then I had finally persuaded the people in charge of the budget that I simply had to have two housemen) and some of our own security people, I finally got the baggage distributed and the Italian security people calmed down. As the butler had reported, they were jittery and no help at all when it came to getting the luggage out. Mostly they created noise and nerves where calm and quiet efficiency were called for.

We were coming into a time when security was getting to be increasingly important. I understood that these people had the awful responsibility of guarding the very lives of their heads of state, and I could see that they often erred on the side of being overcautious. We had similar problems on other visits, but I found our own security people could calm down their colleagues since they shared the difficult job.

There was to be a luncheon at the State Department, and Mrs. Rusk and Mrs. Duke had sent their luncheon clothes over earlier and were in my room changing.

I thought to myself that if we ever got around to enlarging the house we ought to set one room aside just for that purpose.

There were the usual last-minute changes during the Segni visit: a sudden "working breakfast" for sixteen, a more or less impromptu press conference for fifteen that turned out to attract forty-five, and so on. But we had gotten used to swinging with these punches and were prepared for anything.

In addition, Fred Maroon was everywhere, trying to be unobtrusive while taking photographs. Even after the party left on the sixteenth there were more photos to be taken. Mrs. Stewart Udall was being photographed in the library, and Mrs. Rusk and Mrs. Willard Wirtz had their pictures taken in the house in the afternoon after the Segnis took their leave.

Our next guests were Prime Minister and Mrs. Lester Pearson of Canada, here for a working visit that included the signing of two agreements between our two countries. One was for the establishment of an international park at Campobello, the summer estate of President Roosevelt. The other was the Columbia River treaty, which was signed by Secretary Rusk and his Canadian counterpart, Hon. Paul Martin, Secretary of State for External Affairs.

A few days after the Canadian visit, former Ambassador (to Great Britain) and Mrs. Winthrop Aldrich and their daughter came over to see how we were progressing on the redecorating of the Blair-Lee study—often called the President's study because President Truman had used it as his office while he stayed at Blair House. The Aldriches had donated silk damask for the walls and drapes, a double pedestal desk, two leather-covered chairs, and several small pieces for this room.

Although the furniture was not yet in place, the damask had been hung on the walls. It was an exact duplicate of the deep green silk that had given the White House Green Room its name. Originally Mrs. Kennedy had sent over the fabric from that room when she removed it as part of her White House redecoration. But unfortunately the silk had split apart with age and could not be used. The firm of Scalamandré of New York had made the original damask and had duplicated it exactly for us. It arrived from New York in enormous bolts. I had figured out precisely how much we would need to cover the walls, upholster a sofa, and make drapes for the windows. I worried for days that we might have made a mistake in the complicated computations, but everything worked out all right and the Aldriches were delighted.

We were constantly receiving beautiful antiques, lovely fabrics, and decorative pieces of all sorts. But we also appreciated the more practical gift of a much needed Speed Queen washer and dryer, which were quickly installed.

Upstairs in the library Mrs. Udall was working with Mr. Goff of the Library of Congress, selecting books from our collection that were worth keeping and sending others off to be stored. This made way for the many volumes that had been contributed and were just waiting to be put on the shelves. Mrs. Arthur Goldberg, wife of the Associate Justice of the Supreme Court, had designed a special Blair House bookplate to be inserted into each book on our shelves.

The cabinets in the library were made of beautiful wood intricately carved. They lined the walls between the windows and the fireplace. The library, a perfectly proportioned room of generous size, was set off with a rug that had been specially designed to draw attention to its scale. The deep red rug had a border in lighter shades of the same color. Mrs. Averell Harriman was going to provide sheet curtains and new drapes for this room, but except for a few accent pieces, we were going to retain most of the original furniture.

A marble bust of Francis Blair had stood on a marble pillar, and another of his son Montgomery as a young boy, on the mantel. Mr. Keith Irving, the decorator in charge of the room, installed three plaster busts, of Washington, Jefferson, and Lincoln, and banished the Blair family to another location.

In February I was invited to a White House diplomatic reception. I received hundreds of invitations every year to all sorts of events, and although I was always pleased to have been included I just couldn't go to all of them. I did try to accept White House invitations whenever possible, however, and on this occasion I got to dance with Washington's most sought-after dancing partner, the President.

The next day the newspapers were calling to ask me how I felt about dancing with the President, was he a good dancer, and other weighty questions of that sort. I couldn't really tell them if he was a good dancer or not. The idea of dancing with the President had me dancing on air, I just followed his lead, and before I knew it, the music had ended and I was back at the side of the room talking to Robin. It was really a great treat for me and something I still tell my grandchildren about.

Chapter Fourteen

❦ ON THE EVENING of February 12, 1964, during a dinner at
Blair House that Secretary Rusk was hosting for Sir Alec
Douglas-Home, Prime Minister of Great Britain, the phone rang
continuously. Several of the guests were called away from the
table, and at one point Assistant Secretary Phillips Talbot and
McGeorge Bundy from the White House came over to talk to
the entire group.

Something was certainly going on, and several of the dinner
guests continued discussing whatever it was until late in the evening. Although I had security clearance I never did find out
what was happening.

In my years at Blair House I decided that the less I knew
about matters of secrecy the better. Most of the time I didn't
bother to find out the facts, even though I could sense there was
something top-secret in the wind. Frankly, I just didn't have the
time for such things.

However, along with everyone else I was aware of the need
for security. After the assassination of President Kennedy everyone was more conscious than before that protection was important for our guests.

Along those lines we were installing bulletproof glass in the
windows of the front bedrooms. Several companies were bidding
for the job and one had actually installed its glass so that it
could be tested.

Leo Crampsey, a Department of State security officer who
had been a football player, was given the job of lobbing a
dummy grenade at the window to see if the glass would hold.

We all stood anxiously around the sidewalk in front of the house while he raised his mighty arm and threw. The grenade rose in the air, hit the pane of glass, and amid the unmistakable sound of glass breaking, kept right on going until it landed smack in the middle of the bed. That particular kind of glass was not installed in our windows.

My old friend and associate James Stanier was transferred away from his Blair House duties that March and we were very sorry to see him go. Before he left he arranged for fresh sod to be laid in our back garden and created a walk across the rear of the house. Before the visit of King Hussein of Jordan in April we planned to get the front walk in shape as well.

King Hussein stayed for two days and was out for all his meals except for one scheduled luncheon that he gave for members of Congress. This was a relatively simple visit, since all the guests were men, but I have never seen a group more passionate about shopping. They had much more luggage when they left than when they arrived. Among the things they took back with them was a large supply of Chesterfield cigarettes, which I had been asked to get for them. I bought out the local drugstore and ended up with dozens of cartons, which I packed to go back to Jordan.

In April, at the invitation of President Johnson, former President Truman was at Blair House overnight. He had come for the annual Gridiron Club dinner given by the Washington press corps. In addition to good food, the dinner always features a song and dance performance that gently and not so gently ribs Washington's famous people.

Mr. Truman arrived on Saturday. Our regular butlers were not available, so I hired a butler with the usual security clearance. He couldn't have been a security risk since the poor fellow turned out to be almost totally deaf. Luckily I discovered quickly that he couldn't even hear the front door bell. During the entire visit the parlormaid or I had to be nearby, ready to open the door for any callers.

Mr. Truman followed his usual routine, rising early on Sunday morning for one of his famous morning walks. He was accompanied by a small group from the press and was hailed by passersby who were thrilled to see the former President striding by in the manner that had become familiar to everyone all over the country. When he was recognized by people who called, "Hello, Mr. President," or "How are you, Harry?" he would stop and shake hands and chat with them for a few minutes.

Then he came back, had a leisurely breakfast, and left almost immediately for the trip back to Independence. Since it was Sunday the front gate was locked as soon as he left, and a small staff was tidying things up inside when all of a sudden the side door bell rang. Because I was in my office I was closest to the door. I went to see who it could possibly be at that time of day on Sunday. I opened the door and there stood President Truman. He had come back to use the bathroom. I showed him to the elevator and Rigoberto accompanied him upstairs to the room he had vacated only about a half an hour before.

When he came back down, President Truman apologized and said he was sorry to have been "such a nuisance." I, in turn, apologized for the locked front gate. Graciously he said he didn't mind using the side door at all. It saved him from walking up the front steps. But we never again locked the front gate after a departing visitor until we were sure they arrived at the airport.

In May Mr. Truman was back again, this time for a round of festivities in honor of his eightieth birthday. His schedule would have exhausted a much younger man. He was to be honored by the National Press Club, at a Masonic dinner that followed a reception at the Austrian Embassy, and by breakfast at the Capitol given by the Senate. When he was not off at a party somewhere he was hard at work with a secretarial staff in his old study on the Blair-Lee side of the house.

We had a lavish birthday cake for him and he received hundreds of gifts, telegrams, and masses of flowers. Photographers were constantly arriving to take his photograph. Through it all, Mr. Truman was smiling and cheerful and didn't seem the least tired.

The former tenant of Blair House stayed in his old room and told me how much he loved the house. He also kidded me about the rat he had seen on his visit in 1963. I was still embarrassed about it, but he took it as good-naturedly as he seemed to take just about anything.

Our next visitors came from the new African nation of
Burundi. This turned out to be the most confused visit of my entire career at Blair House. Since no one could tell us how large a
group to expect or who was included, we had no way of making
room assignments until the first day of the visit.

No one spoke a word of English and our French interpreter
didn't arrive until everyone had left for lunch.

The same day, while His Majesty King Mwambutsa IV was
still at the White House having lunch, Robin came back to Blair
House with the Burundi chief of staff, a Frenchwoman named
Miss Villacourt. An hour or so later Ambassador Duke arrived
from the White House with the King.

All of a sudden we heard loud shouts in French coming from
Miss Villacourt's room. It turned out that she had locked herself
in. All Blair House doors have a lock equipped with a lever that
is almost invisible unless you know where to look for it. This
lever, when moved into place, slides an extra bolt in the lock,
preventing the door from being opened from the outside even
with a key. Miss Villacourt was screaming so loudly, in French,
that we had a hard time getting her attention. Finally one of the
butlers was able to explain to her how to move the lever that
would open the door. She emerged a bit shaken. But later that
afternoon she managed to do it again.

Although I had prepared lunch for the members of the party
who wouldn't be going to the White House, not a single person
stayed to eat it. I never did find out where they all went.

That evening the King was host at a reception at the Shoreham Hotel in honor of President Johnson. Of course, the entire
staff went along. The King returned to Blair House by about
seven o'clock and went up to his room for a short time before is-
suing instructions for all the members of his party to return to
Blair House immediately. This was all highly irregular because
the Burundi ambassador had arranged a formal dinner for the
King and the ranking members of the party at the Shoreham.
For some obscure reason the King apparently wasn't planning to
be there, and he made it clear that he had no intention of spending the evening alone at Blair House.

After much telephoning back and forth and strong resistance
from the staff, Miss Villacourt and one of the aides returned to

Blair House. She looked as if she wanted to slug the King and marched upstairs to her room. The aide went to his room. The King, who had been waiting downstairs for them, went up to *his* room. In about an hour all three came down and asked that I reserve a table for three at the Shoreham restaurant.

I got Lou Deaner to call the maître d' and as far as I knew they left. A few minutes later, however, the aide came downstairs: he'd somehow managed to be left behind. Although I didn't think he wanted to go to the hotel, he seemed rather miffed about it all. In the end our translator and I had dinner with him. A few stragglers came back from the hotel just about then and they joined us at the buffet.

The King and Miss Villacourt returned around midnight. By then, in ones and twos, the rest of the group came back and everyone settled in for the night.

The next day saw the same kind of disorganized chaos, but finally the entire group left for the airport and New York.

I can't remember a more hectic visit. But another time a group of overseas visitors caused me a different kind of concern when they arrived.

Our official visitor and his party had stopped off in France on their way to the United States. There one of his aides had made the acquaintance of some Frenchwomen and two of these ladies had followed the party to New York, where they spent a few days before coming to Washington. Just before they were due to arrive I had been warned by our security man to expect this unofficial addition to the group.

Sure enough, on the day of arrival, just after the head of state left for lunch, the two ladies appeared at Blair House, were admitted by the visiting aide, and came through the door as if they were authorized members of the group.

Percy, the butler at the door that day, saw the aide escort the ladies to his bedroom and alerted me that they were there. He knew that women who were not members of the official party were not permitted in men's bedrooms.

By that time the aide had left for an official luncheon, so I went up to his bedroom and found the two ladies making themselves comfortable. In a firm but pleasant tone of voice I asked the ladies who they were and what they were doing in the aide's bedroom. They replied that they were friends of the aide and that he had asked them to wait in his room until he returned.

I told them politely that our male guests did not entertain ladies in their bedrooms and invited them downstairs for some tea. Then I left and asked the butler stationed at the foot of the stairs to let me know what they did.

A short time later Percy reported that they had come downstairs to the drawing room, where he had served them tea. A few minutes later they left, and we never saw them again but I heard that they followed the group back to New York and were seen there.

Although they used commercial transportation and never traveled on the plane carrying the official party, they seem to have been hired (perhaps by the aide) to be some sort of jet-set camp followers for the group. I do know for a fact that the head of state never knew anything about this colorful, clandestine addition to his entourage.

Blair House is always the scene of many contrasts. Our next guest, the President of Ireland, Eamon de Valera, had an extremely well organized schedule although he was almost constantly on the go.

The President's visit had been scheduled during President Kennedy's administration and I know that the President would have enjoyed Mr. de Valera, who spoke so often and with such warmth of President Kennedy's visit to Ireland during his trip to Europe. It was obvious that he took some pride in the fact that we had had a President of Irish descent.

In spite of his heavy schedule, President de Valera took time out to call on Mrs. Kennedy, who was living in Georgetown at the time. He was honored at a dinner given by Archbishop O'Boyle and he had dozens of visits from old personal friends from all over the country who had traveled to Washington to see him. The President's personal assistant, Miss Marie O'Kelley (she showed me how to spell it in Gaelic, Maire Ni Cheallaigh), was concerned about her eighty-one-year-old boss's long hours. She had tried to get him to slow down, she told me, but he loved being in America and simply refused to shorten his schedule. I'll rest when I get home, he told her.

President de Valera was one of our most popular guests. You couldn't help liking him. When he left he asked every member of the staff up to his suite and thanked each of them personally for the care he had received.

The Irish visit was followed by Prime Minister Levi Eshkol and a group from Israel.

Of course, for Israeli visitors we served kosher food, but on this visit our lives were relatively uncomplicated since we needed to serve only breakfast. However, the visit taught me an important lesson about appearances.

Mr. Eshkol held a press conference during his stay with us. As usual, we prepared refreshments for the reporters. In addition to coffee, tea, and soft drinks and liquor, we had trays of open-faced sandwiches. I had made sure that we were going to use margarine instead of butter to spread under the roast beef, according to the Jewish dietary laws, which forbid mixing meat and milk. But one of the Israeli press attachés pointed out to me that margarine looks exactly like butter and might give rise to a rumor that would embarrass his government. We solved this dilemma diplomatically by having a tray of meats, a dish of clearly marked margarine, and a basket of bread so that people could make their own sandwiches. And that procedure became standard whenever we had Israeli guests.

A few days later I got a call from Bess Abell. Mrs. Johnson was going to represent her husband at the dedication of the Truman Library in Independence, and I was asked to make a suggestion about something she could take as a gift from the government. The dedication was the very next day, so I tried to concentrate on what might be appropriate. I thought hard, but the only idea I came up with was the presidential flag that flew at Blair House while Mr. Truman was in residence here. To my surprise, everyone thought this was an inspiration, so we unearthed the flag and had it boxed and it went along with Mrs. Johnson the next day.

On August 6, just before we closed the house for that summer's round of renovations, U Thant, the Secretary General of the United Nations, arrived to spend a night with us. Mr. Ralph J. Bunche, undersecretary for special political affairs of the UN, and Mrs. Bunche and our United Nations ambassador, Adlai E. Stevenson, came along with the group.

They were all invited that evening to dinner at the White House and we were going to serve cocktails at Blair House before they left.

It was suggested that Mr. Stevenson stay at Blair House, too, and although that hadn't been planned we certainly had lots of room, so I showed him to one of the second-floor bedrooms.

He then asked for his luggage and I had to tell him that it had been sent to the home of Senator Warren Magnuson, where he had been planning to stay. I assured Mr. Stevenson that it would be no trouble to have the luggage picked up, but he decided to go along with the plans as made and left, promising to come back that evening for cocktails.

At about seven-thirty everyone assembled in the Blair drawing room. Cocktails were just about over when Robin called me over to her.

"I've just noticed that Ambassador Stevenson seems to be missing a button on his evening shirt. Do you think you have one to match it?"

We both went over to where Mr. Stevenson was standing, completely unaware that he was about to be ambushed by two ladies bent on offering their help.

Before he could say more than a word I had produced a short stud that I thought might fit the bill, but it didn't. So we dragged the poor man off to another room where Ingrid waited with sewing kit and button box in hand.

When he was finally permitted to speak, the ambassador said, "Just a minute. I've got the button right here. It only just popped off."

In short order the shirt front was again pristine and the man who had become famous for having a hole in his shoe, a small imperfection that he used brilliantly though not successfully during his campaign for President, was once more restored to perfection.

The tiny drama caused all the other guests to check on their own clothes. Sure enough, one of the ladies confessed to some trouble with a strap. A safety pin made short work of that problem. It was like a family gathering by the end, and when they all went off to the White House a few minutes later, everyone was in a jolly mood.

And now Blair House was officially closed for the summer so our redecorating could begin again.

Chapter Fifteen

By 1964 WE HAD made a lot of progress in our renovation. The President's study and the Blair drawing room and dining room were completely redecorated. It had proved easier to get donations for these first-floor rooms, since they were seen by more people. On the second floor, only the Queen's Suite had been finished.

Now the Lincoln room on the first floor was to be redone. On the second floor the Head of State's Suite, the library adjoining it, and the bedrooms we called by the numbers 21 and 27 were slated for renovation.

Outside of some minor repairs no further work was scheduled for the time being on the third and fourth floors.

Three different decorating firms were involved in these plans: McMillen, Inc., under the direction of Mrs. Archibald Brown, had the overall responsibility for any rooms for which no specific decorator had been chosen by the Fine Arts Committee. At this time, that meant Room 21, the head of state's bedroom, the Blair-Lee drawing room, and the Blair-Lee dining room. *House and Garden* magazine's decorating editor, Mr. Arthur Leaman, was in charge of Room 27. Mr. Irving, Mrs. Harriman's decorator, was still working on the library.

It was my job to coordinate these projects and to see that all the work was done in some sort of order. It was a terribly complex assignment.

Some of the furniture had been sent to New York for reupholstering; some was done in Washington. The fabric came to the upholsterers from a variety of sources. In some cases I had to send it from Blair House.

Mrs. Willard Wirtz had come up with the imaginative idea of having people from the local Goodwill Industries install the needlepoint chair covers that had by now been finished by the wives of President Kennedy's Cabinet. Under each chair we affixed a brass plate with the name of the particular woman who had worked that chair's cover. Since the chairs had identical seats, this was the only way to give each of the women credit for her work. As far as I know, the plaques are still there.

I had to know where every piece of furniture or every yard of fabric was at all times. I was also in charge of scheduling the workmen so that the jobs were completed in a sensible sequence. The inside of the fireplaces had to be finished before the painters got to the woodwork, for instance, and the marble men who took down the old mantels had to have a place to put them until they could be reinstalled.

We had a deadline, as usual. On October 5 we were expecting that fall's first visitor, President Diosdado Macapagal of the Philippines.

All summer long we were busy with the renovation. Robin stopped by frequently to see how things were going; there were new, unforeseen problems nearly every day.

But little by little the work was done and we had the enormous satisfaction of seeing the rooms emerge into an elegance and authenticity born out of careful work and a scrupulous attention to details.

The Lincoln room was the first to be completed. The AFL-CIO had contributed the funds to redo the room. Since most of the furniture was going to remain where it was, the money was spent on other things in the room.

The color scheme came from new silk wallpaper, which was striped and flocked in two shades of beige and a rich gold. Beautiful silk draperies in the lightest of these shades were made for the window and set off with an ornate silk paisley braid-trimmed valance. The valance picked up the color of the ruby glass chandelier, one of the original Blair treasures. The ceiling in this room is about thirteen feet high, which made the window treatment an important focal point.

A new handmade Portuguese rug in colors suitable to the room was placed on the floor. The sofa and two of the chairs were upholstered in a light gold sculptured velvet to harmonize with the gold in the wallpaper. An antique clock and two hurricane lamp candle holders were placed on the mantel.

The fireplace in the Lincoln room has an eighteenth-century mantel, and one of the original Blair pieces of furniture, also from that century, was the desk Francis Preston Blair used when the Lincoln room was his office. President Lincoln used the desk on several of his visits to Blair House, and it was in this room that Blair offered General Robert E. Lee command of the Union Army at the request of the President.

In addition to the oil painting of General Lee that had been donated by the Daughters of the Confederacy, this room contains several other interesting pieces of art. The pen-and-ink drawing of President Lincoln is inscribed "Yours Truly, A. Lincoln," and there is a group portrait of Lincoln and his Cabinet.

The Blair family is represented by a double portrait of Francis Preston Blair and his wife—he is seated, she stands behind his chair.

The door to the Lincoln room, installed when the house was built, had a very large brass lock and a brass key about six inches long. Most of the first-floor rooms had the same sort of splendid hardware.

By this time also the Blair-Lee drawing room had been completely and dramatically transformed with furnishings donated by Secretary of the Treasury and Mrs. C. Douglas Dillon.

The focal point of this handsome room was its unusual wallpaper. Mrs. Dillon had discovered the lovely two-hundred-year-old Chinese wallpaper at the Douglas Gracie importing firm in New York. It had been peeled from the walls of an English house called Ashburton Place. On a green background, variations of the tree of life design had been hand-painted in soft colors, so that beautifully painted birds and flowers covered the walls. To hang this fabulous paper, McMillen had brought in a paper hanger who was also an artist. This was vital, since there was not quite enough paper to cover all the walls completely. The artist painted a matching mural that extended all around the room for three feet above the baseboard. It also covered the heating units in the walls and was so cleverly done, with the colors so perfectly matched, that the heating units look like part of the wall.

Heavy damask drapes in a slightly lighter green were hung at the windows, and valances in a pagoda shape echoed the oriental feeling of the room.

There was quite a discussion and much wringing of hands before it was decided to bleach the oriental rugs Mrs. Dillon had donated. Oriental-rug experts grew pale along with the rugs at the thought, but when the job was finished, those who had encouraged the bleaching were vindicated. The rugs looked perfect and didn't clash with the busy design and bright green of the paper.

Two beautiful sofas, a dainty settee, and a number of tables, all antiques, were brought in. Several lamps with oriental bases were placed around the room. The sofas were upholstered in damask in a shade slightly darker than the wallpaper, while the other pieces were covered in appropriate matching or blending colors. Beautifully framed oval mirrors were hung over the two mantels and two old candelabra were placed at the ends of each mantel. A centerpiece of antique Chinese porcelain stood on each mantel and Chinese decorative pieces were placed on several occasional tables.

This drawing room was the only room in Blair House in which there were no original Blair pieces. So when it was nearly finished the decorators took a bench from one of the other rooms to place in front of the fireplace, and a library table from another room was put in back of the sofa. We often placed a large bouquet on this table.

The other room that had been completed was Room 21, which had been Mrs. Truman's bedroom during the First Family's three-year stay in the house. All the furniture was part of the legacy of original Blair family heirlooms, which we were lucky to have, but the room desperately needed new draperies, hangings for the four-poster bed, a rug, and general overall brightening up.

An Ohio couple who wished to remain anonymous provided the funds for refurbishing Room 21.

The new bed hangings and window drapes were made of

cream-colored wool serge. The valances were hand-embroidered in a design featuring leaves and plants in various colors, with accents provided by bright red embroidered strawberries. The curtains were finished off with colorful fringe, and the bed hangings were lined in a chintz that included some of the colors found in the embroidery.

The quilted bedspread was made from the same chintz. A new easy chair and matching ottoman were brought in and upholstered in a blue fabric with flecks of color. The room's original furnishings included an old tambour desk and chair, which received a new cover; the old lamps were given new shades. Two of these lamps stood on either side of the bed.

Pale beige wall-to-wall carpet was installed. The donors sent eight old English bone china plates and stands for the mantel. An interesting old lintel clock remained on the mantel where it had always stood, but the historical prints that had been hanging on the walls for years were rehung to make them more decorative.

Because of the way the furniture had been replaced in the room, the door could no longer open as it had and so it had to be taken off its hinges and reversed.

The room had been declared finished when Mrs. Clark Clifford found a small handwoven bedspread that nearly matched the embroidery of the curtains in the room. It was cleaned and brought in to be used as a throw on the easy chair. Several years later, when James Symington was chief of protocol, his wife, Sylvia, made needlepoint luggage straps using the strawberry design for the rack in the room.

What we now call the head of state's bedroom had been President Truman's when he lived at Blair House. The massive maple furniture—a four-poster bed, a desk, a beautiful highboy, and several tables—were probably early-nineteenth-century. The room has a handsome fireplace and mantel. Everything was rather large and masculine in scale. Before the end of my tenure the room underwent further changes. But at this juncture the refurbishing was minimal.

New draperies, new hangings for the bed, a new bedspread, and a new rug were obtained, and several of the chairs were reupholstered. The furniture itself was in excellent condition and was retained.

Ambassador and Mrs. Duke and Mr. and Mrs. Harcourt Amory provided the funds for refurbishing this room.

The new rug was similar to the one in the Lincoln room; it had a black background with a beige and red design. The room had traditionally been done in reds. The draperies and hangings were off-white in a weave that resembled crewel embroidery, with red and white ball fringe trim around the hems. The backdrop and hangings on the bed were lined in red to match the color in the rug. The window valance was off-white and was also decorated with fringe. And a chair and a masculine-looking chaise were upholstered in a fabric similar to that used for the drapes, except that it had a red design woven in. The desk chair and one other were upholstered in this fabric.

The lamps all got new shades and a new table lamp made to resemble an oil lamp was added. The bowl of this lovely lamp was made of ruby glass. The old chandelier, which was really too small for the scale of the room, was removed.

On the pale ivory walls there was a series of prints of the Presidents of the United States. A presidential seal in needlepoint and an old barometer completed the wall decorations. An old and valuable clock stood on the mantelpiece and several precious old Bennington pottery pieces were on the highboy and the mantel.

The library walls were painted red, the bookcases white, and the ceiling set off with fine blue lines to delineate its original lines. The furniture and the red rug that were in the room were not removed and the original chandelier also remained, but its chain was covered in red velvet.

Against the wall, above the level of the bookcases that line the room, several portraits of Presidents on loan from the National Portrait Gallery were hung.

New curtains of red and beige chintz with blue piping and matching valances were installed at the windows. The floor-length curtains were tied back with matching strips of cloth and did not traverse. The same chintz was used to upholster several of the chairs in the room and new chair covers of blue Naugahyde were added to the two Queen Anne chairs. The beige velvet sofa and two matching chairs were original Blair House pieces. A Chippendale chair by the desk had been upholstered earlier in a lovely needlepoint that was an exact duplicate of its original Blair House design.

All in all, the library is a very imposing room. Its large Chippendale desk sits in the center of the room, facing the entrance. A fireplace and several chairs are one end of this long room, the sofa and its two matching chairs at the other. Original tables and lamps are placed around the room and two lamps with new shades stand on the desk. It is a masculine and richly colorful room.

In Room 27 Arthur Leaman had kept as many of the good original pieces as he could. The graceful sleigh bed and a large Victorian chest made of matching wood were the eye-catchers here. New wallpaper of deep beige striped alternately with green and blue paisley was hung on the walls. The bathroom walls were painted a deep matching beige, and stripes of the paisley were used in the corners and for a ceiling border. A similar border was used in the bedroom. The windows were hung with deep beige silk to the sill, with draperies of the same material tied back and finished off with silk fringe in a darker shade.

The bathroom window had a single swatch of material tied to the side in a very effective, unusual treatment. The bath linens in this room were green and blue, matching the touches of paisley.

Mr. Leaman had brought in a heavy Victorian desk, which he supplied with a group of current books, and he added some masculine-looking bric-a-brac to the room.

The desk chair got a new green cut-velvet seat. An antique stand stood near the bed to receive the bedspread at night. A large leather chair and ottoman in what Mr. Leaman called a "nothing" color were put in the room "just for sheer comfort." Behind the chair stood a little brass "nothing" lamp that could be turned every way for reading comfort. Mr. Leaman said he could just imagine a tired diplomat collapsing in that chair after a hard day of official duties. I can testify that that is just what happened.

On the floor in front of the bed, on top of the soft beige wall-to-wall carpet, there was an antique needlepoint rug done in rich, dark colors. The bedspread and pillow sham were of heavy quilted cotton lined with green. The bedside table was small and also Victorian, as were most of the furnishings in this room.

The desk and table lamp had glass bases resembling a bowl set in brass. On the wall, near the door, there was a six-foot-long bellpull embroidered with beads and needlepoint in colors close to the greens and blues in the wallpaper. The antique bellpull was handmade in Czechoslovakia.

Two decorative oval plaques of marble were hung one on each side of the chest. The ceiling light was replaced with an ornate Victorian chandelier in black and gold. A brass planter containing real ferns stood on the windowsill.

Today this room remains exactly as this decorator set it up. The window hangings have been replaced once or twice over the years, but the same fabric has been used. The bedspread was also replaced once, but we were able to find something very similar. Room 27 was used for nearly every visit when I was at Blair House, usually by someone very close to the head of state, such as a private secretary. Once or twice the son of the head of state has been put there.

While we prepared for our next visit, photographer Tom Leonard of *House and Garden* was working every day on the article featuring the house which would soon appear. He carefully stepped around the workmen to photograph what had been completed. For every finished room he ordered flower arrangements, and occasionally I was asked to do a bouquet. The last room, Room 21, was not completed until October 2, just three days before the Philippine visit.

Finished or not, these rooms had to be in shape for our visitors. Telephones had to be reinstalled and TV sets replaced on their stands, the rooms had to have lights, and the plumbing in the bathrooms had to be working even if all the furniture had not yet arrived. And where a table or a chair was still missing, I had to substitute another for the comfort of our guests.

The Philippine visit went off smoothly in spite of all the behind-the-scenes juggling. President and Mrs. Macapagal were escorted to Blair House in a small motorcade. During the visit Mrs. Macapagal wore a succession of beautiful Philippine dresses. These traditional dresses hang straight down without a waist and have a special short, open, puffed sleeve that stands out gracefully from the shoulders. Mrs. Macapagal had slippers to match each of her many dresses. Her first day's outfit was pink and white. During her stay I counted twelve different colors. When not on official business, by contrast, the First Lady wore simple tailored suits.

Mrs. Santos, her personal assistant, arrived with the party but was never seen again until the day they left, since she stayed in her room for the entire three days. Even her meals were sent up to her. I couldn't decide why she never emerged. Perhaps she was guarding the First Lady's things.

The minute the visit was over we went back to decorating. Quite a lot of furniture had been delivered during the visit and was now stacked in the basement and in unused rooms on the upper floors.

Mrs. Udall was proceeding with her project of placing a collection of American Indian art on the second-floor landing of Blair House. This landing was large and square, almost the size of a small room, and had an unusual large window of frosted glass, three-sided, with curved tops. The center pane was higher than the other two. The landing made a beautiful background for paintings, pottery, and baskets, each item done by a master artist of an Indian nation. A visit to the Indian art collection at the Department of the Interior would give one an idea of the beauty of the American Indian art at Blair House, since our collection was on loan from the department. The landing was destroyed later when Blair House was joined to the house next door.

Just about this time, several large cartons arrived, and inside, carefully wrapped, was a collection of English porcelain birds of all kinds, fourteen pairs in all. They had been donated by Stair & Company of New York, and although they were spectacularly beautiful and realistic in every detail, I thought I would never find places for all of them. Mrs. Amory and I spent quite a lot of time deciding where to put them; fortunately we found that, with so many rooms in the house, there was a place for each pair.

On October 22 we were planning to have a press reception and a party for the donors to the house. The two weeks between the Philippine visit and "Donors' Day" were busy ones. We wanted everything to be perfect. I suddenly realized that in three of the newly redecorated rooms sheer curtains had not been provided, so once again I called on Camilla Payne, who made them for us in no time.

On the day of the reception, hundreds of carnations had been ordered by Arthur Leaman. We were planning to make arrangements in colors to match each of the rooms. There were eighty-two arrangements in all to be made, and I was about halfway through when Mrs. Amory arrived. She was dressed for the reception, but immediately asked what she could do to help. I gave her an apron and put her to work on the flowers, and they were all in place when the reception began.

The rug for the head of state's bedroom was the very last thing to arrive. It came at four in the afternoon after all the movers had gone home. So two of the butlers I had hired for the reception and two of the decorators, also dressed for the party, hastily removed the heavy furniture and laid the rug. Downstairs the guests were assembling.

More than two hundred people came to see the house that day. But because of the death of President Herbert Hoover, Mrs. Johnson did not attend.

In a charming speech of thanks for all Robin Duke had done to bring about the improvements that were being displayed that day, Secretary Wirtz called the house "Robin's Nest."

Brooke Lee, the great-grandson of Francis Preston Blair, was one of the invited guests that day. As he walked through the house with the other visitors touring it, he mentioned that he had been born in the Queen's sitting room. "Also my brother and I were both in bed with measles in this room," he added.

Immediately following Donors' Day, many articles appeared in local newspapers and magazines all over the country, and we were soon inundated with requests for tours. We had to limit tours severely to people who had given us items of furnishings or who were planning to donate something. Donors were also allowed to bring friends, family, or club members. It was hard to deny these generous people a look at the house.

But by spring I was worried that these tours were wearing out the rugs, and it was very difficult to fit them in since we were back to a full schedule of visits and functions. I spoke to Ambassador Duke about the problem, and he agreed to cut down on tours. He even assigned someone at the department to be in charge of tour schedules, and it did seem that the stream of tourists diminished a bit.

Our next official visitors came from Zambia, the African nation that had been granted its independence from Britain only a month before. Its ambassador, Mr. Hosea Soko, had not yet presented his credentials to President Johnson. Zambia's new leader was President Kenneth David Kaunda, a fighter for his country's freedom from colonial rule.

Since Zambia had no embassy, we agreed to hold a reception for two hundred people at Blair House so that Dr. Kaunda could officially be introduced to the Washington community and to the ambassadors from all the other African states. Only the South Africans were left off the invitation list.

The party severely strained our capacity, especially since, it being November, we could not use our garden, but the Zambians were so appreciative that it made the extra effort worthwhile.

Both the President and his Prime Minister, who usually wore Western dress, put on their country's colorful toga for the party and for other official functions. The toga was a wrapping of a long, wide piece of heavy woven fabric that stayed in place because of the way it was draped. It looked quite comfortable, but the uninitiated might have trouble keeping completely covered. Ambassador Soko remained in an ordinary business suit, which he thought was more appropriate for someone who was planning to stay on here as his country's representative.

Our next visitor, also from Africa, was the Prime Minister of Malawi, Dr. H. Kamuzu Banda, a slight man who carried himself in a very erect and poised manner. In his right hand at all times he carried a heavy cane topped with a horse's tail. This cane was the symbol of his office, and I never saw him use it for support.

Prime Minister Banda's chief of intelligence and security, Mr. Lomax, had been an official of the British Government when Malawi was the British colony of Nyasaland. He had been kept on during the first months of the new country's independence to help make the transition easier. Mr. Lomax acted as a liaison between me and the Prime Minister, who was otherwise surrounded by people too busy with what they thought were the more important aspects of the official visit than to be bothered with the many tiny details that I had to concern myself with.

The visit went smoothly, all in all, and soon after the Malawis left, Mrs. Rusk gave a tea at Blair House for Mrs. Andrei Gromyko, wife of the Soviet Union's Foreign Minister.

The new year of 1965 began with the appearance in *House and Garden* of the picture spread that Tom Leonard had been working on for so long. It was a marvelous piece of journalism; the pictures were extraordinary and really gave one a feeling of having been at Blair House. But many people, after reading the article, wanted to have the actual experience, it seemed. The number of calls and letters asking for tours was almost overwhelming. I referred them all to the Protocol Office.

Our first visitor that year was Prime Minister Eisaku Sato of Japan: he was due on January 10. On the ninth I arrived for work to find that stands were being erected in the street just outside our front door for the January 20 inauguration of President Johnson. It was out of the question for the stands to remain there during the next four days, since no cars could drive up to the front of the house. I immediately called the "powers that be" at GSA, and after about half an hour of explanations to several people they agreed to explain to the inaugural committee, who in turn agreed to get the people building the stands to undo what had been done and postpone the rest of the work until January 14, when the Japanese party would be leaving.

In addition to the renovations, there had been another change at Blair House. President Johnson, who was about to enter his first elected term as President, had appointed Lloyd Hand to be the new chief of protocol. Angie Duke was named ambassador to Spain.

Mr. and Mrs. Hand had been invited to stay at Blair House during the Japanese visit so that they could see for themselves what went on during an official stay at the house.

This would be my first meeting with the Hands, and although I had heard only glowing reports about them, I would certainly miss the Dukes. We had been close friends for many years. They helped me through my first months at Blair House, and Robin and I had formed a particularly deep friendship while working on the Fine Arts Committee.

The Prime Minister of Japan and his party arrived and were shown to their rooms. After changing into their evening clothes, they promptly left for dinner at their embassy.

The Hands were ensconced on the third floor. I was astonished at how young Mrs. Hand looked. She was blond and slim and wore her hair in the bouffant style of the time. I was bowled over when she told me that she was the mother of five children—she looked like a girl herself.

When the Japanese visitors left, the reviewing stands were reinstalled in front of the house. All over the city one could feel the spreading excitement as the day of the inaugural drew near. Hundreds of out-of-town visitors had come to Washington. Some of them had written me asking if they could stay at Blair House. I guess a hasty reading of the many articles that appeared about the house could have given the impression that we were a very fine hotel, not a residence reserved for presidential guests.

In fact, we were preparing for presidential guests of a special sort during the inauguration. (Our old friends the Trumans were also among those expected, but at the last moment they were not well enough to make the long trip in the cold winter weather, so Margaret Truman Daniel and her husband were going to represent the Truman family.)

Bess Abell, Mrs. Johnson's social secretary, was in charge of the arrangements, and she and I were in constant contact. We were arranging things just as we would for any state visit.

Our guests were Mr. and Mrs. Huffman Baines, Mrs. Joseph Saunders (uncle and aunts of the President), and Mr. and Mrs. Sam Fore and their daughter, Mrs. Robert Spruce, who were close family friends. All were expected on Sunday. The Daniel family, including Clifton and William Daniel, and their nurse, Annie Dutelor, were expected early in the inauguration week.

Each of the family groups was assigned a military aide. Mrs. Saunders and the Baineses arrived around 10:30 P.M. in a cold, pouring rain. Mrs. Saunders had gotten her feet wet and was deathly afraid that she was going to get a cold. She was a dear little southern woman with a great deal of the charm ladies were supposed to have in her part of the country. Captain John Heinz, the military aide, hovered by her side as we welcomed her. When she learned that she had been given the Queen's Suite, she was so excited she almost forgot her wet feet. We found her some bedroom slippers to use until her luggage arrived, and she seemed quite content.

Mr. Baines was not in good health, and it had been a long trip for him from Texas. He went to bed as soon as he could and was planning to pass up some of the preinaugural activities so that he could be sure to attend his nephew's big day. Captain Alwain, the aide assigned to the Fore family, arrived with them just as we were getting Mr. Baines settled in his room. Because Mr. Fore used a wheelchair, I had given him a room on the fourth floor, since that was at that time the only place that our elevator opened directly level with the main landing. On both the second and third floors there were a few steps down or up, which led to the bedrooms. I had put Mrs. Spruce, the Fores' daughter, in a room near her parents.

We got everyone settled in their rooms finally, and served them sandwiches, cookies, and warm drinks—tea and hot chocolate, but no coffee since it was quite late by this time. The luggage didn't arrive until well after midnight, so it was a while before everyone was settled in for the night. I went from room to room offering suggestions, answering questions, and giving any help I could.

In the morning the Fores came down for breakfast, but the other guests had breakfast together in the Queen's Suite, which they thoroughly enjoyed because of the fact that so many important people had stayed there.

The women were invited to attend the Distinguished Ladies' reception, which is a tradition at every inauguration. In the morning there was a constant stream of relatives and friends who were staying in other parts of Washington. And the phone kept ringing and ringing with people who thought this would be just the time to come tour the house. The Protocol Office should have known better, but even it called at one point to ask if I was giving a Blair House tour that afternoon. The only tour I was giving was for our guests.

That evening I walked through the house with the little

group. Mrs. Saunders kept saying, "It's like being in fairyland." I almost got caught up in their enthusiasm. After all, these were ordinary citizens, and everything about their trip to Washington, but especially their stay in the house, was an unusual treat for them.

Finally Mrs. Saunders said that she had to go back to her room and "dream that I am a queen," and the rest of the guests also decided to turn in early.

The next morning began badly with a call from Ingrid at seven-thirty saying that the elevator wasn't working. I called for a repairman, since I knew that Mr. Fore was to be at the White House at nine and there was no other way of getting him down from the fourth floor in his wheelchair.

The repairman arrived almost immediately and worked frantically, but he couldn't get the machine running.

I called Captain Heinz, and with several of our housemen and butlers helping, our visitor was carried down four flights of stairs. Mr. Fore took it in good spirit, and the electrician was able to get the elevator working by the time everyone was back from the White House for lunch.

The Daniels were due to arrive by one-thirty, but once again there was some problem with the train they were on, so they came by car from Havre de Grace, Maryland. By the time they got to Blair House at three-fifteen the Washington *Post* reporter and photographer who had been waiting for them had given up and gone home.

I got the Daniels, the children, and the nurse settled, and then was treated to a fashion show as Mrs. Baines and Mrs. Saunders modeled the outfits they had planned to wear to the inaugural concert that night. But when they saw their heavy schedule for the following morning, they decided to stay home instead, and only the Daniels went to the concert.

The next morning, Inauguration Day, everyone was up early. Every Blair House window facing the parade route was filled with children and adults. Mr. and Mrs. Baines and Mrs. Saunders were in the Queen's Suite; Ambassador and Mrs. Duke's children used the President's study window; and the Hand children watched the parade out of the window in an unoccupied room on the third floor.

That evening the Baines and Saunders ladies came downstairs in their long ball gowns. They were as excited as if they were young girls going to their high school prom. It was a touching sight to see them walking down the steps to their waiting cars with their handsome young military escorts by their sides.

Later in the evening, the Daniels decided to walk back from the White House rather than waiting for their car. I was watching the inaugural activities on the TV set in the President's study, but had left word that anyone who needed me could find me there. The Daniels walked up the stairs to the front door just as Rigoberto, the butler assigned to that door, was bringing me a message. So he wasn't there when the Daniels rang the doorbell—which wasn't working.

A few minutes later I got a call from Mr. Carter, deputy chief of protocol, telling me about this little mix-up. The Daniels started out again, and this time they were let in promptly. Margaret laughed it all off with her famous good humor, but I had a feeling that Clifton Daniel was a little miffed.

The next morning everyone left. Mr. Baines was so eager to go home, or so agitated about the long trip ahead of him, that he was up at 4:00 A.M., wandering around downstairs. He had a cup of coffee and returned to his room to wait for everyone else to get up.

When she left, Margaret returned to me a small bag I had loaned to her. A week or so later I opened the bag and noticed a card of some sort lying in the bottom. It turned out to be Margaret Daniel's driver's license. I called her and then sent it back. She responded with a note saying how pleased she was to have her license, since she would have had to take the difficult New York driver's test again and she didn't think she wanted to go through that.

Chapter Sixteen

✿ EARLY IN THE year we had the last meeting of the Fine
Arts Committee with Robin presiding. At that meeting
Mrs. Hand was introduced to all the members. It was at this
meeting, also, that Mrs. Eugene Carusi, a member of the committee, mentioned that Mr. Dominic Tampone, president of the
New York firm of Hammacher Schlemmer, had offered to redo
the closets in the entire house. Mrs. Carusi was already beginning to take the measurements of all the closets so that this project could get under way.

Mrs. Hand was extremely interested in further improvement
and in the renovations. She stopped by frequently with prospective donors. In general, tours had been kept to a minimum, but I
was glad to take these generous people around. And occasionally
the tour business was rewarding.

One day Brooke Lee played host to the Harvard Business
School Club of Philadelphia, of which he was president. They
met in the Blair-Lee drawing room and Mr. Lee told them a bit
about the history of the house. Then they asked if they could
take a quick tour. They asked all sorts of tough questions and
seemed more than usually interested in the answers.

A few days later one of the men who had been with the group
called. Alan Corderman was an officer of RCA, and he wanted
to know if we could use a few television sets. In fact, as he had
probably noticed, we had only four color sets in the whole
house. The rest were our old portable black and white sets. I
didn't want to appear greedy, so I asked for four more sets, one
for each of the suites. But he suggested that we could use a set

for each bedroom. He said I should go to the RCA showroom, pick out what I liked, and let him know. When I got to our local RCA dealer I found that none of the sets would match the dark old wood in the house. They were all light wood designed to fit into a modern decor. I called Mr. Corderman and asked if there might be some darker cabinets available. After checking he found out that there weren't any, but said that if I would get him a sample of the wood I thought would be suitable, he'd have them specially made for us.

I sent him a drawer from a little table, and a few weeks later TV sets in cabinets made of a matching wood were being installed in all the bedrooms. The sets were a real treat for our guests, many of whom did not have television in their own countries.

Our very next visit included a TV addict from an unlikely place. The President of Upper Volta, Mr. Maurice Yameogo, and his wife brought along her sister, Mrs. Yaro, as a companion.

Mrs. Yaro took one look at her room and decided not to leave the house unless she was forced to. She spoke very little English and was shy, but in fact she had fallen in love with television. The set in her bedroom was on all day and much of the night. Toward the end of the three-day visit she was simply not going anywhere. On the night that the group was headed for an embassy reception she refused to change her clothes, claimed that she was not feeling well, and got to have her dinner on a tray in front of the TV set, where she stayed having a lovely time all by herself.

The Volta visit was as colorful as many of the other African visits had been. Both men and women wore the traditional *bou bou:* a long, loose sleeveless dress with a full skirt for the ladies and a long, free-flowing robe for the men. They all topped off their outfits with turbans in matching fabrics.

At a small coffee reception for the ambassadors of African countries, Mr. Yameogo made a short speech and then left the room. The minute the door closed behind him a terrible fight broke out between the members of the Upper Volta group and the Ghanaian ambassador. There was obviously a strong difference of opinion that caused everyone to raise their voices, and they just stopped short of exchanging blows. I was told later that the Ghanaians did not attend the embassy reception that evening.

I had long been hoping that we would finally get a curator for Blair House, someone who could catalog the furnishings we had and see that new acquisitions were properly listed. In 1965 Mrs. Helen Fede, a former curator at Mount Vernon and then custodian of the catalog at the Smithsonian Institution, was assigned on loan to Blair House three days a week. We set up an office for her on the fourth floor and she began her often tedious but vital work. Mrs. Fede was very knowledgeable and for the most part worked alone. But when she was unable to find a piece of furniture that had been listed elsewhere as belonging in the house, she enlisted my help, and together we always managed to discover the missing chair or plate or piece of silver.

(She was with us for a year and then returned to the Smithsonian. On February 5, 1968, just after she had come back to Blair House as curator, she was suddenly stricken with a fatal cerebral hemorrhage. We were all terribly shocked at her death.)

Hammacher Schlemmer's Mary Ellen Bugler and her assistant were already hard at work on the closets, which they planned to refurbish to match the decor of every bedroom. Each closet was to get a new tile floor and new wallpaper selected and donated by Hammacher Schlemmer and installed by the GSA. The work was to be completed during August while the house was closed. The Hammacher Schlemmer people made scale drawings of each closet, and we arranged to have before and after photos made.

Some of the closet walls were to have vinyl wall coverings; others were to be covered with quilted chintz. Many were to have poles on both sides of the closet and others had a rod close to the ceiling fitted out with hangers on long poles so that evening clothes or a sheikh's robes could be hung without touching the floor. Some closets would get shelves and others were going to have built-in cabinets.

There were padded coat hangers in fabrics to match the walls, hat stands covered with the same fabric, luggage racks, special hangers for furs in the ladies' bedrooms, trouser hangers for the men, and even a special hanging rod for saris.

The completed closets were so beautiful that we often deliberately left their doors open when we showed the rooms.

When all the redecorating was done, Ingrid took the scraps of material and ran them through her sewing machine and soon all the dresser drawers were lined, too.

By fall of 1965 Mrs. Hand had become quite involved in the renovation. She had hoped that we could get some of the fireplaces working, but to her sorrow the GSA vetoed that idea after a thorough inspection by the fire department. But we were able to make many other changes she suggested. Several paintings were moved, and at her request we brought a number of potted plants into the house, which added some warmth and charm.

Before they left for Spain, Robin and Angie Duke were guests at a party given by their successors at Blair House. Mrs. Pat Boone, wife of the singer, was the Hands' houseguest at the time and was among the forty guests at dinner that evening.

The menu was particularly sumptuous and included many of Angie and Robin's favorite dishes. I made eight flower arrangements for the mantels and tables. Our candle trees were fitted with scented votive candles, and flowers and greens were entwined around their bases. Other lighted candles stood in candelabra in several places around the house.

I could remember few occasions when the house had looked lovelier. There was to be dancing after dinner, and the atmosphere in the house and around the tables in the Blair-Lee drawing room was gay and festive.

The drapes were drawn to protect the privacy of the guests, but you could see out through the glass panels on the Blair-Lee entrance hall. I was just congratulating myself on how well the dinner party was going when I walked by that entrance hall. Outside on the street I saw what I thought were red lights. I knew what had happened: something had set off the fire alarm. We had been having terrible headaches with that device. It was designed to alert us to any fire in the house, but apparently because it had been set too sensitively, it was always going off for no more reason than a puff of smoke or a bit of grease burning in the kitchen and often we couldn't hear it.

I raced upstairs to go across to the other side of the house so that, without disturbing the party, I could see what was going on. As I passed through the head of state's bedroom, I saw a ladder at the window. I put on an extra burst of speed and ran down the stairs to the Blair House entrance. As I got there I could hear a loud hammering at the door.

I opened it and was staring into the business end of a fire ax that was just about to come crashing through the door.

The steps were filled with firemen and draped with hoses and other equipment. The lieutenant in charge said, "We have been told that you have a fire on the premises." The alarm had rung in the fire station, but in the house the "ping" the alarm button made on our board was too subtle to be heard by anyone.

I assured them there was no fire anywhere, but when they insisted on coming in to see for themselves, I urged them— begged them—to come to the side entrance leading to the basement.

I glanced outside. All traffic was stopped. The street was filled with fire trucks of all kinds, ambulances, police cars, everything. I took one look at all that emergency equipment and raced downstairs to let the firemen in.

The lieutenant and I went down to the fire board, which did show that a "fire" was in progress in the kitchen. The kitchen was only about forty feet away across the hall. We rushed in and found a calm and efficient staff serenely preparing platters to be sent upstairs to the dinner in progress.

The firemen looked at the situation and decided that the extra heat that was being generated in the kitchen during the preparation of the dinner had set off the alarm. They agreed to send the equipment away but decided to leave one truck on the street just in case there was any problem at all.

Just to be super-safe, the lieutenant and I took a tour of the whole house. I had convinced him that we didn't have to go into the Blair-Lee drawing room, where the guests were seated. As we were slowing down on the first floor, quite certain now that everything was fine, I again heard a frantic pounding at the door. I opened it to find a policeman standing there demanding a report on the fire. He insisted he needed a written document even though there was no fire.

The firemen left and I took the policeman into the Lincoln room, where I told him exactly what had happened. A few minutes after he finally left, there was once again a loud knocking. This time I opened the front door to a young reporter who had been sent over by his paper to check out the fire at Blair House that had been announced in a bulletin on local radio. The poor fellow had been having a drink before dinner at home when he had been told to rush over to get the story. He had even brought a camera. Disappointed that there was no story, he thought he might at least get a shot of Blair House just inside the front door. I refused, even though I felt sorry that he had had to miss his dinner. By this time I was also pretty tired of all the fuss about nothing.

When he left I went to check on how our dinner was progressing. The guests were just moving into the Blair drawing room for after-dinner coffee and liqueurs. They had heard none of the excitement. The little orchestra hired for the occasion began to play then, and everyone danced until one in the morning, oblivious to the fact that we had had quite an exciting evening.

On March 18, 1966, Ambassador Hand resigned to return to California, where he was entering the congressional race. The resignation caught me by surprise. For once there had been no rumors before it happened.

President Johnson appointed James Symington of Missouri as the new chief of protocol. His wife, Sylvia, and the dean of the diplomatic corps attended the swearing-in ceremony, which was held at the house, followed by one of my extra-special tours. During the tour I learned that the Symingtons would be staying with us as guests during the forthcoming visit of Prime Minister Indira Gandhi of India.

There was another change in the offing, and this one would be truly hard for me to take. Ingrid's husband was returning to Norway and so she would be leaving us. I was really sad. Ingrid was not only the most efficient housekeeper I had ever had, she had become a dear friend. We were all going to miss her.

I interviewed quite a number of people in search of a replacement for Ingrid and finally decided to hire Wilhelmina Dahmer, who had come highly recommended by Ridgewell's Caterers in Washington. Ingrid was planning to show her the Blair House ropes, but unfortunately she developed pneumonia and was not able to come to the house for several weeks. So we all pitched in, trying to get Wilhelmina acclimated to the way we did things before our next visit.

But Mrs. Gandhi's visit was sure to be a test of everyone's ability. I knew I would have to rely heavily on the parlormaids and butlers who had been with us on previous visits. I had a new chief of protocol and a green housekeeper for one of the most important visits of the year.

We had met Mrs. Gandhi before, of course, when she traveled as hostess for her father, Prime Minister Nehru. So we knew that she was allergic to both strawberries and tomatoes, that she did not eat fried foods, that she drank her tea hot, with no milk and only a little sugar, and that she really enjoyed Western food.

We put red roses in Mrs. Gandhi's room. When her father, Jawaharlal Nehru, had stayed with us, I had been told to provide pink rosebuds for him, since he liked to pin them on the famous "Nehru jacket" he always wore. Although I had put a large vase of pink rosebuds in his bedroom on the day of the visit, I found that he preferred the red roses we had put in the library. Mrs. Gandhi commented that the red roses reminded her of her father.

Everyone wanted to know whether Mrs. Gandhi was going to sleep in the Head of State's Suite or in the more feminine Queen's Suite. In fact, she used both. She held meetings in the library, but she slept in the Queen's Suite and had her tea and smaller, more informal meetings with friends there.

After her arrival at the White House, Mrs. Gandhi walked over to Blair House with President Johnson. All traffic stopped as the two walked across Pennsylvania Avenue, and the drivers had a front-row seat from which to watch these two highly recognizable world leaders strolling along, chatting together like old friends out for a walk.

Mrs. Gandhi's two sons, Rajiv and Sanjay, who were college students in London at the time, had flown over with her to the United States and were also staying at Blair House. They had breakfast with her each morning in the library, but then went off on their own sightseeing while she fulfilled her heavy schedule of official functions.

Sanjay later became an active and controversial member of Mrs. Gandhi's administration. He was his mother's closest adviser, and during a time when she was out of power he was sentenced to two years in prison for destroying a film critical of his mother and of his growing power. His political excesses were said to be partially responsible for her defeat. In June of 1980 Indira Gandhi was again Prime Minister, and Sanjay, still a person around whom much controversy swirled but once again on the ascendancy, was killed in an airplane crash. Seeing the photographs of Mrs. Gandhi sitting next to the body of her son as she took him from the hospital to his cremation, I remembered those happy breakfasts at Blair House.

While Mrs. Gandhi presented an imposing, dignified exterior publicly, I found her personally quite accessible and warm. Ambassador and Mrs. B. K. Nehru were in and out of the house often during the visit and were very helpful. They came to escort the Prime Minister to many of her appointments. Mrs. Gandhi was dressed in beautiful saris at all times, plain ones during the day and lavishly embroidered ones of silk for the evenings.

The Symingtons, as planned, had moved into the house for this visit. They took a room on the fourth floor and ate several meals with us. Both the ambassador and his young wife seemed quite at home in their new duties. I had heard that Jim Symington played the guitar very well and that he often entertained at parties by singing folk songs, but he didn't get a chance to show off this talent during the Gandhi visit.

The only person who had a really hard time while Mrs. Gandhi was with us was poor Wilhelmina. She seemed bewildered and spent most of her time just observing. She appeared to be too nervous to do much of anything.

On the morning after the Indian party had left, I came to work and was told that Wilhelmina had had a heart attack. Cora had taken her to the hospital but no one seemed to know which one. I finally tracked her down at George Washington University Hospital by checking with the ambulance dispatcher at the fire station. I called the emergency room at the hospital and was told that what had looked like a heart attack was just an attack of nerves. I spoke to Cora and suggested that they take a taxi and come home.

It began to dawn on me that Wilhelmina was a very high-strung person and that she had not been prepared for the stress that went with her new job at Blair House. It looked as if it was going to be up to me to get her settled in the job. It had become clear that Ingrid was never going to recuperate in time to do any of the training.

Ingrid did get to come to a farewell party we gave her. It was a warm and loving gathering. Not only the permanent Blair House staff but many of the part-time people who had worked with her arrived with presents. The food was provided by the kitchen staff, and it was a lavish spread. We managed to surprise her with the party, which was planned for the day on which she was coming by to show her sister, her niece, and her husband through the house. For all of us Ingrid's leaving was a great loss and the party, while gay and festive, was a poignant occasion.

Then, a few weeks later, we had some more unhappy news. James McHaney, the marvelous houseman who had had such a long career with Blair House, complained that he wasn't feeling well. In fact, he said, he'd been feeling poorly for some time and his doctor's treatment didn't seem to be working.

I insisted that James go to the doctors at the Department of State for a complete physical. They examined him and immediately ordered him into Georgetown Hospital for an operation. After the surgery, Dr. Coffey called me to say that there was unfortunately nothing to be done for James: he had cancer, which had spread beyond any hope.

We were all very sad. James had lost his wife the previous year, and since her death he had been spending more and more time at Blair House. He would come to work early, eager to stay as late as anyone needed him. He treated Blair House as if it were his own home, caring for it in many ways that were beyond the call of his duty.

After recovering from the surgery James came back to work, but he was unable to do the heavy work he had done before. We hired another houseman to replace him, but when James returned to us we were glad to see him and he worked side by side with the new man, even though he had to curtail his activities severely.

Chapter Seventeen

❧ THE SPRING AND EARLY SUMMER of 1966 saw a veritable avalanche of guests, including King Faisal of Saudi Arabia, Prime Minister Harold E. Holt of Australia, Prime Minister Forbes Burnham of Guyana, Prime Minister Harold Wilson of Great Britain, and the elderly President of Israel, Zalman Shazar. Then in August our attention turned to domestic affairs. We began to plan for the wedding of Luci Baines Johnson to Patrick Nugent.

The Shazar visit came only four days before the wedding and the presidential state dinner at the White House became part of the prenuptial celebrations. The groom's parents were among the guests, and the Shazars came to the United States with wedding presents in their luggage.

On Saturday, August 6, the day of the wedding, all the male members of the wedding party dressed at Blair House. It was not as simple as it sounds to arrange for twenty military aides, thirteen ushers, eleven groomsmen, and the groom and his father to get into their wedding clothes. Lieutenant McNamara, one of the White House military aides, helped with the arrangements. Every single bedroom was in use. Pat Nugent and his father shared the Head of State's Suite and the rest of the group was assigned by fours, threes, and twos to the other rooms.

We checked everything as carefully as if we were planning a military campaign. There were a room assignment sheet and a timetable listing the times of arrival and departure for each person. Every member of the party got an information sheet.

Lynda Bird Johnson was escorted to the wedding by the

handsome film actor George Hamilton. I noted that Charles Robb was one of the military aides, but I never thought of the name again until sometime later when it was announced that he and Lynda were getting married.

Bess Abell was handling arrangements at the White House. She was planning a luncheon and a huge wedding reception, and the only role for Blair House was to act as the dressing room for the men. Bess thought it would be a good idea for me to have a seamstress and a tailor on hand in case of emergencies.

For refreshments we planned to serve only coffee, tea, fruit juice, and soft drinks. Absolutely no alcoholic beverages, said Bess, and there was no need, she thought, to serve any food.

I saw to it that every bathroom was supplied with plenty of towels and a good supply of toilet articles. The day before the wedding, Lieutenant McNamara and the man from the tuxedo rental place came over and placed the suits in the proper rooms. That alone was a formidable task, demanding careful coordination.

The next morning when I arrived at eight I found the lieutenant and some of the military aides already there and then the rest of the party began to straggle in. Percy, the butler, was trying to handle the heavy traffic at the door and Helen Delamiason, one of the parlormaids, was setting out drinks and serving coffee to the early arrivals. But she looked concerned. "These boys haven't had any breakfast," she told me. "Don't they look starved to you? I think we should give them something just to tide them over until the wedding."

One look at all those hungry young men and I told Dallas to warm every bit of pastry he had in the freezer and then sent out for more. In truth, the members of the wedding not only had not had breakfast, but were suffering from the aftereffects of a late-night stag party for the groom. I can tell you, they were really grateful for just a little danish pastry.

They also all needed help of some sort with collars, ties, and boutonnieres. Finally, with the help of all the butlers, we got everyone ready to go. By ten o'clock all the ushers and military aides had to leave for the church. A little before eleven Pat Nugent and his father and the groomsmen left.

I found it very pleasant to have all those young men around. They reminded me of my two sons and their friends.

At about twelve-thirty the military aides came back to change into their uniforms for the reception. Each time any of them came in they made straight for the refreshment table to refuel.

By three-thirty many of them began to drift back for the last change of the day. Quite a few brought their wives or girl friends. By the time they had all gone, the staff was quite tired out. The house was still filled with reminders of the wedding. In each room rented tuxedos were hung awaiting their return to the store on Monday morning, which was also the first day of my vacation.

By now plans were progressing for the building that was to be constructed between the Carnegie House and Blair House in order to make the new addition part of the whole complex. This severely affected the garden in the rear of the new addition.

When I got back on August 21 we began meetings about the garden. Mr. Michael Painter, the garden architect from John Carl Warnecke's office, was assigned to the project. Warnecke was responsible for the overall design of the Lafayette Square renovation project, and since the Blair House garden was adjacent to the square it became part of the project. We spent a great deal of time outlining plans to make the garden a place where our guests could find some relaxation on a nice day. It was decided that the garden was to be floored in red bricks to match the bricks that were the hallmark of the Lafayette Square renovation.

The remainder of the year we had a number of guests, including Ne Win, the Premier of Burma, President and Mrs. Ferdinand Marcos of the Philippines, and President Léopold Sédar Senghor of Senegal and his wife. President Senghor, a poet, was in town to receive an honorary degree at Howard University in recognition of his poetry. Our last guest for the year was Prime Minister Souvanna Phouma of Laos.

Between visits, work was proceeding on the Victorian Room on the third floor. And gifts for the committee continued to come in from generous donors. Two lovely antique sconces arrived, gifts from Mr. and Mrs. Harold F. Linder. Mr. Linder was president of the United States Export-Import Bank. The Linders had also sent two chairs, but they had not met with the approval of the committee because they did not fit into the decor and they had been returned with thanks.

The furniture for the Victorian Room arrived, and it was enormous. The intricately carved bedroom set had won first prize at an exhibition in Philadelphia in 1876 and was on loan to the house from the Smithsonian Institution. Dr. Richard Howland of the Smithsonian had arranged for the loan. When the headboard of the huge bed was put into place, it nearly grazed the eleven-foot ceiling. The bed came in two massive pieces. The top fit into the bottom with wooden dowels, and I thought it was frighteningly wobbly. I had visions of the whole thing falling over onto a sleeping guest, so I insisted that metal braces be put behind the headboard. The foot of the bed was somewhat lower than the head, but it was still the largest bed I'd ever seen, larger even than the Spanish bed at the Renchard house.

The combination bureau and dressing table was also very ornate and heavy. A matching washstand, not as large but also ornate, was brought in, as well as a table desk that looked as if it belonged in the room, even though it didn't match. Two Victorian occasional chairs completed the room.

Dr. Howland loaned the room one of his own footstools to go with one of the chairs.

When I first saw the paint samples and fabric swatches that were to be used in the Victorian Room, I couldn't imagine that they would look good on the walls and the furniture. Every color in the rainbow was represented in the strongest shades. But when the upholstery and drapes were made and in place, I saw that they offset the scale of the furniture perfectly.

It took several days for us just to get the furniture clean enough to install, since it had been in storage for such a long time.

Some time before this, Mrs. Merriweather Post had given us a rather large and unusual framed needlework picture of a parrot. I had put it in storage until I could find a place where its strong colors wouldn't be overpowering. As the work proceeded on the Victorian Room, I could see that I had found a perfect place for the parrot. Mr. William Pahlmann, the decorator in charge of the room, agreed that the bird seemed quite at home there.

At the end of 1966 Dr. Coffey called to say that James seemed to be responding to the cobalt treatments and that it would be good for him psychologically to work as much as he wanted to. This was good news, and with a glass of sherry we toasted the end of the year and looked forward to a busy schedule for 1967.

Chapter Eighteen

ONE OF THE first visitors in the new year was King Hassan II of Morocco. Arriving with him, in addition to a large official entourage, were Prince Sisi Mohammed, aged three, and his sister, Princess Lalla Merinn, aged five, and their governess and nurse.

We decided that the two small royal visitors would use one of the bed-sitting-room suites on the third floor of Blair House with their nurse and governess in the adjoining rooms. But when I looked into the rooms we had assigned the children I thought, "This surely doesn't look inviting to a child."

So I had all the breakable little knickknacks removed and spent a happy afternoon buying a few toys for the prince and princess to play with.

On each bed I put a stuffed animal and on the floor I placed a wagon full of blocks, some coloring books and crayons, several books of paper dolls, and a little cloth doll. I also bought cookie cutters in shapes children would like. Lillian Brown, the "cookie baker *extraordinaire*" for Blair House, immediately set about turning out gingerbread men and animal cookies.

Two days before the visit the snow began to fall, and by midmorning we were having a mini-blizzard. I prepared to stay in the house during the entire visit.

Before His Majesty came, on the day of his arrival a chartered bus pulled up in front of the house and a large number of Moroccans—many of whom were undoubtedly supposed to be staying at the hotel—got out with their luggage. While I was trying to make some sense out of where the various people were to stay, the two children and their entourage slipped into the house. When I was later able to go up to their suite to welcome them, the children were already playing with their toys. The governess had prepared a list of what they would like to have for lunch, which she gave me verbally. It was a normal menu for children, with soup and meat and vegetables, and puddings or fruit for dessert. The only item that might not have appealed to American children was plain yogurt at meals and then again in the middle of the afternoon.

The prince and princess had impeccable manners. They spoke Spanish and French and were the most polite children I have ever met. Every morning they had a visit with their father just before he left on his round of official functions. The minute they entered his suite the formal atmosphere melted away and the sounds of happy laughter could be heard throughout the house.

At all other times, however, formality was the keynote. Even in the children's room we were entertaining royalty, as Rigoberto learned when he went upstairs to serve the children lunch the first day. He was roundly scolded for serving the little princess before her brother. In Morocco, men are served first even if they are only three years old and particularly if they are going to be King someday.

I had saved several toys in order to give the children a new plaything on each day of their visit. One morning I gave the prince a toy car carrier complete with tiny cars. He was thrilled with this toy, and I was puzzled that he wouldn't shake my hand when I was about to leave the room. But he steadfastly refused, keeping his hand behind his back. The governess kept trying to convince him with words and then finally she yanked him into the bathroom and gave him a quick but firm paddling. He came out a little tearstained, but he did shake my hand. It turned out that he thought I wanted to take the truck with its little cars back. He had it clutched tightly in the hand behind his back.

I thought it strange that the King didn't bring any toys with him for the children. But perhaps he had arranged to have some toys brought to the house. On the first day of the visit Mrs. Laraki, wife of the Moroccan ambassador, brought over a large doll carriage containing a beautiful doll and some things for the little prince also. The toys were all too large to use in the house and so they were packed up and shipped home to Morocco.

In contrast to the pleasure of having the children in the house there was, on this visit, a troublemaking security man who traveled with the party. Since we were all snowbound by one of Washington's unexpected mini-blizzards, I had prepared some extra bedrooms for my staff, but when I went to check on them I found that a group of Moroccans had moved in. These rooms, on the fourth floor, were almost never used by guests since they were smaller and not as comfortable as those on the lower floors. We reserved them for the sort of emergency we were now facing. So I asked the Moroccans to leave. They were part of the large unofficial group that had arrived in the bus, and once they understood the situation, they graciously left for the hotel.

But the next morning the security man complained to an interpreter who had never been to Blair House before that I had thrown some of the guests out. He also told her that one of our security men had wakened the King during the night because of a false alarm. In fact the alarm had been set off inadvertently by the Moroccan security man himself when he opened one of the windows in his bedroom.

When I heard about the flap he was creating, I called the Moroccan to my office and told him that I would be happy and eager to apologize to His Majesty and would discuss with the King any of the complaints the security man had voiced. At that the man practically begged me not to say anything to the King. "It is unimportant," he said, "nothing to trouble His Majesty about."

I told him then that I knew he had made those stories up to make himself important, and that if I heard any more from him I would go straight to the King. There were no more complaints.

But there was a sudden, unusual request from the children's doctor, who was a member of the party. On the day before they were to leave, he said that the little prince seemed to be coming down with a cold and that he needed some beef blood to help prevent the infection from developing further. It took some doing, but our butcher was able to get us the blood, and I assume the little fellow drank it. When they left the following morning, he looked none the worse for the experience.

After the weekend, Emperor Haile Selassie arrived for a two-day stay. We had not seen him since his visit at Renchard house. The visit began in some confusion because there were no room assignments in advance. Perhaps this time His Imperial Majesty wanted to make sure he got a bed that suited him. At any rate, there was a certain amount of chaos before we got everyone settled and the many pieces of luggage correctly delivered. The Emperor left for luncheon with the Secretary of State shortly after getting settled, and I checked his room just to make sure everything was in order. There, sitting on the chaise, was an adorable little brown dog, watching me solemnly. He was our first canine visitor.

Somehow the dog had been smuggled in by the Emperor, under the watchful eyes of our security people. I kidded them unmercifully, I admit, about this extra member of the party who escaped their careful scrutiny.

His Imperial Majesty was devoted to the little animal. He walked him in the garden every morning between six and six-thirty. Several times when we were expecting the Emperor to descend the staircase in the careful, regal manner he had, the little brown dog would come bounding down the stairs, into the hall, and through the door the butler was holding open, and with one leap past the chauffeur into the waiting limousine. Whether the dog accompanied Haile Selassie into the White House or not I never did find out, but he was certainly in the car on almost every official journey His Imperial Majesty took.

The Emperor's valet did double duty, seeing to the well-being of the royal pet as well as that of the King. He took the dog for walks during the day. Once in a while he would ask for a little ground beef for the dog's dinner, but his diet consisted mainly of Ethiopian dog food that came with them in their luggage. One of our large ashtrays got broken during this visit when it was used as a water dish for the dog.

As always, there was a great deal of protocol and formality attached to the visit of the Ethiopians. When the African ambassadors came to Blair House to call on Haile Selassie, they were ushered into the Blair-Lee drawing room in order of precedence to be received by the Emperor, who was standing in full dress uniform. They all stood in a circle while he spoke to them briefly, and then they filed out exactly in the order in which they had entered the room. There was only time to serve them a glass of champagne before they left in complete silence.

Minutes later, a group of Ethiopian students arrived. His Imperial Majesty spoke to them even more briefly and then left the room to return to his suite. Unlike the ambassadors, the students stayed and, like students everywhere, admitted that they were hungry and happy to eat the food we had prepared for both groups of visitors.

When it came time for His Imperial Majesty to leave for his trip back to Ethiopia, I was once again summoned to his suite for the Formal Farewell. I remembered not to address him before he spoke to me. I stood respectfully in front of his chair while he graciously told me how much he had loved his visit and the house itself. His attendants and his little dog looked on. Then I was dismissed and free to leave the room.

The Prime Minister of Korea, Chung Il Kwon, came in the middle of March, and the Prime Minister of Afghanistan, Mohammed Hashim Maiwandwal, came at the end of the month. President Cevdet Sunay of Turkey came at the beginning of April, and then we had almost a month before welcoming the Prime Minister/Vice-President of Nationalist China, His Excellency Yen Chia-kan. We played host again to Prime Minister Harold Holt of Australia, and Dr. Banda of Malawi was also with us again (he was now President) for one night at the beginning of May.

In June I got a letter from my friend Nina Lytle at the Plaza Hotel in New York. She wrote:

"Just a few brief lines to give you some information on the King and Queen of Thailand which I think you might find useful.

"Her Majesty's preferred flowers are Lilies-of-the-Valley; however, she does like Yellow Roses and Orchids. She was fascinated by Dogwood, as were the other ladies of the party, for it appears they have not seen it before.

"Their Majesties are served breakfast in bed by their own servants. She takes soft boiled eggs every day, while he takes soft boiled, or fried, or scrambled.

"Her Majesty likes fresh orange juice as a refreshment.

"His Majesty does take an occasional Scotch, while it seems he is allergic to Champagne.

"By the way, Her Majesty likes her beef well done, while His Majesty likes it rare.

"They steadily ordered French Fried Potatoes, so I presume they liked them.

"They like melon in season and Her Majesty loves fresh strawberries.

"They are very punctual and quiet. The Lady-in-Waiting, Her Serene Highness Princess Vibhavadi Rangsir, can give you almost any information, and either Mr. Uthai Suwanchinda or Mr. Subhakdi Suwanchinda, who is the personal valet, will take care of all the food and other details. His English is rather poor—his French, however, is good.

"Hopefully this skimpy information will be of some assistance.

"With best of Wishes,

As ever,

[signed] Nina"

"P.S. Their Majesties also like to have flower arrangements in the national colors of Thailand, with blue in the center, then white, and then red around the outside. We used blue peonies, white snowdrifts and red carnations. In some cases, for variation, we used white lilac."

I was grateful to Nina for all the information she had sent. One thing I knew after reading her letter. I was going to be relying on people's titles this time around. With names like "Devaluka," "Sarsikanchua," and "Wongsanuvatra" I knew I'd be saying, "Yes, Your Serene Highness," and "Of course, Your Majesty" on this visit.

King Bhumibol Adulyadej and Queen Sirikit arrived on June 27 with a group of nineteen. The Queen dressed in Western clothes made of beautiful Thai silk, and at night she had a fabulous wardrobe of elaborate gowns of Thai silk satin.

The King and Queen were a handsome young couple and obviously very fun-loving. Unlike many royal visitors who have separate press conferences, Their Majesties met the press together. I didn't think it would be a particularly substantive meeting—but I was not prepared for the King's relaxed manner with the press, and neither were they.

The Queen mentioned at the beginning of the conference that the King had been up all night writing a speech he was going to deliver later. He was asked, "Don't you have a speech writer?" to which he replied with a smile, "No, we are perhaps a little primitive." "How do you write?" he was asked. "With a ball-point pen," he responded.

The King said that other rulers he knew had "talking chiefs." "What is a talking chief?" "If you have to talk but you don't want to, you say to your talking chief, 'You talk.'" So of course he was asked, "Do you have a talking chief?" "Oh yes, I do," the King said with a straight face. "I have a talking chief. He's allowed to speak but I forbid him to think."

By that time everyone had given up suppressing laughter. Someone asked about the couple's four children. One of their daughters was sixteen and had wanted to study science since she was eleven. She was thinking of coming to the United States to study nuclear physics. And a son was in school in England. When asked what the prince was studying, his father replied, "He's learning to be lazy like his father."

The press was completely won over by the royal couple and they got a great deal of coverage. The whole mood of the visit was light and pleasant. That evening at the White House dinner the King, who is a well-known jazz saxophonist in his own country, was entertained by Duke Ellington, Stan Getz, and other jazz performers. The Marine Band played one of the King's compositions, a march, when the party arrived, but the King, as far as I know, did not play the saxophone at the White House.

The year 1967 was a busy one for us. We had twenty-seven visits in all, and many functions. The staff was on duty nearly full time. The house was constantly in use. In September, during the visit of President Hamani Diori of Niger, our beloved houseman James McHaney died. He had been readmitted to the hospital earlier in the month and I had visited him several times, but it was clear that his condition was terminal. He was going to be missed deeply.

By the beginning of December we were finished with that year's visits. And at the last moment we were told that the house would not be needed for the wedding on December 9 of Lynda Bird Johnson and Charles Robb. The papers were full of wedding preparations, pictures of the wedding dress, lists of the guests, and on December 5 there was a photograph of Lynda and her wedding cake, along with Chef Clement Maggia, who had baked it.

The cake Chef Maggia made for Lynda was six feet high and weighed 250 pounds. It was his last creation: he died suddenly the next day. Maggia had been the executive pastry chef and instructor at the Greenbrier Hotel in White Sulphur Springs, West Virginia. He had made cakes for four Presidents and for a visiting King and Queen. For Lynda's wedding, in addition to the extraordinarily beautiful cake, he had made hundreds of heart-shaped petit fours iced in white and five hundred pale yellow mints topped with lilies of the valley made of icing. He had worked in the White House kitchen with executive chef Henry Haller all week before the wedding. His death shocked a city that was getting ready for a gala event.

The morning of the wedding I received a call at home from Joe Rosetti, chief of physical security at State.

"How would you like to have some visitors this evening?" he asked. Since Joe and his wife were personal friends, I thought they wanted to come over to my house.

"Sure," I said. "I'm free, when do you want to get here?"

"I don't mean at your house," he said. "I mean, how would you like some very special guests at your other house?"

I didn't have to be a psychic to know it must have something to do with the wedding.

"This is top secret," Joe said. "We got a call from the Secret Service. President Johnson called them with the idea that Blair House might just be the perfect place for Lynda and Chuck to spend their wedding night in complete privacy. They don't leave for their honeymoon until tomorrow morning."

I agreed that Blair House was a splendid hideaway. Joe told me I was to meet Lynda's personal Secret Service man at Blair House later that afternoon to make arrangements. Even Joe was not in on the details of the plan.

I called Dallas and Cora, two people I knew I could trust, and told them to meet me at Blair House at 4:00 P.M. I said I would explain what it was all about when they got there, and they were not to tell anyone where they were going.

The Secret Service man met me at three at the house and informed me that we should set up one of the bedrooms, that we didn't need to serve dinner, but that it would be nice if there were fresh orange juice for breakfast. No lights must show in the house except those we normally left on when the house was empty.

The Secret Service didn't know the best way to sneak Lynda and Charles into the house. I suggested that they come in by the side door to the basement and take an elevator straight up to their room.

We decided to turn the Queen's Suite into the Honeymoon Suite, and I showed the Secret Service the quickest way to get there.

When Cora arrived she made up the bed and put linens and toiletries in the bathroom. Dallas made a tray of fancy little open-faced sandwiches and got out some of our best cookies. We set up a tea table in the room with the sandwiches and cookies and added a bottle of champagne in a cooler. Dallas also put out everything they would need for breakfast and showed the Secret Service where it was in the kitchens.

The three of us, feeling like conspirators, made a date to meet at Blair House the next day at four to clean up the room and put everything back as it had been so no other member of the staff would suspect that anyone had been there.

I stayed on to make a few last-minute checks to be sure that everything was in order and to get some additional briefing from the Secret Service.

As I left, I could see the cars at the White House, where the wedding was in full swing.

The next day, as planned, we met at the house. It was deserted, but there were signs that we had had guests overnight. The breakfast food had been eaten and the champagne bottle was empty. But standing next to it on the little tea table Cora had so carefully set up, there was something we had not arranged for. It was an empty carton from the local Kentucky Fried Chicken outlet. It was the one and only time that Colonel Sanders had ever prepared a meal for Blair House.

We laughed about that and then put everything back in place and quietly sneaked out of the house.

The Monday morning papers were filled with details about the wedding as well as quite a bit of conjecture about where the young people had spent their wedding night. Rumors abounded and several hotels were mentioned as places where Lynda and Chuck had been seen by "reliable sources."

But until now the secret had never been revealed publicly. Mrs. Lyndon Johnson told me several years ago that even she wasn't told until some weeks later where her daughter had been that night.

The year had ended on a note of playful intrigue and happiness; 1968 was to bring an election and some surprises.

Chapter Nineteen

As the new year began, Mrs. Symington and her decorator, Mrs. Philip Geyelin, completed work in a suite of rooms on the third floor. These rooms, which did not need any new furniture, were refurbished with new draperies and upholstery. The suite included a sitting room furnished for the most part as the Blair family had left it. Because the walls were lined with cabinets holding a superb collection of old glass, it had always been called the "glass room." In addition to examples of pressed and Sandwich glass, there were also several valuable pieces of pottery from Bennington, including an unusual pottery spittoon. A dozen pairs of antique whale oil lamps made of various kinds and colors of glass were the most remarkable part of this collection. The room, with its ornate woodwork and lighting, designed to highlight the treasures kept there, was a small and cozy museum.

We had a visit, just for the day, early in the year, from Secretary General U Thant of the United Nations. Occasionally we had this sort of working visit. The Secretary General and his staff were assigned bedrooms where they could rest in between meetings. A switchboard was set up to take calls, and butlers and maids were assigned to take care of the guests' personal needs. Of course there was round-the-clock security. In every way this sort of stay was a mini-visit.

Our next overnight guest was Prime Minister Mohamed Ibrahim Egal of Somalia. He was accompanied by his young wife. She was his second but not his only wife. The first Mrs. Egal, to whom the Prime Minister was still married, stayed behind in

Somalia. The second Mrs. Egal had been married to the Prime
Minister for five years. When someone asked her if the two
wives lived together with their husband she threw up her hands
in horror.

"Good heavens, no!" she said. "That sort of thing only happens
in books. We each have our own house."

Mrs. Egal was a midwife and, although the wife of the head
of government in her country, worked at her profession, which is
in heavy demand in her country.

The President of Liberia, William V. S. Tubman, a frequent
Blair House visitor, was our guest a few weeks later. He arrived
with a large party and had many visitors during his stay, including a large group of Liberian students from schools in Washington. Many of them claimed to be related to the President, and
Mr. Tubman cheerfully acknowledged this, saying, "All Liberia's
children are mine." Liberia, founded in the nineteenth century
by freed American slaves, was ruled for generations by the descendants of these slaves, many of whom were related to each
other. Until a recent coup, the ruling class of Liberia represented a close-knit elite, all claiming ties to these original set-
tlers.

President Tubman shared with many of our other African visitors a deep affection for children. Several of our African guests
told me they could not understand such American institutions as
foundling hospitals or homes for abandoned babies. Children are
considered a national treasure in these countries where life is
hard and many children still die in infancy or early childhood.
As a member of a Nigerian delegation said, "Africans measure
their wealth by the number of their children."

In April, Ambassador Symington resigned to run for Congress.
Sylvia and Jim had become very involved with the running of
and renovations at Blair House and I was sorry to see them go.
But the blow was softened when I learned that Angie and Robin
Duke were coming back.

At a dinner honoring both the outgoing and incoming chiefs
of protocol, given by Leonard Marks, the head of the United
States Information Agency, Liz Carpenter arrived wearing a
button from a long-past campaign of Jim Symington's father,
Senator Stuart Symington of Missouri. Mr. Marks saw it and

grew pale. He begged Liz to take it off, saying, "You'll ruin my toast." He had found the same button and was planning to give it to the younger Symington at dinner.

The first guests Ambassador Duke welcomed in his new term as chief of protocol were Chancellor and Mrs. Josef Klaus of Austria. The party also included the Austrian Foreign Minister, Dr. Kurt Waldheim, who is now Secretary General of the United Nations. Since both Dr. and Mrs. Klaus were devout Catholics, their schedule included a visit with Washington's archbishop, Cardinal Patrick O'Boyle.

One afternoon Mrs. Klaus and I discussed plans for the Blair House garden, which was now in the process of being installed. It had been decided to soften the red brick of the walls surrounding the garden and its brick floor with as many plantings as possible. Three fountains were also planned. Ivy was to cover the walls of the adjacent Renwick Gallery and the New Executive Office Building. One of the fountains was installed on the walls; the others spouted from the two pools, one circular, the other rectangular, cut into the brick floor. Later, Mrs. Sidi Parker of the Perennial Garden Club was to place white flowering plants in tubs and flower beds throughout the garden. While we were discussing it, Mrs. Klaus and I looked out over a rather blank and bare expanse, but soon trees and shrubs would be in place, and within a few years the little city garden was transformed into a lovely oasis offering some outdoor relaxation space for our visitors.

King Olav V of Norway came in late April, followed the next month by Prime Minister Thanom Kittikachorn of Thailand and his wife, Chongkol. Her title was "Thantuying," and we were specifically asked by the Thai Embassy not to change that. Once again I found that I had a little trouble getting my tongue around the mellifluous-sounding Thai names, but I managed to call her "Mrs. Prime Minister" only when referring to her. In her presence, I struggled with "Thantuying Kittikachorn."

As chairwoman of her country's National Council of Women and editor of several magazines of interest to women, Thantuying Kittikachorn was one of the most influential women in her country and, indeed, in all of Asia.

Dallas had an easy time during this visit since, with one exception, every bit of the food the visitors ate came already prepared from their embassy, including an entire meal that was served very late one evening after there had been a state dinner at the White House.

Dallas prepared the food for a party the Thais gave for four American couples, including Chief Justice and Mrs. Earl Warren, and four Thai couples.

Ten minutes after the guests had gathered in the Blair drawing room, the Thai ambassador came to me and asked that we serve dinner. It was only about eight-forty, and dinner had been planned for nine, after a half hour for cocktails. But I instructed the butler to announce that dinner was served.

The Prime Minister promptly said we should wait until the guests had had more time for cocktails. The butler withdrew and the guests continued their cocktail hour.

After ten minutes the ambassador again drew me aside and suggested that it was time for dinner. I told him I thought we should wait for a signal from the Prime Minister, and although the ambassador still insisted, I managed, as diplomatically as possible, to stall him until the Prime Minister let it be known that now it was time to eat. They all went to the table at nine-fifteen.

Later I found out that the ambassador was worried that the Prime Minister would have too much to drink. But his worry was completely unfounded. The Prime Minister gave no evidence in any way during our stay that he had any sort of a drinking problem.

One of the Prime Minister's daughters was the wife of the naval attaché at the Thai Embassy; she had a ten-year-old son. Every night the little boy slipped into Blair House and slept in his grandmother's suite. He must have camped out on the chaise. When the Prime Minister was out on official business, the little boy, who was taking piano lessons, would practice on our piano. It was obvious that his grandmother doted on her grandson, whom she did not get a chance to be with very often.

(While the Symingtons were at the Protocol Office, Mrs. Symington, an accomplished pianist, noted that there was no piano at Blair House. The president of Steinway & Sons donated a small movable upright piano to the house. Later a Steinway grand was given to the house and put in the large reception room in the new Jackson Place addition.)

President Bourguiba of Tunisia returned to Blair House a week after the Thai visit. He appeared to be in perfect health this time. The President's son had returned to Tunisia and was now Secretary of State for Foreign Affairs. He traveled with his father, and his wife served as her father-in-law's official hostess on this trip.

President Bourguiba also brought along his valet and his own chef, who served him his meals no matter where he was eating, although, to tell the truth, the chef did very little of the cooking. He would appear in the kitchen about twenty minutes before dinner and watch Dallas prepare the food. Although the Tunisian chef spoke only French and Arabic, neither of which Dallas could understand, they seemed to understand each other over the cooking pots.

President Bourguiba was even planning to bring his own food —prepared in our kitchen by Dallas under the supervision of his chef—to dinner at the White House. I arranged for a car to pick up the chef and the President's valet along with the food about half an hour before the dinner was to take place. I had cleared them through the White House security, and I knew that there would be no problem.

At seven-thirty the car was waiting, but no one could find either the valet or the chef. The food had also vanished. We called the White House kitchen, but it was still waiting for them. Finally our security people ran them down. The chef and the valet had left in an embassy car, which had taken them to the wrong gate at the White House. There they were being held, food and all, until it could be discovered who they were and why they were bringing food into a house with one of the best kitchens in Washington.

Otherwise the visit from President Bourguiba went along uneventfully.

But the whole country was going through difficult times. Although the Vietnam peace talks had begun, the antiwar demonstrations that had been part of our landscape for a long time were at their peak that spring. I don't think I ever looked out the window during the early months of 1968 without seeing a large group of demonstrators in front of the White House holding their placards in a silent vigil or shouting their opposition to our country's policies. They were a constant presence in Lafayette Park or in the streets. And peace was not at hand.

In April Dr. Martin Luther King, Jr., was assassinated in Memphis. Washington was the scene of one of the most terrible and tragic riots the country had ever seen. The smoke from those parts of the city that had been set afire blew over the White House and could be seen from our windows. It was a devastating time.

The city of Washington shut down early the day the riot started so that workers in the various government agencies could get home before dark, but I was busy in the office and it was quite late before I was ready to leave. Dallas appeared at the door to my office and told me that he was taking Stewart, the houseman, home and that they would not leave until I was ready to go. Everyone else had left, I realized.

The streets were full of traffic. The trip home, which usually took half an hour, took three hours, but it was not the length of the trip or the traffic tie-ups that distressed us but the force of what was going on. It was a terrible and sad sight to see the city in such turmoil, made even more tragic by the conviction I had that the destruction and violence would solve nothing.

I had been in the riot neighborhood that morning before I knew how serious it was, to attend the funeral of our longtime friend and butler Rigoberto Rodriguez, who had died very suddenly. He was living alone and had fallen into a diabetic coma from which he didn't recover. Once again we had lost an irreplaceable member of the Blair House family.

The Monday following the start of the disturbances, the fires were still smoldering and there were pockets of violence in many parts of the city. We had a dinner scheduled. I was afraid that some of our staff would find it hard or impossible to get into town, but we decided to have the dinner even if we had to pick up the people at their homes.

Much of the rest of official Washington had slowed to a crawl. The hotels had been reduced to serving only sandwiches, since a large percentage of their work forces had been unable to come to work, and many business establishments were operating part-time. So it lifted everyone's spirits to be at Blair House that evening. Most of the staff had been able to get there, and although there was an air of solemnity in the group at dinner, the evening went well.

Then on the fourth of June I spent the night at Blair House. In the Head of State's Suite, President José Joaquín Trejos Fernández of Costa Rica was bedded down for the second night of a three-day visit. At 4:00 A.M. the telephone rang by my bed and the telephone operator gave me the terrible news that Senator Robert Kennedy had been shot in Los Angeles. I could not go back to sleep, so I went downstairs to have a cup of tea and look at the next day's schedule. I knew that the Costa Rican ambassador and Mrs. Ortuño had planned a huge reception in honor of President Trejos that night. Six hundred guests were expected at the Pan American Union.

In the morning, when President Trejos arose, there was a great deal of discussion about whether or not to cancel the evening's event. President Trejos was in favor of canceling. But other members of the party thought they should have the reception on a smaller scale, just for diplomats and members of the Costa Rican community. They wanted to switch the party to Blair House. I didn't think we could manage such a huge crowd. They cut the guest list down to three hundred, but it was still a lot of people for us to handle. Ambassador Duke asked me to try to do it, and I agreed.

We took as much furniture out of the downstairs rooms as we could, and I assigned butlers and parlormaids to take wraps and direct people as they came in.

The Costa Ricans had engaged Mr. Erich Braun, one of Washington's best caterers, and he brought the food they had prepared for six hundred guests. It was hard to find a place to put it all in our small pantry. Washtubs filled with ice were put behind the bars on pads so that the rugs would not be ruined. We managed to get everything organized by six o'clock, when the first guests arrived.

There were about three hundred fifty people and it was a very warm June evening. Our air conditioning was unable to cope with the crush of people, but somehow we managed. The crowd was very subdued under the tragic circumstance of the day, and by nine-thirty President and Mrs. Trejos went to their rooms. They asked that we serve dinner to about eight people in the library adjoining the Head of State's Suite. They had been scheduled to go to the Embassy for dinner, but those plans had been canceled. We managed to improvise a semiformal dinner.

The housemen worked until early the next morning to put the house back into shape.

The Trejoses and their party were sincerely grieved at the death of Senator Kennedy, and what had been a happy group enjoying their stay with us became a sober collection of people, just waiting out the time until they could return home.

On June 11 the Shah of Iran came for an overnight stay. Mr. Cyrus Farzaneh, who had often accompanied the Shah on his visits, inquired about my youngest daughter, Jenny. He had met her on his last stay at Blair House when she came to bring me something I had forgotten at home. I was happy to announce that she was getting married the next week.

The wedding was at Fort Sill, Oklahoma, and I was able to get away for a few days to help with preparations and to see my last child leave home. She was radiant with joy, even though her husband, a young marine lieutenant, was leaving for Vietnam before the end of the year. That was another reason I was hoping the Paris peace talks would be successful.

Angie and Robin had once again left for another assignment. This time Angie was named ambassador to Denmark. Tyler Abell, whose wife, Bess, was Mrs. Johnson's social secretary, took Angie's place. His father, George Abell, was an assistant chief of protocol and administered the oath of office to his son, who had been an assistant postmaster general.

President François Tombalbaye of the African country of Chad and his wife were the first guests Tyler Abell welcomed to the White House. Mr. Abell accompanied President Tombalbaye to Blair House, and after I greeted the President, the three of us and the French interpreter went upstairs so that the President could be settled into his room. As we were walking up the stairs, Tyler suggested that I tell the President something about the history of the house. I'm always glad to answer questions like that, but the opening minutes of a visit are not the best time for a history lecture. There's just too much else to do. Besides, I had noticed something quite alarming.

As we got to the top of the stairs, I saw that the door to the Head of State's Suite was closed. And the key normally found in the door was not there. Sure enough, when I tried the door, it was securely locked.

Luckily the door leading to the library was open, and as if it were routine, I showed the President and Tyler into that room. I was glad it was Tyler's first experience as chief of protocol because he also thought this was part of every visit. I made a bit of welcoming small talk through the interpreter, and then I asked the President if he would like some tea. I don't know how I would have gotten out of there if he had said no, but when he accepted the offer I left the room slowly and with dignity and then flew down the stairs into the pantry to ask the staff why the door to the Head of State's Suite was locked. They looked at me as if I had taken leave of my senses. I ordered a tea tray for the library and then tried to unravel the mystery.

I checked first with our security men, thinking that maybe they had some special orders, but they knew nothing. They promised to check with Chad security. I went out into the front hall thinking, "*Now* what do I do?" Just then I saw a member of the Chad party coming down the stairs swinging a large brass key. It looked suspiciously like the key to the Head of State's Suite. I grabbed an interpreter and one of our security men and explained that we didn't lock the doors to the rooms before the guests had been installed, and then only if a guest requested it.

It turned out that this zealous Chad security man had come over to the house early and had locked all the bedroom doors, taking the keys with him for safekeeping. By this time the other members of the party began to gather around, wondering why they couldn't get into their rooms. Fortunately Mrs. Tombalbaye and Mrs. Massabi, another lady in the party, had come over earlier in the afternoon and were safely settled in.

Eventually we got everyone into their rooms, but it was not an easy task since all the keys had to be sorted out before this could be accomplished.

In a house like Blair House there are a lot of keys. The enormity of the situation in which I found myself will become clear if you realize that in today's Blair House there are seventy-three rooms, nineteen closets, and ten outside entrances—and *each one has its own key*. Luckily there is a master key that can be used for about forty of the inside locks, and I was able to use this key to open several of the bedrooms for the Chad visitors.

There was a large key cabinet in my office where the keys to each room were hung. Another complete set of keys was kept in a vault whose combination was known only to the housekeeper and me. The combination was changed every time there was a change in housekeepers, and it is never written down. The two people entitled to know it memorize it and keep it to themselves. The only record of the combination is kept in a vault in the Department of State. If all of this sounds like something out of a spy thriller, remember that the security of a great many of the world's most important people was in our hands while they were at Blair House, and the tightest controls were necessary.

The head houseman, Dallas, and I had a key to one outside entrance, and the same key was also in the hands of the Department of State and both the White House and the General Services Administration security people. This key opened the only entrance that could be opened from the outside with a key. All the other entrances could be opened only from the inside. Just to be extra careful, there was also a padlock on the front gate.

It took quite a bit of time before everything was back to normal. The first thing I did, of course, was open the door to the suite and show the President in.

Ambassador Abell came downstairs to wait for him in the sitting room before they went off together for the first official meeting of the day. I don't think either one of them ever realized the problems we had had.

It turned out that the chaos that began the visit continued almost without letup. For example, that day a reception was scheduled at Blair House for the ambassadors from the African nations. The reception was to begin at five-thirty. An hour before that time, it was discovered that someone had forgotten to invite the guests. Sam King, assistant chief of protocol, hastily called all the embassies and ten of the ambassadors arrived shortly after the appointed hour.

Later that evening, when the visitors assembled in the drawing room to await the signal to go across the street to the White House for dinner, I noticed that the President's wife was not there. It was getting late, and it was important that the party leave the minute the White House called. I asked Jeanine, our interpreter, to go upstairs to see if she could hurry Mrs. Tombalbaye along. And on an impulse I followed her up the stairs. When I got to the landing, Jeanine was just rushing out of the Queen's Suite. Her face was that of someone in mild shock. "She doesn't know she was invited," she announced, "and so she hasn't planned to go. She isn't even dressed."

Through Jeanine I informed Mrs. Tombalbaye that indeed she had been invited and was expected. She was a little chagrined, I think, since her husband had not bothered to tell her about the invitation. I got a parlormaid up to the room and she and Jeanine somehow managed to get her dressed. Jeanine even put up her hair for her, since she had been planning to wear a kerchief. I explained to Ambassador Abell what had happened and asked our security officer to leave a car for her because I was certain she wouldn't be ready in time for the call from the White House. I informed the rest of the party that Mrs. Tombalbaye would be coming along in a short time.

When she finally came downstairs, the First Lady was quite nervous, petrified really, so I sent Jeanine with her to make sure that she would be turned over to someone at the White House who would make her comfortable. It was all new to Mrs. Tombalbaye, and the fact that she spoke no English at all made it more of an ordeal for her. But when she returned after dinner she was smiling happily. She had had a lovely time, she said. The next evening she was downstairs, dressed beautifully and with her hair freshly done, ready to go to an embassy reception. I felt we had helped her over a difficult few minutes and was pleased to see that it had all turned out so well.

Soon we were plunged into the hard-fought national election of 1968, and the number of visitors to Blair House dropped off sharply. With the election of Richard Nixon we anticipated quite a few changes in Washington, including a new chief of protocol. I asked Wiley Buchanan, a good friend of mine and chief of protocol under Eisenhower, if he was coming back as chief in the Nixon administration. But he answered, "No, you have to work too hard in that job."

I have seen many chiefs of protocol come and go. Of course, one can't help having special favorites, but I always worked under the rule that whoever was in office as President, whoever was Secretary of State, and whoever was the chief, I was going to do as good a job as I could. Still, I would miss Secretary and Mrs. Rusk, who were so helpful during their term of office, and I had grown very fond of the Johnson family.

In December we had two visits, the first from Amir Abbas Hoveyda and his wife. Mr. Hoveyda was a Prime Minister of Iran who was subsequently executed by the Khomeini regime. He was a very brave man who, when offered exile from his country after the Ayatollah Khomeini took over, refused to leave.

Our last official visit during 1968—and the last visitor for President Johnson—was Sheikh Sabah al-Salim al-Sabah, the Emir of Kuwait. The Emir was personally very austere in his taste. However, after their Sheikh had retired, many of the other members of his party would party until the early hours of the morning.

The Kuwaitis arrived with a large sum of money, which they gave for safekeeping to a security man. On their last day the entire group went to a mosque in the Washington area and the security man gave me the money in a Federal Reserve bag to hold until they returned. I couldn't wait for them to get back so that I could be rid of that little bag.

Chapter Twenty

ONCE AGAIN a new Administration was taking over. On the Friday before the inauguration of Richard M. Nixon, Clem Conger called to say he was bringing over our new chief of protocol designate, Emil (Bus) Mosbacher, Jr., and his wife, Pat. I liked them both immediately, and we sat down and talked easily together for about two hours and then toured the house. The Mosbachers had many questions and seemed to be really interested in what had been going on at Blair House. I knew that Pat Mosbacher would be an active participant in the renovation.

Our friendship lasted and deepened during Bus's entire two-and-a-half-year term as chief of protocol. But at the time of our first meeting I wasn't even sure that I would be staying at Blair House. I had been hearing rumors—not for the first time—about someone who wanted my job. I knew that if either the chief of protocol or the President had another candidate for the position, I could be transferred back to the Department of State. But as it turned out, although I had an uneasy week or two, those who were campaigning behind the scenes to change things at Blair House lost out, and I stayed on.

Inauguration Day was bitterly cold. The usual arrangement had been made on the street so that guests and visitors could see the inaugural parade. There were loudspeakers set up in front of the house, and tight security arrangements had been made. Antiwar demonstrators had contributed to the feeling of tension that hung in the air.

On Inauguration Day we would be serving as a way station

for the diplomatic corps, providing coffee and refreshments and
opening the Blair House guest rooms.

The diplomats began arriving in shivering groups around 2:00
P.M. They came and went all day and, to be truthful, many of
them stayed in the warm house and watched the marchers
through our windows. The Jamaican and Chilean ambassadors
and their wives seemed nearly frozen when they arrived. They
simply took off their coats and stayed.

Mr. Whitehead, a protocol officer, came with the wives of the
astronauts who were the highlight of the parade. They were getting the same sort of attention that John F. Kennedy's PT-109
crew received during his inauguration.

The parade was very colorful, with floats from every state in
the Union and bands and military groups from all over the country, and there was the usual air of expectation that always sur-
rounds a change in administration.

Pat Mosbacher plunged right into her role as the wife of the
chief of protocol. In an interview given to the Washington *Star's*
Marian Burros in April of 1969 Pat stated, in her straightforward, no-nonsense manner, "Protocol is a frightening-sounding
word, but it is really just manners. It's nothing new. You just
have to remember what your mother told you." It was as good
a description of protocol as I have ever heard.

It was Pat's idea to try to solicit gifts from donors for the dec-
oration of whole rooms. People who wanted to make a very visible contribution could be persuaded to give the furnishings for
some of the rooms that were still not finished.

But the first task of the year was linking Blair House to the
Carnegie House next door on Jackson Place. There was some
fear that funds would run out before we could carry out the
plans, and so we met to decide on priorities.

It was clear that the matter of the greatest importance was the
pantry on the Jackson Place side, since the linkage would destroy our old pantry as well as the bathrooms all the way up the
house on that side. On February 15 the demolition of the outside
wall of Blair House began. We were being closed in about three
feet inside that wall, and another inside wall would be cut off
the back hall during the demolition. We would have to store the
things from the Blair pantry in the Blair-Lee pantry or send

them to a storage warehouse. The rooms adjoining the new
house all the way up to the fourth floor were to be closed off,
which also meant that we would lose our elevator temporarily. It
was going to be a long walk up to the fourth floor for a while.

Another casualty was our wine cellar. The wine was carefully
moved to another room in the basement. We were assured that
everything would be finished and back to normal by July 15.
Secretly I decided that I could count on completion by October
15, and until then we'd have to make do with a greatly
decreased amount of space and comfort.

Mrs. Nixon came by one day in February with a friend, Mrs.
Jack Drown from California. They spent over an hour walking
around the house through rooms that were already refurbished
and even picked their way delicately over the demolition in
progress. Mrs. Nixon was a gentle and very shy woman, soft-
spoken and extremely careful about the feelings of other people.
She was familiar with Blair House from the days when her husband had been Vice-President. Now she expressed her concern
about the wreckage, which seemed to her to make it much more
difficult to entertain visitors. I tried to reassure her that we
would manage. But she was right. This phase of the renovation
process was the most difficult for all of us at Blair House.

In March, Prime Minister Trudeau of Canada was President
Nixon's first state visitor. The whole visit was a joy as well as a
comedy of errors. First there was the matter of the room assignments. Through some foul-up, Mr. Mitchell Sharp, the Canadian
Secretary of State and the ranking member of the party after the
Prime Minister, had been given a more modest room than the
Secretary of the Cabinet. But luckily they were all very amiable.
Mr. Sharp came downstairs after being shown his room and said
jokingly, "How come Secretary Robinson got the room with all
those lovely antiques?" I mumbled something about a typing
error.

Then late one afternoon the parlormaid came into the dining
room where a meeting was in progress. She asked everyone
seated around the dining table to please sit in the drawing room
so that she could set the table for dinner. They all collected their
papers and trooped meekly out before the error was discovered.

When I heard about all of this and went up to apologize, they
said that their meeting had been nearly over anyway.

The Prime Minister was a charming man who had simple
tastes. He didn't smoke and he drank only a glass of wine or a
bottle of beer with dinner. His warm and witty manner made it
easy to be with him. One evening the butler was helping him
into his coat as he was preparing to leave for the White House
when he turned to me and said, "What time should I be home?"
I was a little startled and so I stammered, "I leave that to your
good judgment, Mr. Prime Minister." And he replied, "Oh, my
mother often tells me what time I should be in."

I was still laughing when I went down to my office after the
door had closed behind him, but my laughter quickly died when
I saw that my office had flooded again from one of the recurring
problems in our laundry room. Luckily the GSA was able to get
a night plumber to come fix the mess before our visitors returned.

Another day during the visit, while everyone was out, thank
goodness, we had one of our false fire alarms. And so it went
during the whole time they were with us. But since they never
experienced these emergencies and were such a happy group
anyhow, I remember that visit as one of the most pleasant we
ever had.

When the Prime Minister and his party were about to leave,
he gave me an autographed picture of himself that I still treasure, and then with a twinkle in his eye he said, "I hope I have
not been too difficult a guest."

"On the contrary, Mr. Prime Minister," I said, "you have been
very well behaved."

"I wish you would tell that to my mother," he replied and
then, to my complete astonishment, kissed me good-bye.

Later that week, just as the guests were arriving for a luncheon, I got a call from the office saying that former President
Eisenhower had died. We were to go on with the luncheon, but
the upcoming visit of Prime Minister Gorton of Australia was
postponed.

President Nixon had invited both former Presidents, Johnson
and Truman, to stay at Blair House over the weekend and on

into the following week for President Eisenhower's funeral. I was told about this on Friday and arranged for a staff to be ready at the house for the visits. On Saturday I learned that the Trumans, on the advice of their doctor, were not coming, but I heard nothing further about the Johnsons' plans, so I kept the staff and was prepared for a visit.

It was not until Monday that I heard the Johnsons would be staying at a hotel. Someone had forgotten to tell the Johnson staff people that I needed to be informed. We had no guests for the funeral at all.

A week later we were once again hosts to King Hussein of Jordan. He brought along his brother, Crown Prince Hassan, who shared the King's fondness for hamburgers. By now we knew to lay in a good supply of chopped beef whenever the Jordanians were expected. As usual, they called for a double order of hamburgers almost as soon as they arrived and ate them just before leaving for a state dinner. Knowing how often the head of state is interrupted during those formal meals, I could understand why the King and the Crown Prince had a snack before leaving. But two hamburgers apiece were quite a hearty snack.

The work was proceeding on the renovation next door and I found myself exploring new territories in connection with the changes we were making. One day, with a mask on my face to protect me from the marble dust that was everywhere, I walked through a marble warehouse to select the material for the tops of the vanities in the bathrooms. It was fascinating, like being in another world. There were slabs of marble as tall as a room stacked wherever you looked. We wanted an off-white for all the vanities. A lot of the marble looked white until you got close to it, and then little veins of color—tan, green, or gold—were revealed. I picked the purest white they had. I felt as if I had stumbled into an alien world. There were no windows, and an otherworldly light pervaded the place, and in addition, I was the only woman there.

I also went to a wholesaler in beauty supplies because so many of the hairdressers who came to Blair House had complained that we had no shampoo chair. It was really quite difficult to shampoo comfortably the hair of a woman sitting in a straight chair. I hoped I could get the chair in time for the now rescheduled visit of Prime Minister and Mrs. Gorton. I got the price on the chair and was given the clearance to order it, but it wasn't delivered in time for the visit.

We were going to have a great many visitors in the next few months. Quite a number of foreign guests came to meet the new President, many of whom were interested in effecting a change in our Vietnam policies. I knew that we were in for a busy time.

The Gorton visit went off without incident until the morning when Mrs. Gorton woke to find that she had somehow dislodged the cap on her front tooth overnight. She was due at the White House that morning and was understandably a bit upset. Luckily my dentist had arrived at his office early that day, and he was able to make a temporary replacement in time. He was so pleased to have been able to help one of our distinguished visitors that he didn't even charge for his services.

Mrs. Gorton was American-born and had met her husband when they were both students at Oxford University in England.

Our next guests were the young royal couple from Belgium, King Baudouin and Queen Fabiola. When I showed them to their rooms, His Majesty informed me that they would both be sleeping in the Queen's Suite.

From the beginning I felt that I had always known them. They were as unpretentious and easygoing as the "couple next door." Queen Fabiola was very shy and reserved and quite beautiful.

They had been at Cape Kennedy witnessing the Apollo 10 moon shot launch before coming to Blair House, and after spending one night with us they went to the Goddard Space Center in Beltsville, Maryland, for a tour of those facilities. But before they left, a Belgian priest came to the house and served Mass in the library. I believe that this was the only time a religious service had been held there.

A regularly occurring event during this time was a luncheon meeting of the Foreign Intelligence Advisory Board. This group —usually numbering about twelve people—met every other month for two days at the Old Executive Office Building and came over to the house for lunch since they could be sure not only of a good meal but also of guaranteed privacy. The board was under the chairmanship of General Maxwell Taylor. The members included Governor Nelson Rockefeller, Clare Boothe Luce, and several eminent scientists. The board was disbanded when President Carter took office.

In 1971, during one of the meetings at the house, there was a call for Governor Rockefeller on the phone in the pantry. The caller said it was urgent that he speak to the governor. So we interrupted the meeting and he went into the pantry on the other side of the house where he could speak in absolute privacy.

I stood outside the door so that he would not be disturbed, and when he came out, after ten minutes or so, he said, almost to himself, "This can't go on forever. Someone had to do something." I had no idea what he was talking about until the next day, when it was revealed that Governor Rockefeller had given the order to break up the riot at Attica prison. I realized that the order must have been given over the Blair House pantry phone that afternoon.

In 1969 the entire country was excited about our country's exploration of outer space. When Ambassador Mosbacher asked me if I'd like to witness the Apollo 11 launch on July 16 I didn't hesitate for a moment. Even though it meant I'd miss out on a night's sleep, I was eager to go. At four o'clock on the morning of the launch I was handing out literature to a group of diplomats and their wives. We were going to board a plane which would take us to Cape Kennedy. We were airborne at 5:00 A.M. and had breakfast on board. By seven, when we arrived, we were all terribly keyed up. We were driven out to an auditorium and briefed by astronaut Tom Stafford for about an hour.

By the time we got to the moon shot site and were sitting in the grandstand, the Florida sun had made its appearance. I seemed to be the only person who had brought a hat. The others were soon decked out in makeshift hats made from newspapers. The men had taken off their jackets. It was refreshing to see the usually impeccably dressed diplomatic corps in their shirt sleeves.

A loud boom came from the rocket and after a breathtaking second it rose into the sky amid clouds of steam, and we all felt we had witnessed a historic event.

Then we were taken on a tour of the space center and back to our waiting plane. By three we were back at Andrews Air Force Base, exhausted but exhilarated.

Back in my little corner of this planet there was a great deal of progress. The exterior work of the Jackson Place renovation had been completed and it was now possible to walk from Blair House into the new addition, although the work inside was continuing. Actually, because of the terrible dust everywhere, we tried to do as little commuting as possible to the new addition. But it was nice to see the work proceeding on schedule.

Meanwhile, Mrs. Jane Fitch of Hudson, Ohio, a suburb of Cleveland, was ready to complete a project that had taken three years of planning and work. Room 36 was ready to be transformed into one of the most unusual and beautiful rooms in the entire house. Mrs. Fitch had been collecting furniture for the room and was now prepared to move it in. We had had the walls painted off-white in preparation for her refurnishing.

The focal point of what came to be known as the Needlepoint Room was a fabulous rug that covered the floor. Anne Hopkins Burnham, a fellow Ohioan who had heard of Mrs. Fitch's project, designed the rug and had selected sixty-four expert needle-pointers to translate her graphs and drawings into a series of squares that were joined together. Mrs. Fitch made the needlepoint border. The predominant colors were soft blues, pinks, and greens on a blue-gray background. The squares and border were joined so beautifully you could not see the seams.

The rug depicted a woodland scene with a pool at its center. Water lilies, frogs, dragonflies, and even a little snake were found in the pool. Around its edges and scattered over the expanse of the rug were all the flowers, ferns, and creatures of the forest. Rabbits, mice, chipmunks, birds, and butterflies frolicked among the leaves and blossoms, and as you looked it seemed that new little animals emerged from hiding. The detail was incredible, the artistry extraordinary. The rug was almost too beautiful to walk on, and nearly every visitor commented on its unique beauty.

Mrs. Fitch had created the overall design of the room, including the crewel embroideries that were used for draperies at the two windows and as hangings on the unusual beds.

Ohioans George Shephard and Sydney McKenzie converted an 1860 four-poster bed, which had been donated for the room, into two twin beds, using the original four beautiful carved posts for the headboards of the new beds. New footboards were designed. To make sure that everything was just as he wanted it to be, Mr. Shephard came to Blair House personally to oversee the installation of the beds.

The lamps in the room were the work of another Ohio artist, the late Virginia Clark Ellis, whose work is now highly prized by collectors of folk art. The lamps had hand-painted bases and shades in colors that complemented those in the rest of the room.

Between the windows, a full-length mirror made the room seem larger and reflected its treasures. Mrs. Fitch brought in a new easy chair with a crewel-embroidered cushion, but she retained the antique chest that had been in the room originally. The adjoining bath was not overlooked in the redecorating effort, and Hammacher Schlemmer contributed a splendid closet design to complete the room.

Since it had been in the works for three years while chiefs of protocol came and went, the people involved in this project have not until now received the credit due them for their extraordinary gift.

The Needlepoint Room became a peaceful oasis in the busy house, and often when things went wrong I would wander up there for a moment's rest. It never failed to build up my morale to spend a few moments looking at that restful yet active woodland scene.

The day I came to work to find new awning frames being installed outside was such an occasion. The new awning was wider than the old one, and the holes for the frame had to be set back farther on the sidewalk so that people could get their car doors open. But that morning, to my horror, I saw that the new holes were being placed in the same position as the old ones. Luckily I had come upon this disaster before the awning had been completely installed, and by making a few phone calls I was able to forestall catastrophe. Then I went up to sit in the Needlepoint Room for five minutes of relaxation and peace.

Mrs. Arthur Gardner had agreed to refurbish Rooms 33 and

34, the suite on the third floor that we had always called Margaret Truman's room because Margaret had lived there during her years at Blair House.

There were two rooms and a bath. Mr. Glenn Smith of Palm Beach, Florida, the decorator, wanted to use as many of the original furnishings as possible, but he made one radical change. The suite's sitting room became the bedroom, and the bedroom was turned into a sitting room. Since the bedroom would then connect to the bathroom, this seemed quite logical, and I often wondered why no one had thought of it before.

Because the two rooms were of about the same size, it was no problem to change their functions while retaining their furnishings. In both rooms the walls were painted pale yellow and the woodwork and ceilings were white. A white wall-to-wall carpet decorated with little gold fleur-de-lis went on the floor. I was certain that rug would be gray in no time, but it has held up amazingly well.

Pale yellow and apricot chintz printed with a leaf design was made up into bedspreads. A quilted version of the fabric covered the headboard, and chintz draperies and a valance hung at the windows.

A lovely carved wooden mantel was brought in for the sitting room fireplace. The wood was left in its natural state and waxed. In the bedroom the original mantel of marble with a touch of apricot was retained. A large framed portrait of the Dearborn children, ancestors of the Blairs, hung above the fireplace.

On one side of the fireplace Mrs. Gardner placed a dressing table, and on the other, a small cabinet that had been in the room all along.

A Queen Anne–type easy chair was reupholstered in pale yellow, and several reproduction Lowestoft china pieces with deep apricot borders were put on tables and on the mantelpieces.

The lamps in the room got new shades, and one new lamp, which was attached to a small round table, was brought in.

Two of the original straight chairs in what was now the bedroom were reupholstered in a white and rust fabric.

In the sitting room two settees faced each other over a Chinese lacquer table. They were upholstered in the same chintz, and two new club easy chairs were upholstered in a luscious apricot velvet. On one side of the fireplace there was a lowboy that had been in the room, and against a back wall, a tall cabinet with a glass front. It contained pieces of porcelain from the Blair House collection.

A smaller table desk and the little armchair that Mrs. Kennedy had admired on her first visit were also placed in this room. Over the sitting room mantel there was a gold-framed mirror, and a large oval painting of a young girl who was a Blair relative was hung above the sofa.

Double doors opened from one room to the other so that there would be privacy in the sleeping quarters. As a final authentic touch, Mrs. Gardner added old brass hardware, similar to that on the first and second floors of the house, to all the doors in the newly refurbished suite.

The whole effect was light and extremely elegant. The room was, from then on, reserved for the second-ranking guest in the head of state's party, which was most often the Foreign Minister. Of course, on several occasions, it was once again Margaret Truman's room.

In August, Kurt Georg Kiesinger, Chancellor of the Federal Republic of Germany, was our guest. Chancellor Kiesinger had been at Blair House in 1967, but on that occasion he had spent only two days of a four-day visit with us; the other two days he was at the home of his daughter, who lived in Washington. The papers had been full of pictures of the Chancellor playing with his grandchildren. He was photographed eating dinner with them, playing outside with them, and having a wonderful time just being "Opa" instead of Chancellor.

This time, when Chancellor Kiesinger was invited to the White House, Dr. Wernher von Braun, the German-born rocket expert, was one of the guests. In his toast to the Chancellor, Dr. von Braun predicted confidently that both the United States and Germany would have "men on Mars by 1982."

In September, Prime Minister Golda Meir of Israel came for an overnight stay. She gave the appearance of being a grandmotherly sort of woman, but beneath that warm exterior, I knew, she was a fierce champion of her country's cause and had a strong sense of what she wanted in every situation. She was accompanied on this trip by her Foreign Minister, Abba Eban,

and his wife, Susan. Mrs. Yitzhak Rabin, wife of the Israeli ambassador to the United States, was extremely helpful in the planning of this visit, and Mrs. Meir's longtime companion, Mrs. Lou
Kaddar, tried every way she could to find some time in Mrs.
Meir's busy schedule for a few rest periods.

Mrs. Meir had other plans and no intention of slowing down.
When she returned at 11:15 P.M. after a White House state dinner, she did go immediately to her suite. A few minutes later,
Henry Kissinger, who was not at that time Secretary of State but
was already beginning his diplomatic activities in the Middle
East, arrived to keep an appointment made over the dinner
table. He left after midnight, but Mrs. Meir was still not ready
for bed. A few minutes later her sister, her son, and her
daughter-in-law came over for an hour or two. It was a day that
would have exhausted me. But Mrs. Meir seemed to thrive on it.

Early next morning there was a breakfast for a selected group
of congressmen. And so it went until the Prime Minister left for
the trip home. She later sent me a thank-you note in which she
said she was only sorry she didn't get enough leisure during her
stay to see more of the house and really enjoy her visit.

We were experiencing a very busy time, a flurry of visits.
Prince Souvanna Phouma of Laos was followed by Prince Fahd
Ibn Abd al-Aziz, Second Deputy Minister of Saudi Arabia. The
Shah of Iran arrived for a short stay without the Empress, who
was expecting a child, and the Prime Minister of Japan, Eisaku
Sato, was our last guest for the year.

But when there were not guests, there were many functions.
The house was in daily use. In addition, there was a lot to do
concerning the house's expansion.

Sometime in November, Ambassador Mosbacher came over
for lunch and we talked about the increased use Blair House
was getting. I told him that I could predict with certainty that
as soon as the Jackson Place connection was completed, we
would be using the house even more often. It had been no secret
that I wanted to have additional help: I had been campaigning
for this for some time. Now I said that I would need at least one
more chambermaid and another permanent houseman for the
present, but most important of all, I wanted an assistant to take
some of the burden of the paper work off my hands. I needed

someone whom I could train to take over some of the supervisory duties as well. Since Ingrid had left I had had no one to whom I could entrust some of the details of a reception or a visit if I was busy with other things.

We had a good discussion and I managed to describe in some detail what I thought the future staffing of the expanded house would look like. When Ambassador Mosbacher left, he said he would be back with Frank Meyer, assistant secretary of state for administration, who could approve the allocations for extra positions. I was already feeling more optimistic just discussing the subject. I had even managed to put in a word about the much needed appropriations for finishing the interior work on the Carnegie House. I was afraid that when the exterior work was completed, the inside of the house might not be done.

A few months later I took President Nixon on his first real tour of the renovated Blair House. He was very impressed at what had been accomplished since he last saw the house.

When we came downstairs he turned to me and said, "Mrs. Wilroy, are you sure we can afford all of this?" He was joking, but to many people it probably seemed that Blair House was an extravagance, a frill that could be dispensed with in a time of tightening budgets. But Blair House is not a luxury. It is necessary for the President to have an easily accessible, elegant house in which to receive and entertain the guests of the nation.

The problem with the Blair House budget has always been that it is administered both by the State Department, which is in charge of the overall operation, and by the General Services Administration, which handles the maintenance. This arrangement results in many gray areas. Often the funds that are so desperately needed are not allocated because they fall somewhere between the two departments. It was for this reason that I was always very vocal, quite open, and sometimes I guess even a wee bit aggressive about voicing our needs.

Early in December Mrs. Spiro Agnew held her first press party at Blair House. Seventy-five newspaper, magazine, and television reporters were invited to meet informally with the wife of the Vice-President. They were given a tour of the house and a chance to meet informally with Mrs. Agnew, who answered questions about her family, her Christmas plans ("No, I haven't decided what yet to give my husband. If you have any ideas, you'll let me know, I hope"), and her preference in fashion. Those were the days when what a woman wore was as important as what she said. Mrs. Agnew was dressed in a "smooth black wool dress with a gay scarf at the neckline."

The women had just about finished their coffee when the butler responded to the front door. There stood the Vice-President.

He had walked across the street from his office in the Executive Office Building, probably anxious to see how Mrs. Agnew was doing at her first meeting with the press.

Mr. Agnew seemed quite at home among all those ladies. He stayed about fifteen minutes, during which time he was asked what he thought of this group of press people. He had already created quite a bit of controversy by outspoken criticism of the media. These are "my favorite kind of press people," he was quoted as saying. "They are prettier, nicer, more objective . . . what else can I say?"

The highlight of the Vice-President's visit, however, was not what he said but what he did. He was persuaded to sit down at the piano and render the Agnew version of "Sophisticated Lady." Then, amid applause, he ended his little impromptu visit.

On the first anniversary of his inauguration President Nixon was given a party by Secretary of State and Mrs. William P. Rogers. The entire Cabinet and their wives were invited. I checked with Lucy Winchester, Mrs. Nixon's social secretary, at the White House about the menu and made sure that I'd have the best parlormaids and my pick of butlers for this very special party.

The menu featured Mr. Nixon's favorites: quail with white grapes and Madeira sauce, wild rice with truffles, baked eggplant provençal, green peas with water chestnuts, and a watercress and avocado salad served with pâté. For dessert we served one of Dallas' rich chocolate desserts.

The mood of the party was relaxed and happy, a group of friends celebrating together, but the plans had been elaborate. The forty guests came early so that they could rehearse their big number, the Whittier College song.

Bryce Harlow, President Nixon's counsel and one of the wittiest men in Washington, was the master of ceremonies. And the high point of the evening was a film specially made for the evening. It was a little hard to describe. Imagine, if you will, a football game with ballet music as a background and a ballet teacher's commentary as the spoken sound track. Anyhow, everyone found it hilarious.

The football theme continued in a picture given to the President at the dinner. This was a photograph of a football team with the faces of the Cabinet members substituted for the real players; the photo was labeled "The President's First Team." Mr. Nixon in turn gave each member of the Cabinet a framed photo of himself, with the presidential seal and the motto "Forward Together" set into the frame. Each of the women received a pin decorated with the presidential seal in blue enamel inside a circle of pearls.

The Cabinet members gave their "boss" a golf putter made of wood from the inaugural stand. Mr. Nixon's signature had been engraved in the putter's blade. Mrs. Nixon was given a jewelry box made of the same wood, lined with silk.

There was informal seating, with several Cabinet members at each of the four round tables. At Mrs. Nixon's place we put a nosegay of her favorite flowers, daisies. The other tables had bunches of spring flowers.

After dinner there were many toasts. Betty Beale reported in her column in the next day's Washington *Evening Star* that Mr. Nixon had responded to the toasts by saying that he didn't want to say anything meaningful or he wouldn't have anything left for the State of the Union Message, which was scheduled for a few days later.

By now Pat Mosbacher had formed a new Fine Arts Committee. She had kept most of the experts who had served on the original committee but had added many new people. Right from the beginning, Pat had put her own personal stamp on the renovating process. She had quite a number of good connections, both with large companies, such as Bloomingdale's, and with people who might be interested in helping in the work. Pat also came up with one of the best ideas for a new room for the house. Why not have a beauty parlor, she said. And Elizabeth Arden, who had contributed so much to the house and from whom we almost always got our hairdressers, would probably be pleased to contribute to this room. She was right.

The new beauty parlor was to be situated on the third floor of the new Jackson Place House. It would have all the facilities of a professional salon. There were to be built-in cabinets, dressing tables with excellent makeup mirrors, a shampoo room, hair dryers, manicure tables, and all sorts of toiletries and the equipment to give almost any kind of beauty treatment.

The room was decorated in soft pinks, flattering the complexion, and like all the Elizabeth Arden salons in the world, it was to be found behind a red door.

When his wife told him about the Elizabeth Arden project, Bus Mosbacher quipped, "Well, I hope they will give you the room, seeing as you've already paid for it many times with your constant visits to Elizabeth Arden salons."

Early in 1970 we were expecting a visit from President and Mrs. Georges Pompidou of France, and I was sorry that the new beauty parlor would not be finished in time. Mme. Pompidou was bringing her own hairdresser from France, we had heard, and there were going to be many ladies in the party in addition to the elegant wife of the President.

When they arrived, the daily press was there in force. They were there because M. Pompidou was the head of one of the most important countries in the world. But the main focus of their attention was not on NATO or French atomic energy developments. It was centered on what Mme. Pompidou was wearing.

She was a tall, slender woman with blond hair and a dimple in her cheek who wore the clothes of most of the French designers, Dior, Cardin, Chanel, Saint Laurent, and Mme. Rochas. Her hats were by Paulette of Paris; her perfume, Chanel No. 5.

When she stepped off the plane for the official welcome, the press noted with enormous excitement that she was wearing her skirt at a new longer length. In America some women were still in miniskirts and most of us wore knee-length. The shortest skirt Mme. Pompidou wore was mid-calf, and her coat was just a few inches above the ankle.

The flashbulbs popped, the pencils flew. Matters of state were ignored while the press reported that Mme. Pompidou (she was quickly called Claude) wore a hat to every daytime occasion. The reporters were entranced that every day she had on the same pair of beige peau de soie pumps with medium boxy heels and rounded toes that she wore on her arrival. But she changed her clothes constantly. There was a new outfit for every function, and every single dress, suit, gown was photographed and photographed.

Picture after picture recorded the ensembles. Paragraph after paragraph was devoted to the hemline. One *Star* photographer got the brilliant idea of photographing Mrs. Mosbacher, Mme. Pompidou, and Mrs. Agnew in a row—from the knees down. By then everyone knew that the one in the longest skirt was the French First Lady.

For the Pompidou visit we were finally able to use all the Blair House bedrooms again, and seventeen members of the Pompidou party stayed at the house. Security and protocol offices were hastily set up on the first floor of Jackson Place in space that had just been completed, and on the second floor of the new area we established offices for M. Pompidou's staff. The furnishings were haphazardly assembled and temporary, but it was grand to have so much room. I couldn't imagine how we had ever managed without it.

For the security people, the expanded space meant that they had to increase their area of surveillance. Now they had to secure the Jackson Place House and its entrance, which was around the corner from the Blair House entrance.

As usual, during a visit there were some unexpected requests. President Pompidou's Water Pik broke down and we had to send it out for a quick repair. Mme. Pompidou ordered some pieces of luggage to be sent over so that she could select several new suitcases.

During the visit I was working with the telephone company to iron out the wrinkles that had appeared in our new, expanded intercom system. Calls meant for the pantry were finding their way up to the third floor or the kitchen. But we soon had everything in working order.

After the large French party left, the house seemed quiet and almost empty. We spent every minute getting the new areas of the house furnished so that we could use it as much as possible as soon as possible. Pat Mosbacher was getting increasingly involved in soliciting contributions to that end. Although she worked much more behind the scenes than some of the other protocol wives, she was every bit as energetic and successful at finding generous donors.

On the first Saturday in April we had some visitors about whom I had heard such a lot that I was filled with anticipation of their overnight stay as the day approached.

The Duke and Duchess of Windsor were coming as guests of the Nixons. The first question I had was how were we to address them. The Duke, it turned out, was called Your Royal Highness; the Duchess was simply Your Highness.

When they arrived I showed them to their rooms, and tea was served. They were to go to the White House for a dinner in their honor and after breakfast at Blair House the following morning would be off for Palm Beach, where they were to be the guests of Mrs. Arthur Gardner.

The Duke and Duchess were escorted to Blair House by Ambassador and Mrs. Mosbacher and by British Ambassador John Freeman and his wife, who had greeted them on their arrival at the railroad station. The Duke was staying in the Head of State's Suite and the Duchess was in the adjoining Queen's Suite. Both loved their rooms and kept running back and forth between them showing each other the little things they had found there. The Duchess checked to see that her luggage had been sent to her room. I was amazed to see that they traveled with only two small bags.

When we sat down to tea the Duke asked me directly and in a very forthright manner where I was from. When I told him Maryland, the Duchess chimed in, saying that she was from Baltimore, and we talked about that city and the "white marble steps." This row of town houses with steps that were scrubbed every morning used to be a Baltimore landmark. He had just said, "Maryland people are quite clannish, in my experience," when the tea arrived—luckily, since I couldn't think of anything to say in response.

I poured for them. The Duchess took hers plain, but the Duke asked for milk. Neither ate more than a mouthful from the amply stacked tea tray. They were both extremely slender and looked very well. Although the Duke was using a cane, he was really quite spry. He refused to use our elevator, choosing the stairs although he was seventy-five years old at the time.

The Windsors traveled with a small staff. He was accompanied by his secretary, Miss Jacquet, and the Duchess had a lady's maid with her. But the Duke had no valet, and so I sent Domenic up to help him dress that evening. A hairdresser and a makeup man came at six to assist the Duchess in her preparations.

When the Duke and Duchess came downstairs, His Royal Highness said that, by helping him dress, Domenic had saved his life. Just then he noticed Domenic in the dining room. He called to him rather loudly and Domenic came running, more than just a little startled by the Duke's tone. But the Duke, smiling broadly, said he only wanted to thank him for his help. The expression of relief on poor Domenic's face was something to see. The Duke was having a little joke.

The Mosbachers came to escort the Windsors to the White House, and after they left, Miss Jacquet came down with the Duchess's jewel case to be put in the safe.

They returned around midnight and I escorted them to their rooms once again. They said they had had a marvelous time. The Duke had brought me the evening's printed program as a souvenir.

The Duchess insisted on putting out some of the lights herself. "You know," she said, "I pride myself on being a meticulous housekeeper."

I noticed that she was quite apprehensive about their trip the next day. She admitted she hated to fly. Someone had offered them a private plane for their trip to Palm Beach. I'm sure it had been meant as a special favor, but the Duchess was praying for bad weather so that they would have to take the train.

The next day dawned beautiful and clear, however. The makeup person and the hairdresser came immediately after breakfast and I sent Domenic upstairs to help the Duke get ready for the trip.

When he came downstairs, Domenic said the Duke wanted to

see me in the library. When I came in, His Royal Highness looked as if he had lost something. I asked if I could help.

"Domenic got me all dressed except for my coat and tie," he said, "and now I'm afraid I can't find my tie."

It was hanging on the back of a chair, hidden behind a partly open door. At that moment the Duchess came in.

"Darling, Mrs. Wilroy was nice enough to help me find my tie," the Duke called out as she came through the door.

"Oh, David," she said. "You are always losing things."

They were dressed just as they had been when they arrived. I had always heard that they were internationally famous fashion plates and had expected them to arrive with many changes of clothes. Instead, I found them to be a very modest, unassuming, and rather touching elderly couple.

Some newspaper people were outside on the sidewalk waiting for them when they came out a little later. The Duke and Duchess chatted with them briefly and then got into their car for the trip to the airport. I felt sorry for the Duchess, who was really quite visibly anxious about the plane ride that awaited her.

A few days later Mrs. Dwight D. Eisenhower came by to chat about the room she was going to contribute in honor of her late husband.

We all hoped that she would choose to do Room 26, the one next to the Queen's Suite that was reserved for the ranking woman or the lady-in-waiting. It was badly in need of refurbishing.

But Mamie Eisenhower had another idea and she was not to be budged. She was going to transform the head of state's bedroom into a monument to Dwight David Eisenhower.

Her decision caused quite a bit of consternation behind the scenes. President Eisenhower had never stayed at Blair House and had visited only two or three times. The head of state's bedroom was full of marvelous furniture, and because it had been for so long the bedroom of former President Truman, many people thought it should become a room to honor him. Unfortunately, no one had come forward with the funds that would be needed to do that. Besides, one doesn't argue with the wishes of a former First Lady. Mrs. Eisenhower had her way.

With the assistance of decorator Elisabeth Draper, Mrs. Eisenhower had all the elegant furniture removed from the room. It was placed in one room on the fourth floor. In the back of our minds, I think, was the notion that if we kept the furnishings together, there might still be a chance that in the future someone would come forward to endow a Truman room and then we could replace them.

In the meantime, floors were laid in the head of state's bedroom. The overmantel that had graced the fireplace was removed, and it too was put on the fourth floor with the other furnishings from the room. The way was clear now for the Eisenhower renovation to begin.

The work progressed steadily, and on December 4, 1970, the room was dedicated in a brief but impressive ceremony. The proceedings began with a prayer by Senate chaplain Edward Elson, who had been the Eisenhower's pastor at the National Presbyterian Church. Both Ambassador and Mrs. Mosbacher spoke, and so did the Eisenhowers' longtime friend General William Westmoreland. Two West Point cadets solemnly placed the former President's West Point swords above the mantelpiece. A tearful Mrs. Eisenhower, dressed in a purple suit and hat, made a short, graceful speech, ending the moving ceremony.

The room was filled with Eisenhower memorabilia, not only from the President's public life but from his personal collection as well. There was the wooden stand used at the Capitol during his inauguration upon which was placed the illustrated 1885 Bible he had used for the Oath of Office. The former President's eyeglass case, on which his initials were stamped in gold, and the small framed photograph of Mamie Eisenhower in a straw hat that he took everywhere with him were on the night tables on either side of a huge mahogany four-poster bed. His silver cigarette case with his initials and a sterling-silver inkstand were on the desk.

The walls of the room were covered in gold damask and the rug was maroon, blending with the tones of the fabric used for the curtains and bedspread.

It was this fabric that caused the most comment. Known as the Eisenhower toile, it was printed with scenes from the President's life. Hardly anything had been omitted. Here was the

President's boyhood home in Abilene; his Gettysburg farm; the White House; Columbia University, of which he had been President; and even Mamie Eisenhower's home in Denver. Symbols of his career were interspersed. The insignia of his wartime command in Europe, the five stars of his rank, a Republican elephant, a Nazi flag lying trampled beneath the flags of the triumphant allies, and a paint box and brushes to represent President Eisenhower's famous hobby. The fabric was copied from one that had been used at Gettysburg except, as Mrs. Draper explained to the press, the new fabric was aubergine instead of gold, because aubergine was a "virile, resiliant color with all the patina he brought to his life." The heavy mahogany furniture, which was criticized by some as being too massive, was chosen, Mrs. Draper explained, because it had a "deep gloss that is strong with the weight of integrity that I think reminds you of the man." She had decided against "Mr. Chippendale's best," she said, "because Mr. Chippendale's best was not President Eisenhower."

Two flags, a large American flag with heavy gold fringe and Eisenhower's presidential flag, flanked the fireplace. On the mantel beneath the crossed sabers was a selection of the President's favorite books between heavy bookends.

Several original Eisenhower paintings hung on the wall along with a framed copy of the President's prayer, dated January 20, 1952, the date of his inauguration, at which it was a part of the ceremony. A ceramic bull, sculpted by Edward Marshall Boehm, in a one-of-a-kind edition inscribed to President Eisenhower, stood on a table.

A large carved eagle graced the entranceway that leads to the hall, and in one corner, on a pedestal, was a bronze head of the former President, sculpted by Nicholas Tregor in 1945.

The room was certainly a shrine to the memory of President Eisenhower and it caused a great deal of comment. Many people thought it was inappropriate for the country's visitors of state to be welcomed into a room that so definitely bore the stamp of only one of our Presidents. But until now the head of state's bedroom has remained virtually as Mrs. Eisenhower designed it.

While the work on the room was going on, we had several visitors. The largest personal staff ever to accompany a head of

state was the one President Joseph-Désiré Mobutu of the Congo
brought with him in August of 1970. (President Mobutu, whose
country is now called Zaire, is now called Mobutu Sese Seko.)
There were two full-time interpreters, since French was the only
European language anyone in the party spoke. Mrs. Mobutu
traveled with a personal companion, a sort of lady-in-waiting,
two wardrobe maids, and a hairdresser. The President had a
valet and three aides-de-camp, who stayed at a nearby hotel.

The Mobutus were a young couple and very handsome. She
wore the long dresses traditional in her country. For daytime
they were made of a simple, heavy handwoven fabric, but at
night they were satin and silk. "I have no problems with skirt
length, midi or mini," she said. "Mine have always been and always will be long to the floor."

While he was with us, President Mobutu received an honorary
degree from Duquesne University, which was presented to him
at Blair House by the university's president, Rev. Henry
McAnulty, in the presence of the chiefs of the African missions
in Washington.

In October we had a strenuous visit from His Excellency
Nicolae Ceauşescu and his wife, of the Socialist Republic of
Romania.

Before this time, State Department security officers had been
in charge of guarding our guests. From this visit on, the Secret
Service from the White House and the White House police as
well as the District of Columbia police were also involved. The
police from both forces were on the street outside the house, and
White House police were stationed in the garden. And all
through the house the Romanian security people kept watch.
One security man was stationed on each stairway landing, and
there was a guard on duty twenty-four hours a day in front of
the President's bedroom door. It was the most security we had
ever seen.

A Romanian-born employee of the Voice of America had been
sent over as our interpreter, and I had planned to have her stay
with us during the visit since no one in the party spoke any English at all. I also wanted her to answer phones for the visitors.

Just before the Ceauşescus' arrival she was sitting in the Lincoln room, which I thought would be a good central location for

her. I walked by at one point and noticed that the top Romanian security man was just going into the room. He closed the door behind him and I could hear him talking in a loud, stern voice. Even though I couldn't understand a single syllable of what he was saying, it was quite clear that he was raking her over the coals.

When he left the room, I went in to find a very shaken woman. Although she is now an American citizen, at that time she had been in this country for only six years. She asked that she never be left alone with any Romanian, and so I stationed her in my office or in the pantry, and we never left her side. During the entire visit we really watched over her. I also reported this incident to our Secret Service, which may have talked to its Romanian counterparts about it.

The Romanians seemed to be under a certain amount of tension. They smiled very little, spoke even less, and seemed to be somewhat wary, even of each other. I was convinced that the interpreters they had brought along with them were members of the secret police, since they seemed to have the group under surveillance the entire time.

One morning, for instance, Miss Groza, who acted as Mrs. Ceauşescu's personal interpreter, came downstairs a few minutes before they were to leave for lunch and stopped to use a powder room on the first floor. A few minutes later another interpreter came down, looking plainly worried, and asked if I had seen Miss Groza anywhere. When I told her where she was, she looked relieved. It was as if they needed to know exactly where every single person was at every single moment.

Although the visit went better than I had expected, the tension infected everyone in the house. When the Romanians were ready to leave, their staff people acted as if they couldn't wait to get the baggage out of their rooms and onto the trucks taking them to the airport. The trucks were due at two forty-five, but they began bringing baggage down shortly after breakfast. To be honest, the rest of us breathed a sigh of relief when they were all gone.

That fall, Pat Mosbacher and Martha Mitchell, the wife of the Attorney General, planned a luncheon to announce the needlepoint project that had been decided upon by the wives of the

Nixon Cabinet. It had become something of a tradition for Cabinet wives to contribute some sort of needlework to the house. Some of these ladies had already fashioned a needlepoint carpet, but now they wanted to make needlepoint representations of their husbands' official Cabinet seals. Initially, the idea was to make these into seat covers, but, as Martha Mitchell explained to a member of the press, "We learned you couldn't sit on an official seal, it wouldn't be respectful, so we're framing the seals and they will be hung on a wall in Blair House."

The luncheon was to be held on November 19; on the day before, a little flap broke in the newspapers which, by then, had found Martha Mitchell a source of good copy. It seemed that Mrs. Mitchell had read in the *Star* that Connie Stuart, Mrs. Nixon's press secretary, had made it sound as if *all* the Cabinet wives were co-hostessing this luncheon when, in fact, she and Pat were in charge.

Mrs. Mitchell told Isabelle Shelton of the *Star* that when she had read this error in print, she had "cried my eyes out."

I thought it was really just a little oversight, but when Mrs. Mitchell arrived for lunch, she was still a little weepy, and the press simply surrounded her and bombarded her with questions. I had to actually shoo them away so that we could get lunch on the table.

All the Cabinet wives were there, and so was Mrs. Nixon, who ate like a bird, as usual, although afterward she said everything was delicious. Each of the ladies was given a very pretty canvas bag containing all the materials and instructions for her own project.

Several months later the seals had been made, and the fuss about Martha Mitchell had been forgotten. But on that day I felt very sorry for her. Mrs. Mitchell was so often in the spotlight during those years, and I thought that she suffered a great deal because of it.

By the fall of 1970 we had added a new and very welcome member to our staff. Mary Schenke had become my assistant.

Once I had received approval to hire someone, I had interviewed many candidates for the job. Then my next-door neighbor's daughter told me about a friend who was looking for something to do now that her child was in school.

Mary was well educated, in her middle thirties, and had had an assortment of jobs. She was a good typist and knew how an office should be run. From the start I found her easy to be with, and I was especially drawn to her quick sense of humor.

She gave the appearance of being small and rather delicate, but in fact she had enormous strength and was extremely capable. Almost from the first day I found that she could take over some of my duties. I showed her how to set up a reception, told her what we needed for a press conference, and explained about room assignments; and having told her once, I knew that she would remember and that I could go off and do something else.

Her greatest asset was the way she could make any crisis seem temporary or trivial. I'd come into the office with some horrible tale of woe and she would turn it into a joke. That was just what I needed, and as we entered the new year I felt that some of the burden of my job was being shared.

Chapter Twenty-One

IN FEBRUARY OF 1971 Mrs. Agnew gave a tea for the wives of the nation's governors who were in Washington at the annual midwinter Governors' Conference.

Among the guests was the wife of California's governor, Ronald Reagan. At that time the Reagans were living in a rented house in Sacramento because the antiquated governor's mansion had been declared a firetrap. Governor Reagan had been in office for four years, and they were hoping for a new mansion before long.

As Mrs. Reagan toured the house with the rest of the governors' wives and several reporters, she declared that she was "thinking house" in anticipation of being able to move to new quarters soon. As we now know, Nancy Reagan is very interested in interior decorating and has a very sure sense of what she likes.

She admired many of the furnishings in the house and, in fact, thought that the needlepoint rugs in the Queen's Suite would be "just right for the new mansion." She found Blair House "enchanting," she said.

Another governor's wife made news that day. Mrs. George Wallace, newly married to the governor of Alabama, came to the tea with her own photographer. This did not endear her to the other ladies, according to a story by Isabelle Shelton that appeared the day after the tea in the Washington *Star*. Mrs. Wallace explained that the pictures were for the monthly newspaper her husband sent to his contributors. He just wanted to introduce his bride to his supporters, Mrs. Wallace explained. The photographer was not there to steal the spotlight away from anyone else.

Blair House and its renovation were featured in the Washington papers with some regularity. Pat Mosbacher came up with the splendid idea of refurbishing the Blair dining room in honor of President Franklin Delano Roosevelt. She thought that the President's son, Franklin, Jr., would probably be interested in such a project, and she was right.

A luncheon was held which Franklin Delano Roosevelt, Jr., attended. Also invited was Mrs. Felicia Sarnoff, former wife of the president of RCA, and an old friend of Pat Mosbacher's. The papers announced Mr. Roosevelt's donation of the room and, in a box on the same page, also announced Mr. Roosevelt's divorce. I thought at the time that this was a strange combination of news stories.

Elisabeth Draper was chosen as the room's decorator, and I hoped that we were not going to have another monument like the Eisenhower room.

For some time I had thought that the white paint on the mantel in the dining room and on the wooden trim above the door to the room might be hiding some sort of beautiful wood. Mrs. Draper thought so, too. I contacted James Swan, an expert in refinishing who had worked for GSA, to remove the paint. What emerged after several weeks of painstaking work was a lovely golden oak, intricately carved in a design of Greek columns entwined with tiny animal heads, leaves, and fruit on the mantel, and above the door there was a small bust of Lafayette. The wood for both the mantel and the overfacing above the door had come from an old house in Portland, Maine, belonging to relatives of the Blairs, which had been built just after the Revolution, shortly after General Lafayette had visited the city.

Pat Mosbacher thought it might be more practical to have the Waterford crystal chandelier in the Blair-Lee dining room wired so that the brackets that now held real candles could be converted to electric light. I personally loved the candlelight glow the chandelier cast. It bathed the room in a soft, flattering light, and when we lit the candles on the tables along with the candles in the chandelier a marvelous special effect was added to any dinner party.

When Pat saw how the candlelight transformed the room she decided that we should have the best of both worlds.

Mr. De Lisa, owner of a local antique shop and an authority on the subject, was called in for consultation. He suggested concealed electric light bulbs around the interior and none in the top of the chandelier where they could be seen from below. This way, when we used candles, the bulbs would be hidden, but on dark afternoons or on those occasions when candles were not appropriate we still had light.

Mr. De Lisa refused to charge for his work, explaining that he had come to this country with seventeen dollars in his pocket. "America has been good to me," he said, "and I want to do something in return."

Mr. Roosevelt was not going to turn the dining room into a Roosevelt shrine, but he did want to hang a portrait of his father above the fireplace. He commissioned Elizabeth Shoumatoff to make a copy of her famous portrait of the President on which she was working at Warm Springs when Mr. Roosevelt was fatally stricken. Mme. Shoumatoff had done a small portrait of the President before she was asked by her friend, Lucy Rutherfurd, to come to Warm Springs in April 1945 to do another, more ambitious painting. There were to be four sittings. She was working on the second sitting when the President complained of feeling ill. He died a short time later. She finished the portrait from memory and gave it to the Roosevelt family. The Warm Springs painting and the copy that hangs in the Blair House dining room show Mr. Roosevelt in his naval cape.

Mme. Shoumatoff came to Blair House about a month before the dedication of the new room to see where the portrait was to be hung. After she finished painting it, she and I spent several days seeing that it was placed and lighted to her satisfaction.

On the day of the dedication several hundred guests, including many members of the Roosevelt family, assembled in the new room. The walls had been covered with a lovely brick-colored silk in a flocked design known as "Beau Brummell" because it resembled the pattern in a dandy's striped waistcoat. The color blended nicely with the brick of the garden floor, which could be seen through newly hung french doors. The windows were hung with off-white silk taffeta curtains, set off by a swag valance decorated with unusual woolen ball fringe attached with brown velvet ribbon.

A plain sand wool rug covered the parquet floor. There was a new sideboard and a lovely new dining room table. We had set the table with the vermeil that had been donated to the room by the president of Cartier, Inc., the New York jewelers. He and his wife were also at the ceremony.

The Reverend Francis Sayre, dean of the Washington Cathedral, gave the invocation. Ambassador Mosbacher made a brief acceptance speech for the Department of State. Mr. Roosevelt made a few remarks and told the famous story of how his mother was really responsible for the purchase of Blair House in the first place. At Mr. Roosevelt's side was his new bride, Felicia Sarnoff Roosevelt. They had met for the first time at the Blair House lunch Pat Mosbacher gave to discuss the possibility of his donating this room. It was, as far as I know, the only time that the Fine Arts Committee had resulted in romance as well as renovation.

The next wedding Blair House had a part in came later that spring when Edward Finch Cox was introduced as the man who was going to marry Tricia Nixon. The engagement was announced at a White House dinner honoring the visiting Prime Minister of Ireland, John M. Lynch. Prime Minister Lynch was asked if he minded sharing the limelight, and he graciously said he'd be pleased to be part of the happy event.

The wedding was scheduled for June. The rehearsal dinner was to take place at Blair House the night before the ceremony. A reporter called a day before the party to ask who would be paying for the dinner, and I answered that the groom's parents were and that permission to hold the dinner had been received from the White House, as was always the case when we had a nonofficial function.

Because there were going to be forty guests, we set up our usual four tables for ten in the Blair-Lee drawing room, using small gold chairs for seating. The color scheme was pink and green, but since the groom was allergic to flowers, the centerpieces were variegated pink- and green-leafed plants. Pink candles and greens stood in the candle trees around the room and these, we felt, could be decorated with flowers. A large bouquet of daisies with white ribbons hung on the front door.

The security was very tight. The Secret Service came over several times during the day of the dinner to check the entire house.

In the afternoon Mrs. Cox, her daughter, Maisie, and her son Howie came by with the wine, which the Coxes insisted on providing. They also brought the place cards and seating charts.

Of course, the neighborhood was swarming with reporters. In the afternoon, as her mother was seeing to the table arrangement, Maisie Cox wandered out to the garden. By accident, the gardener had left the door to the garden open and an intrepid newspaper woman had slipped in. When I walked by the door from the Blair dining room, I saw her engaging Maisie in conversation. I hurried out and shooed her away and quickly locked the door.

The rug in the Blair drawing room was taken up after dinner for dancing to the Lester Lanin combo, which also played during the meal. I thought the young people might have preferred a rock-and-roll band but they did dance to the more decorous Lanin sound.

Dallas had taken special care with the dinner. With drinks there were delicious hors d'oeuvres of all kinds. The dinner itself began with seafood Newburg, one of Dallas' specialties. The entrée was a perfectly cooked filet of beef with truffles, wild rice, fresh asparagus, and cauliflower Polonaise. The salad of Bibb lettuce was served with a lovely runny Brie and the dessert was a combination of pineapple and strawberries with Kirsch presented in pineapple shells. It was a comparatively simple, but elegant meal and Dallas' extra loving attention to the details showed.

The front of the house was roped off to allow the guests to enter comfortably. This was made necessary because of the large number of people who had gathered on the sidewalk to catch a glimpse of the engaged couple and their guests. Some of the spectators were reporters, but in the main they were just ordinary citizens who had come to see such celebrities as the President and Mrs. Nixon, Mrs. Mamie Eisenhower, and Mr. Nixon's friend Charles "Bebe" Rebozo.

After the party was over, at about eleven-thirty Tricia and Edward walked back to the White House hand in hand, but the crowd had hardly shrunk. A little later the President and Mrs. Nixon also walked home, stopping to shake hands and talk with some of the people in the street.

Blair House was not involved at all in the wedding itself.

However, it was a time for parties. A week or so later the Mosbachers gave a surprise birthday party for Secretary of State Rogers. It was the first dinner we had in the newly finished garden and we were all praying for good weather. We had received a present of cast-aluminum garden furniture from Mr. and Mrs. James Josendale of St. Joseph, Missouri. The furniture was painted black and so resembled the much heavier, more unwieldy cast iron that you usually find in formal gardens. There was enough furniture to fill a large room: a group of small tables, five or six large tables, many chairs, a chaise, and tier tables for plants. The tops of the tables were openwork, however, so we were not able to use them for dinner parties. Instead, we brought out five tables from inside the house and put a wooden dance floor down over the brick floor. Our portable piano was set up for Howard Devron and his orchestra.

On the tables we placed small globes encircled by spun glass, which contained small electric lights surrounded by lighted candles. The lamp bases were decorated with fresh flowers. Lighted candles in hurricane shades were put on spikes around the garden, and potted flowering plants surrounded the pool near the dining area. Several tables that were not used for dining were used to hold large bouquets. With all the flowers on the tables and in the garden, the setting for the party was spectacularly beautiful.

Secretary Rogers had been enticed to the house the evening of the surprise party by his wife under the pretext of showing him the needlepoint rug that the wives of President Nixon's Cabinet had made. The rug, which was something like a tapestry and really very unusual and handsome, was usually in an upstairs hall, but we had placed it near the front door so that Mr. Rogers could look at it. As he stood there gazing down at it, the guests rushed in from the Blair-Lee side singing "Happy Birthday."

I think he had no idea that a party had been planned. But everyone was taken by surprise some time later in the evening when the President suddenly appeared in the garden. He promptly sat down at the piano and played the birthday song again. Of course, everyone joined in.

President Nixon spent about half an hour at the party and was backing up to take his leave when Ambassador Mosbacher noticed that he was about to step into the pool. He quickly grabbed the President's arm and saved him from a wet finale to the evening.

Mrs. Rogers had had a cake made from an old family recipe. At the stroke of midnight we brought out a second cake. This one was for Pat Mosbacher, whose birthday was the next day. I think we succeeded in surprising the hostess.

On October 27, 1971, President Josip Broz Tito of Yugoslavia, Mrs. Broz, and a party of seventeen stayed at Blair House.

Both Yugoslav and United States Secret Service people were assigned to the house for President Tito's first visit to the United States.

The Yugoslav leader was a very friendly and outgoing man and his wife was a charming, tall woman with a lovely open smile.

Both spoke excellent English and were surprisingly easy to talk to, but there were several interpreters in the party including Miss Liljana Tanboco, President Tito's personal interpreter. When he made an official statement of any sort, the President spoke Serbo-Croatian, the language of his country.

President Tito and his wife had the usual hectic round of official duties. He was occupied with a tight schedule of meetings with our government officials, while she went to the Smithsonian Institution and to Mount Vernon with Mrs. Mosbacher. There was a well-attended press conference at the house presided over by the Foreign Minister, and Mrs. Broz was hostess to the ladies of the press. Through it all, I noticed that our officials made a special effort to entertain these particular visitors a bit more lavishly than usual.

We were now using our new beauty parlor as if we had always had it. Mrs. Broz had her hair done several times, and she mentioned what a "most useful and attractive place" it was. It was certainly a great convenience for us and for the hairdressers who came to take care of our guests.

We thought we had every bit of equipment we could possibly need in the beauty parlor until a visit from Prime Minister Golda Meir in 1972. Mrs. Meir wanted to have a pedicure. I looked in the beauty parlor but couldn't find anything that looked like a pedicure bowl. So I went to the kitchen and, under the horrified eyes of Dallas, borrowed a stainless-steel mixing bowl. When he heard it was going to be used for a pedicure— even though the feet belonged to one of our favorite guests—he said he could never again use the bowl for food. I assured him that running the bowl through the dishwasher would render it sterile and fit to use again. And I made a note to order something more suitable for the beauty parlor.

When the Yugoslav party left, Prime Minister William McMahon of Australia arrived with his lovely blond wife. The Prime Minister was obviously devoted to his somewhat younger wife and very proud of her. They had barely gotten settled, however, when he became ill. I called Dr. William Lukash's office at the White House and found that he was at the Redskins game. I didn't think it was serious, but because Prime Minister McMahon said he was really feeling awful, I sent a message over to the stadium, and after a while Dr. Lukash came by. Mrs. McMahon was also ill by that time. She was suffering more from jet lag than from the flu, which her husband had. Dr. Lukash ordered a vaporizer put into their room, and soon both were feeling much better.

For the White House state dinner, Mrs. McMahon wore a dress that caused quite a bit of comment. It was white peau de soie slit up both sides to above the knee and decorated with a ladder of rhinestones up both sides and on both sleeves. Mrs. McMahon was tall and had a marvelous figure, and I thought the dress looked quite striking, but she felt it was too revealing and said she wouldn't have worn it if her husband hadn't insisted on it.

The McMahons left on the morning of November 3, and at ten-thirty that evening Prime Minister Indira Gandhi arrived. As she had in the past, she used the Queen's Suite for her private rooms and the library for business meetings. This time she had a fairly large contingent traveling with her, as well as personnel assigned to her by the embassy.

During this visit there were severe tensions between the Indian Government and our own since it had come to light that the United States had given aid to Pakistan in a border dispute between that country and India. The strained atmosphere could be felt and there were more meetings than usual, in addition to the social functions that are part of any state visit.

About a week after the Gandhi party left, former President and Mrs. Lyndon B. Johnson stayed with us at the invitation of President Nixon.

It was a great pleasure preparing for our former first family. We were very accustomed to their likes and dislikes and looked forward to seeing them.

President Johnson liked a weak Cutty Sark and soda before dinner. He ate a late breakfast after he'd been up for a while and he preferred decaffeinated coffee. Mrs. Johnson usually skipped cocktails, but occasionally she had a scotch and water. She ate breakfast with the former President and often had orange juice and poached or soft-boiled eggs on toast with bacon. They both liked whatever fruit we were serving. And we always had lots of sugar-free soft drinks for the Johnsons.

The other people in the Johnson party were Tom Johnson (no relation), the President's former press secretary, and his wife, and Helen Lindau, Mrs. Johnson's secretary. Secret Service agents Tom Mills and Mike Howard also stayed with us. At first we thought that Lynda and Charles Robb would be coming, but at the last moment they changed their plans.

The first evening of the Johnsons' stay, Bess Abell arranged a reception at Blair House for about one hundred of their old Washington friends. It was a happy reunion for the First Family with many of the people who had been at the White House during the Johnson administration. Among the guests were Senator and Mrs. Hubert Humphrey, Mr. and Mrs. Clark Clifford, and General and Mrs. William Westmoreland.

The next evening the Johnsons were to have a few friends in for drinks. That afternoon Mrs. Johnson called from Charlottesville, Virginia, where they were visiting Lynda, to request that we be sure to have some of Dallas' special lobster canapés. They really were scrumptious and relatively simple, just a subtle combination of seasoned lobster on a cracker topped with melted cheese and served hot from the broiler. For some obscure reason, Dallas called these tidbits lobster Lorenzo.

After drinks the Johnsons went out for dinner. They came back early in the evening and we all sat in the drawing room talking. He told me that he had a great many Republican friends. "Politics wouldn't be very interesting if everyone thought the same way," he said. "We'll never have a better world without an exchange of ideas. That's how new ideas grow." We talked about some of the changes he had tried to make while he was in office. He was particularly proud of what he had done in the field of civil rights. "You and I are both southerners," he said, "but you and I both know that we have to do something about this situation."

We talked for quite a while like old friends. I had always liked President Johnson. It's difficult not to feel drawn to a man who is so very persuasive and outgoing. He made a sincere effort to make people like him, it seemed to me.

Mrs. Johnson was very concerned during this visit about her husband's health. It was obvious that she was looking after him with special care. She was the sort of woman who put her needs after those of her husband and her two daughters. If she had any problems, she never mentioned them. The Johnsons were a devoted couple and it was touching to see them together. He called her "Bird" much of the time and seemed to pay attention to her when she told him how to take care of himself. I was certain he wouldn't listen to anyone else. But I noticed that Mrs. Johnson's technique was to give him a great deal of room, and then when she felt he really needed to rest or slow down, she would gently urge him to take a nap, and surprisingly he would meekly obey.

Tom Johnson and Helen Lindau kept things moving smoothly during the two-day visit and even the Secret Service men assigned to the Johnsons seemed to be part of what looked like one big happy family.

The visit to Washington and Blair House with all the parties and receptions meant a lot to President Johnson. He told me he loved having the chance to see so many old friends. For a while, I imagine, he felt as if he were back in Washington for good. He was one man who liked being President. As an activist who loved being in the thick of things, he found it hard to give it all up and to go back to living as a private citizen. Although we didn't know it, this was to be President Johnson's last visit to Washington.

Chapter Twenty-Two

℘ BECAUSE 1972 WAS an election year, we expected fewer
guests than usual. Secretary General Kurt Waldheim of the
United Nations and his wife, Prime Minister Nihat Erim of Turkey, and President Luis Echeverría Álvarez of Mexico were our
only visitors.

We were busy, however, with a series of functions. And the
refurbishing went on.

The needlepoint seals were finished, framed, and ready to be
hung along the Blair House stairs, beginning on the first floor
and extending up to the second-floor landing. They can be seen
from both floors. Again Martha Mitchell and Pat Mosbacher
were co-hostesses at a party for the Cabinet wives. This time
there was no misunderstanding and there were no tears, just a
great deal of pride on the part of the ladies who could see how
well their project had turned out. Mrs. Nixon came to the tea,
but explained that Lucy Winchester, her social secretary, had
done her needlepoint seal for her. First Ladies don't have much
time for handicrafts.

Early in 1972 Frank Klapthor from the Smithsonian came to
be in charge of the Blair House inventory and act as curator. In
addition to his skill at identifying furniture and other antiques,
Frank turned out to have a certain flair for getting contributions
for the house. He soon managed to find some lovely antique
chairs for the new dining room in the Jackson Place addition.

For the last three years of my time at Blair House, Frank was
a constant presence, dropping into my office two or three times a
week to look for some item or check an identification.

He often asked if we wanted a certain kind of lamp he'd been offered or if we needed another small table for this or that room.

He was in great demand as an appraiser and often came across things he thought we might need. If I said yes, he would try to get the owner to donate whatever it was to Blair House, rather than sell it to a dealer or at auction. Sometimes he took me along to look at a prospective gift. In this fashion we acquired quite a number of useful things, including a good bit of antique silver.

Outside of the house, there was renovation of a sort going on at this time. The sidewalks had all been replaced with brick on Lafayette Square, and now the bricks were being extended around the corner to the front of our house as well.

In the fall of 1972 Donald M. Kendall, the chairman of Pepsico, Inc., was a guest at one of our functions. We had a pleasant, lighthearted discussion about the relative merits of Pepsi and Coke, both of which he had noted we served.

"How would you respond to an offer of all the Pepsi products you could use?" he suddenly asked me. This was a very generous offer, since it included not only Pepsi-Cola but all of the products of the company, which meant we would have its entire line of soft drinks and mixers as well. I was delighted, and said so.

The next day a representative of Pepsico, Inc., called on me, and from then on, all I had to do was let the company know whenever we ran short of anything and whatever we needed was immediately delivered.

We were in a period of generosity directed our way. A few days later I was escorting a tour through the house when one of the men said, "Aren't you going to show us the kitchen?" I was a little taken aback. I had never had a man make such a request, but of course I took him downstairs and he inspected not only the kitchen but the laundry room with great interest and an attention to detail that surprised me.

When he was through, he made some very complimentary remarks about all the rooms, the dinner he had just eaten, and the house as a whole.

"There's one thing I could mention," he said; "how come you don't have any Sears, Roebuck appliances in your kitchen or laundry room?" It turned out that he was a vice-president of

Sears, and my response to him was quite direct: "We don't have any Sears appliances because no one has ever offered us any. Almost everything you see has been donated." His immediate response was, "What would you like?"

I didn't have to search for an answer. For a long time we'd been struggling with our laundry room, which was badly underequipped. The appliances we had were in need of replacement. The washers and dryers were always breaking down, and they couldn't keep up with the greatly expanded demands that our new space made on them.

"Decide what you need and it will be installed as quickly as we can get it to you," he said. "We'll also keep your appliances in good working order with a lifetime service contract on everything we send you."

Several weeks later we had two new washers and two new dryers. Sears, Roebuck would have been happy to send more, but there was just no more space in our laundry room.

We were delighted to get these generous gifts. Somehow it was always easier to get people to donate valuable antiques to Blair House, and although we loved having them, we were always badly in need of the practical items without which we would not have been able to run the house.

At the beginning of President Nixon's second term in office there was a party for some of the people who were or had been members of the Nixon White House. The party was given by Leonard Firestone, president of the Firestone Tire & Rubber Company. Among those invited were Counsellor Robert H. Finch, Dwight Chapin, Bob Haldeman, communications director Herb Klein, and press secretary Ron Ziegler. Former Secretary of Commerce Maurice Stans, HEW Secretary Caspar Weinberger, and budget director Wally Ash were also invited.

This was to be a stag party, and the entertainment featured several comedians, among them Foster Brooks, who did his famous drunk act. Jonathan Winters was to be master of ceremonies. He came to Blair House on the afternoon before the party to check the microphones and other equipment. He was still talking about how brave he had been to fly from California. He was absolutely terrified of airplanes and never stepped into one if he could help it. I guess a command performance from

the White House couldn't be denied. He hoped he'd be over the
jitters by that evening, he said.

During the cocktail hour the Air Force Strings played and
their excellent harpist provided music during dinner. Everyone
arrived around seven-thirty, and a few minutes later President
Nixon appeared. He circulated among the guests, chatting with
each of them. He left just before dinner was served but stayed
long enough to make a welcoming speech.

The day after Christmas, President Harry S. Truman died. A
memorial service was held for the former President at the Washington Cathedral some time later. Although President Nixon had
invited Margaret Truman Daniel and her family to stay at Blair
House, she elected to stay with her friend Florence Mahoney in
Georgetown. Again Margaret was plagued by travel difficulties.
Her plane arrived two hours late because of a snowstorm. I had
been informed by the White House that she would like to have
lunch for a few friends at Blair House after the memorial service.

There were about sixty for lunch, including Senator and Mrs.
Humphrey; Mrs. Dean Acheson, whose husband had been President Truman's Secretary of State; and Governor and Mrs. Nelson Rockefeller.

After lunch, when the guests had all left, Margaret and Mrs.
Mahoney took a tour of the house. Margaret was calm and composed and displayed her usual commonsense view of the world.
She was a little dismayed at the changes in what had been her
father's old room, but she loved the way her old suite had
turned out.

In July the Mosbachers left the Department of State and
Marion Smoak became acting chief of protocol. Soon after her
husband took over the job, Francie Smoak, like so many of her
predecessors, took an active role in helping to run the house and
continue with the renovations.

Once again, on Inauguration Day, Blair House was at the dis-
posal of the diplomatic corps. It was no small matter to provide
refreshments and bathroom facilities for three hundred, and we
made elaborate arrangements to prevent bottlenecks by having
the various groups assigned to the several Blair House entrances.
Several members of the protocol staff were to be on hand to help

maintain the flow. Inside, we planned to have all three dining rooms set up with refreshments. We also set up various places where people could hang their coats and opened all the bathrooms.

On Inauguration Day the diplomats were bused to their seats, most of which took up the block across from the house. Somewhere along the route they had had a box lunch, but by the time they got to their seats all they could think of was getting out of the biting cold and into Blair House. Since they had all been to Blair House at one time or another, they thought the only entrance was the main one. No one had been assigned to brief them about our entrance system, and so they fairly exploded into the house. The protocol people managed to herd a few dozen through the other doors, but most of them were milling around in the Blair dining room. There was real chaos at the refreshments table and lines formed outside the bathroom.

Several groups came inside and watched the whole parade from our windows. Ambassador Egidio Ortona of Italy had the right idea when he suggested that a spot of brandy would have been more warming than the coffee we were serving.

It was so cold that the White House buildings manager called us and asked for as many blankets as we could spare for the people sitting in the VIP stands, which were not enclosed and were also in the shade, making them even colder.

The house was a whirl of activity for several hours, and then as suddenly as they had burst into the house, the visitors were gone. The parade was over, the buses pulled up in front of the stands, and our guests vanished into them. By now it was five in the afternoon. They had been involved in the festivities for about seven hours and I think they were glad to go home.

The week after the Inauguration we had planned quite a number of functions, but on January 22 Lyndon Johnson died, and even without being told, I knew that the Johnson family would be staying at Blair House at the invitation of President Nixon.

The former President was to receive a state funeral, and his body would lie in state with the casket on a catafalque in the Capitol Rotunda. President Nixon sent Air Force One to bring the casket and the Johnson family to Washington. The plane landed at Andrews Air Force Base, where a waiting honor guard placed the casket in a hearse, and a motorcade carrying the family and other dignitaries followed it into Washington. Not far from the White House the casket was placed on a caisson drawn by six white horses and followed by the traditional riderless horse, its stirrups carrying the riding boots placed backwards to denote a fallen leader. At this point President Nixon's car joined the motorcade and the caravan proceeded down the streets of Washington, which were lined seven and eight deep with people all the way to the Capitol.

In addition to Mrs. Johnson, her daughters, Luci and Lynda Bird, and their husbands, President Johnson's sister and her husband and their son, Philip, were our guests as well. The Nugents had brought their little son, Lyn. Tom Johnson and Mike Howard were also with the party. We remembered the last time they had stayed with us, in 1971, when the Johnsons had spent such a happy time with old Washington friends.

A strenuous afternoon had been planned for Mrs. Johnson and I was concerned about her. She looked a little tired when she arrived, but by the time she began receiving her visitors at six o'clock she was composed and seemed more rested. The heads of state were greeted by the former First Lady in the Blair-Lee drawing room for forty-five minutes and then, at seven, American callers were ushered into the new Jackson Place sitting room. The new press room was used for the overflow.

There must have been about three hundred people streaming through the house and Mrs. Johnson received them all, standing straight and dignified, accepting the expressions of sympathy so gently that it seemed almost as if she were consoling the callers rather than the other way around. When she arrived, I had asked her if she wanted anything special, but there was nothing she needed, she said. Bess Abell and Liz Carpenter and the Johnson daughters all tried to get her to rest for part of the afternoon, but I know she had very little time for that before she came downstairs dressed and ready to meet her guests.

When I commented on how composed and controlled Mrs. Johnson seemed to be, Lynda remarked, "Whenever there was a crisis, my father would always say, 'Girls, go comb your hair, put on fresh lipstick, and show your prettiest face to the world.' " It was obvious that Mrs. Johnson was showing her bravest side, and she appeared every bit the gallant and gracious lady of whom the President would have been proud.

All of the old Johnson friends came by. Mrs. Johnson had told Leonard Marks, "The one thing Lyndon hated most was to be alone." So a number of his friends had arranged to keep watch over the coffin during the night in groups of four.

I tried to recall what Mrs. Johnson particularly liked in the way of food, but to my chagrin, I could remember only LBJ's favorite dishes. I did recall that she once mentioned cream cheese and watercress sandwiches, and so we did have those. But as usual, she really didn't care what we served as long as the others were pleased.

The next morning the three Johnson women were in Mrs. Johnson's bedroom choosing from a number of black dresses that had been sent from designer Mollie Parnis in New York.

The funeral service was to be at ten o'clock at the National City Christian Church. From there the family would go directly to the plane and home to Texas, where the President was to be buried in the family burial ground on the LBJ Ranch. It was hard for me to control my tears when Mrs. Johnson said good-bye.

A day or so later, we got the following telegram:

"On behalf of Mrs. Lyndon Johnson and the Johnson family, you have our heartfelt appreciation for the final courtesies you extended my boss. [signed] Tom Johnson, Executive Assistant to President Lyndon Baines Johnson."

Only a few days later, of necessity, we were back in the whirl of Blair House activities and functions.

Mrs. George Romney, wife of the former secretary of HUD, was giving a lunch for a group of women and had thought up a novel and charming way of doing the seating. As each guest arrived, she was given a single spring flower from a silver basket. There was a different kind of flower for each guest, which was matched by a similar flower at her particular place at the table. It was not easy, believe me, to find thirty completely different flowers. I admit that I had to give in and use several different kinds and colors of roses. All those flowers created a lovely table and caused quite a bit of conversation.

The next week we were hosts to our old friend King Hussein of Jordan. He brought his bride of six weeks, Queen Alia. The young Queen was a radiant twenty-five-year-old beauty with dark, flashing eyes and long, thick, wavy hair. She was the daughter of the former Jordanian ambassador to the United Nations and had been educated at Hunter College in New York. She had gotten her first job, at the American Express Company, with the help of our ambassador to the United Nations, George Bush.

The King and Queen were obviously very happy. They spent the first three days of their visit in the usual routine of receptions, luncheons, and dinners and then checked into Walter Reed Army Medical Center for complete medical checkups. From there, with the word from their doctors that both were in excellent health, they went to Connecticut, where the King's two sons were in school.

Early in April President and Mrs. Nguyen Van Thieu of South Vietnam were our guests. This was President Thieu's first visit to the mainland United States since taking office. The Vietnam cease-fire had been signed in Paris that January, and President Thieu's visit was designed to give the American public and its leaders a chance to see the South Vietnamese President close up.

The Thieus' first stop had been California, where they stayed at the Century Plaza Hotel, Los Angeles. President Thieu had gone by helicopter to San Clemente several times to confer with President Nixon, then staying at his Western White House. Because of President Nixon's absence from the capital, Vice-President Agnew served at the official host when the Thieus arrived in Washington on April 4 for a visit filled with activities.

President Thieu addressed the National Press Club, met with members of Congress, saw representatives of the World Bank and the International Monetary Fund, and spoke with leaders of organized labor. A group representing the families of our prisoners of war also spent some time with him.

There was a reception for the Thieus at the Vietnamese Embassy, and Mr. Agnew hosted a dinner at the Department of State on April 6.

President Thieu's visit coincided with his fiftieth birthday, so we had a birthday cake for him at a lunch attended by Carol

Laise, our ambassador to Nepal, who is the wife of Ellsworth P. Bunker, then our ambassador to South Vietnam. The National Press Club also gave him a cake, which had one candle on it.

The Thieus left Washington for Texas, where they were the guests of Mrs. Lyndon B. Johnson on the LBJ Ranch.

There were several other visits that spring, including one from Chancellor Willy Brandt of West Germany. As usual, he spent every moment he could in the garden. His Imperial Majesty Emperor Haile Selassie, who arrived in May, was also pleased to see that the garden was now finished. And President William Tolbert of Liberia came in June with a very large group. He had a great many visitors, and the ladies in the party made good use of the beauty parlor.

But all spring we were beginning to plan for the middle of June. The Russians were coming.

Chapter Twenty-Three

₰ IT WAS TO BE the longest visit we had ever had, lasting ten
days. And every bed was going to be filled. Since it was
the first visit to the United States of His Excellency Leonid
Ilyich Brezhnev, General Secretary of the Central Committee of
the Communist Party of the Union of Soviet Socialist Republics,
the planning went on for months prior to June 16. On that date
an advance party of Russians was to take up residence at Blair
House. Brezhnev was due to arrive on the eighteenth.

We were in constant consultation with the Russian Embassy
over plans for the visit. One afternoon while Emperor Haile
Selassie was still with us, eighteen people from the embassy
came over to check out the accommodations and discuss our
plans. And nearly every day during President Tolbert's stay
there were calls with special instructions from this or that Russian. Obviously this was going to be an all-out visit.

The room assignments were changed almost as often as the
Russians came over to check on them. Extra beds were requested for two of the bedrooms, and we installed five additional beds in one of the large offices. This was where the Russian security force would be stationed. I had always in the past
turned down that sort of request, but I had been told that the
word for this visit was "yes." We were meant to be very accom-
modating, and so we were.

While Blair House was fully booked for the visit, an even
larger contingent was staying in a nearby hotel. I knew that
these people would be coming over to the house for meetings
and meals during the visit.

The embassy had assigned us a chef for the duration of the visit, and Dallas and I spent a lot of time with him, weeks before the arrival date, planning the meals. In addition to the regular breakfast, lunch, and dinner, Secretary Brezhnev was giving a luncheon on the day after his arrival for the members of our Senate Foreign Relations Committee.

The chef was never alone with us. Because he spoke mainly Russian—although he and Dallas managed to speak a little English together in the manner of people who have a common interest—he was always accompanied by an interpreter. And standing next to us there was also the usual KGB man.

One morning during the preliminary planning stage, the chef mysteriously appeared alone. I didn't know how he had managed that, and I didn't ask him. It wasn't long before the phone rang and a voice with a Russian accent inquired about the chef's whereabouts. Within minutes of my telling the caller that, yes, the chef was right here, two Russians, visibly disturbed and out of breath, arrived. They looked as if they had run all the way to Blair House. It turned out that the chef had simply gotten tired of waiting for his chaperons.

Our discussions in the kitchen were endless even though the chef was not involved in most of the food for the visit. But he was planning to prepare at least some of what we were serving at the Foreign Relations Committee lunch and we went over every tiny detail of that meal. When we had decided on what was to be served, the Russians would retire to a corner of the kitchen and discuss the plans among themselves. Then they would change everything and we'd start all over again. This went on until the day came when we simply had to order the food. That put an end to all discussion.

Before the visit, we also planned a large press conference to be held in our new Jackson Place press room. We had endless conversations about what kind of electronic system would be needed, and so on. We finally got that settled to everyone's satisfaction.

As expected, on June 16 a small group of Russians arrived. The group included His Excellency Nikolai Semenovich Patolichev, Minister of Foreign Trade, and His Excellency Boris Pavlovich Bugayev, Minister of Civil Aviation.

Later in the day two women came with the luggage for part of the group. After the women had dinner they asked to have their own personal luggage brought down, and off they went in an embassy car. We didn't see them again until Monday. When I inquired who the mysterious ladies were, I was told that they were there solely to look after the clothes of Secretary Brezhnev and Foreign Minister Andrei Gromyko, who would be the ranking member of the party. Their clothes were not going to be touched by our people.

Secretary Brezhnev had both the Head of State's and the Queen's suites. An ironing board was set up in the Queen's Suite and another in the bedroom on the fourth floor where one of the women was sleeping. They never used our laundry room. Perhaps they just rinsed things out in the basins in the bathrooms.

We were asked to put a carafe of very hot tea in the Secretary's bedroom at night and to make sure that there were lemon and sugar on the tea tray. The Secretary also requested a carafe of very cold milk and a dish of yogurt and one of honey.

The Lincoln room had been transformed into a KGB command post. Most of the furniture had been removed, and instead of Montgomery Blair's famous desk there were file cabinets, tables, and straight-backed office chairs. Chairs and tables were put on each of the landings on all sides of the house, and these landings also became KGB lookout posts, which were manned around the clock.

By Monday all was in readiness for the arrival of Secretary Brezhnev. He was to be addressed as His Excellency or Mr. General Secretary, the State Department informed us. We had set up the Blair-Lee drawing room with our finest crystal and linen, and the Blair Lowestoft was ready to receive the Secretary's lunch, since he was expected at one o'clock. Another seated meal was to be served in the Blair dining room, and there was a gigantic buffet ready in the Jackson Place dining room for those who were not to be seated. The food was prepared and waiting only for Mr. Brezhnev's appearance.

One o'clock came and went, but no Mr. Brezhnev. Everyone was getting pretty hungry, so we began to serve in all but the Blair-Lee drawing room, which was where the ranking members of the party were to eat with the honored visitor from the Soviet Union.

I thought everything was going along well, although I was wondering where the Secretary could be, when Domenic came in quite agitated because several people had simply gone into the Blair-Lee drawing room and were sitting at the table demanding their lunch. I asked Viktor Isakov, a protocol officer from the Russian Embassy, our liaison with the Russian Embassy, what I should do, and he said they might as well eat since the Secretary wasn't going to be eating lunch at Blair House that day.

I was rather taken aback. Before I knew what I was doing, I was asking in no uncertain terms why I hadn't been informed about this change in plans. Furthermore, I added, if Mr. Brezhnev did suddenly arrive expecting lunch, I planned to go directly to Ambassador Dobrynin for an explanation.

Ambassador Smoak witnessed this highly undiplomatic little encounter and several months later kidded me in a conversation with someone at the department, saying, "Don't cross Mary Edith. I saw her stand right here and shake her finger in the face of a Russian protocol officer and tell him where to get off. And this was in the presence of any number of KGB men."

The Secretary did get to Blair House, finally, at around five o'clock. He had been welcomed on the South Lawn of the White House and had been quite openly pleased about his arrival. He had come, in part, to sign an agreement between our two countries on the peaceful uses of atomic energy. Smiling broadly, he had addressed the group welcoming him: "This is my first visit to your country, my first direct acquaintance with America and the American people. . . . Our two capitals are separated by over six thousand miles. But international politics has its own concept of relativity not covered by Einstein's Theory. The distances between our countries are shrinking . . . because we share one great goal, which is to ensure a lasting peace for all peoples of our countries and to strengthen security on our planet."

When he came to Blair House accompanied by Foreign Minister Gromyko and Secretary of State Rogers, the Secretary went immediately to his room to get ready for the state dinner at the White House that night.

While White House state dinners are always formal affairs, the Russians did not wear black tie. Instead, Secretary Brezhnev wore a dark business suit. Over the breast pocket he hung two star-shaped Russian medals.

The Foreign Relations Committee luncheon was to be the following day. The morning of the lunch we had a visit from Ambassador Dobrynin, the Russian chief of protocol, Mr. Dmitri Nikiforov, and several people from the KGB who were to be in charge of security during the lunch. I was rather surprised to see Ambassador Dobrynin, since it was unusual for the ambassador of a visitor's country to trouble himself with this sort of detail during a visit. But the Russians were obviously eager that every aspect of Mr. Brezhnev's stay and every event be handled with care.

Everything had been planned. The Russian Embassy was sending its maître d' and two wine stewards who were to supervise setting up the tables so it would be done their way. The maître d' was to supervise the Russian wine stewards, but we would have to augment their staff with our own butlers.

We thought we would have our usual four round tables of ten in the Blair-Lee drawing room. But I received word that someone had decided that the drawing room wasn't big enough and it had been suggested that we serve lunch in the large press room in Jackson Place. The trouble with that idea was that, in addition to the room's being a little bare since the decorating was not in any way finished, I needed it for the buffet to serve the large contingent of security and embassy people who were to be there while Mr. Brezhnev was hosting the Foreign Relations Committee. But I had begun to have it all set up.

I took Ambassador Dobrynin over to Jackson Place and showed him the press room. Both he and Mr. Nikiforov agreed that it was stark and bare. Then I showed them what I had planned to do in the Blair-Lee drawing room, and they agreed that it would be a much better place for lunch. I asked them if I could just get on with it, please, and although they wanted to stay on and talk about other plans, they could see that I was working against a busy schedule and they left.

The maître d' and his staff set up the tables. They wanted to
do it "as we do it at home," they had told me. It was quite a
table setting. At each place there were five glasses (red wine,
white wine, champagne, brandy, and vodka) plus a water gob-
let. They used up every piece of flat silver we had. The knives,
forks, and spoons lined up at each plate took up the space we
usually allotted to two place settings. For the buffet next door
we had to borrow one hundred place settings of stainless-steel
flatware from the State Department cafeteria.

The luncheon guests arrived at one. Lunch went on for most
of the afternoon. Every once in a while one of the guests would
get up to telephone his office that he might be a bit delayed.
Blair House lunches usually lasted an hour and a half. The
Brezhnev lunch was over at five-thirty.

Later that day there was a state dinner with President Nixon
as the guest of honor at the Russian Embassy. On Wednesday,
Secretary Brezhnev, Foreign Minister Gromyko, and several of
the highest-ranking members of the party were to go to Camp
David for an overnight stay. But most of the other guests were
not invited to any of these functions. We had a house full of
people to take care of. And what a houseful it was.

During the entire ten days not one of them left Blair House
for so much as a stroll around the garden. The public areas
looked like waiting rooms in a railroad station, and we served
three meals a day to dozens of people. The meals themselves became a problem because Dallas suddenly announced on the day
after the Foreign Relations Committee lunch that his mother
was desperately ill and that he would have to go to Detroit to be
with her. I felt sorry for him, but no emergency could have been
more poorly timed. Until he returned, we hired a chef for meals,
but that night's dinner had to be catered since he left so
abruptly.

To say that the Russian visitors taxed our facilities and our pa-
tience would be a diplomatic understatement. For instance, they
had a very peculiar sense of time. If I announced that lunch
would be at one—a time chosen with their schedule in mind—
they would arrive at the table at noon or they wouldn't get there
until two. The same thing happened at dinner.

I decided I would ask them when they *wanted* their meals

served. But the results were the same. If they said dinner at eight, they'd be in the dining room at six-thirty. When they found out that there was nothing prepared as yet, they'd leave and come back at nine-thirty to be served.

It was frustrating and eventually infuriating.

We were always prepared to serve refreshments in our guests' rooms, and several of the Russian visitors asked that drinks be brought up. We soon learned that when they asked for a drink they didn't mean a couple of martinis on a tray. They wanted a full, unopened bottle each time. It didn't make any difference whether it was scotch or brandy or Pepsi-Cola. They didn't want the liquid poured into a glass over ice.

One day the butler reported that he had just sent four six-packs of Pepsi, two six-packs of mixers, and two bottles of whiskey up to a certain room. When he went up a little later, there was no one in the room and none of the drinks were to be seen. We never did solve that mystery.

The Russians drank scotch, bourbon, and of course vodka. But they really adored brandy. We couldn't keep the brandy decanter on the refreshment table filled. They drank it in water glasses. It was a little scary to see how much the KGB consumed while Secretary Brezhnev was out. They seemed to drink continuously, but they never appeared to be drunk. When the Russians left and we did our usual inventory, we found that we had used six cases of brandy during the visit, an amount that normally lasted us about six months.

My orders were to give the Russians anything they wanted. But one day I was standing in the dining room chatting with Assistant Chief of Protocol Nicholas Ruwe, when one of the Russians came up and said he would like a quart of brandy to take to his room. Before I had a chance to say anything at all, Nick said, "No. If you want brandy served in your room, let us know your room number and we'll have a butler bring you up a glass of brandy." The Russian meekly did just that and went off to his room.

I was never able to deal so firmly with the Russians. They were extremely demanding and it was hard to fill all their orders. But what annoyed me most was the way they treated the staff. The top-ranking people were very polite and extremely friendly, but the rank and file (and there were a great many of those) spoke rudely to our butlers and parlormaids, ordering them around. Several times members of my staff would come to me with complaints that they had been threatened by the guests.

This was too much. On the second day of the visit I called in the embassy counselor and told him that the Blair House staff was made up of professionals and that I expected them to be treated like professionals. Any orders were to be given through me. After that our people had it a little better, especially when I was around.

Because there was so much work and a great many problems connected with this visit, I was very pleased when Mr. Gromyko, who had come back from Camp David on Thursday, came downstairs and told me how much he enjoyed Blair House and how happy he was to be there. It was kind of him to have made the extra effort to tell me this at a time when I really needed a compliment.

Over the weekend Secretary Brezhnev was scheduled to go to San Clemente as Mr. Nixon's guest, along with Mr. Gromyko and other high-ranking members of the party. They planned to do some sightseeing in California. In the meantime the remaining members of the party were going to stay at Blair House.

The Secret Service was talking about leaving the White House police in charge of this much smaller group. But I knew that the police would not be in the house. They would simply patrol the entrances, and that meant that since the top-ranking KGB people would be in California, I would be left with the underlings who had already proved themselves to be difficult.

I announced that I would not stay in the house and be responsible for the whole thing. I suggested that one Secret Service officer stay in the house at all times so that I could have some help in dealing with the KGB. We had often found a KGB man asleep on a precious damask or satin upholstered sofa with his shoes on. Naturally the butlers would be ignored if they asked him to get off the furniture. The Secret Service had to be called in for that little job.

It was agreed that the Secret Service would stay in the house. On Saturday morning I decided I simply had to get out of the house for a while. I got in my car and started driving, enjoying the beautiful Washington springtime scenery, which buoyed my spirits, and I was ready to face the next crisis.

It was not long in coming, but it added the only light note to the whole visit.

On Sunday morning the ministers who had remained behind were to be taken for a drive to Camp David. In the morning, when they were getting dressed, they discovered that their trousers, which had just been cleaned by our cleaners, could not be worn since all the buttons on the flies had simply dissolved in the cleaning somehow. At any rate, they were not there.

Our button box contained nothing we could use as substitutes. We rarely got a call for a fly button. I was just about to give up in despair, since this was Sunday and the stores were closed, when Manuel, one of the butlers, said he had some very old European trousers at home. If his wife hadn't thrown them out, he thought that they all had buttoned flies and he was willing to go home to get them.

By luck, the pants were still there. While parlormaids armed with needles and thread stood waiting, we sent him home in a car to get the pants. A half hour later the Russians were buttoned into their trousers and ready to go. We never found out what happened to those buttons. They must have been made of some very sensitive material that couldn't stand the onslaught of our strong cleaning fluid.

It was the first time in a week that the Russians had left the house. Of course they weren't allowed to leave alone. The cars taking them to Camp David were driven by American military men and one Secret Service man and KGB officer were in the seat next to the driver.

The Russian visit, although it had its light moments and some truly pleasant people, was the most difficult of my entire stay at Blair House. I tried to understand the way the Russians behaved. Perhaps their treatment of our staff was a way of lashing out at the ever-present restrictions of the KGB. Maybe they were all suffering from a form of cabin fever after being cooped up all that time. I don't know. Whatever the explanation, it was a trying time for us all.

It took two weeks to get the house back in order again. One of the most annoying things during the visit had been the refusal of most of the guests to let the maids into their rooms with fresh linen. Most of the rooms had only been sporadically cleaned over the ten-day period of the visit. Consequently, we had a lot more to do than usual.

We all felt we had been through a long and trying time. But soon we were back to normal again.

Chapter Twenty-Four

♦ DURING THE REST of 1973 we had visits from several of our
old friends. Our first guests after the Russians left were the
Shah and Empress of Iran. The Shah was in this country shopping for military equipment. He went to Andrews Air Force
Base one day for a demonstration of some of our newest fighter
planes. But there was still time for socializing. I was among one
hundred fifty guests who attended a performance of *The Desert
Song* at the Kennedy Center for the Performing Arts.

Before we left for the theater, the Shah and Empress Farah
and I sat in the drawing room talking about simple things. By
then we had really come to know a great deal about one another. We spoke often about our children. I know that Moslem
men are supposed to be partial to their sons, but when the Shah
talked about his youngest daughter, it was clear that she was
very precious to him by the fond look he got in his eye.

The Empress was trying to give up smoking, but as she lit up
a cigarette, she mentioned that she thought it was easier for men
to give up this bad habit. She never smoked in public, of course,
but she had found it impossible to quit altogether. As I smoked
my own cigarette, I could only agree with her.

The evening was a gala one, planned and executed by Ambassador Ardeshir Zahedi of Iran, one of Washington's most famous
hosts. During his term as ambassador his lavish parties were the
talk of the town. So I was flattered when he asked if he could
stay in the Blair House during this visit of the Shah so that he
could observe how we did things. After the visit was over, he

asked me to try and find him someone who could help him out at his embassy.

The following week we had a visit from His Excellency Prime Minister Kakuei Tanaka of Japan, who arrived with Foreign Minister Masayoshi Ohira and a group of high-level diplomats. The visit was preceded by a bit of a snafu. The Japanese had come to the house over the weekend, while I was at home, to see about setting up offices for this visit, which would concentrate on work and negotiations instead of social functions.

They were not aware that since the last time a Japanese visitor had stayed with us we had greatly expanded and now had many rooms in the Jackson Place House specifically designed for offices. It was a little embarrassing to have to tell them on Monday morning that their plans were all for nothing. As always, the Japanese were very polite and simply changed their plans. In fact, they were delighted with the new offices.

Over that summer Secretary Rogers announced that he would be leaving the Administration to go back into private practice. The Rogers announcement had been rumored for some time and so I was not surprised when it finally came, but my farewells to the Secretary and Mrs. Rogers were nonetheless very sad. I still get pictures of the entire Rogers family every year at Christmas.

When Dr. Kissinger became Secretary of State in September, he was not yet married, and Mrs. Kenneth Rush, wife of the deputy secretary, was called upon to be his official hostess.

Early in September, Prime Minister Zulfikar Ali Bhutto of Pakistan arrived with his wife and two of their children. Be-Nazir, their daughter, had graduated from Radcliffe the previous year. Their son Mir, who was studying at Harvard, came from Boston to be with his family at Blair House. Begum Bhutto, daughter of an upper-class Iranian, met the press at tea, and she was quite at home in this capacity.

Prime Minister Bhutto was later jailed by a new government in Pakistan, and in spite of the objections of many other countries, he was hanged in 1979. Both the Begum and her daughter have since taken an active part in leading the opposition party in their country. Early in 1981 the Begum was jailed for a time and then exiled to an outlying province for her outspoken opposition to the present government of Pakistan.

But at the time of their visit all that was far in the future. The visit was a busy one, and both the Begum and Prime Minister Bhutto had a busy schedule.

As always, I admired the beautiful saris the women wore, but I mentioned to Ambassador Khan that I couldn't imagine how they were kept on. It looked to me as if some kind of magic formula was used. "You'll have to come over for a sari-wrapping party one of these days," he said. "Then you'll see that it's very easy to do and very comfortable."

I never did learn how to wrap a sari.

Some months later we had another visit from President Félix Houphouët-Boigny of the Ivory Coast. He had come to the United States for a round of important meetings concerning aid for his country, which was in the grip of a terrible drought.

On the day President Houphouët-Boigny was to leave, he had an appointment at Blair House with Vice-President Agnew. But the day before, the Vice-President had announced his resignation. The meeting with the President of the Ivory Coast had been hurriedly canceled and there had been no time to substitute anything else, leaving us in the awkward position of having a stretch of unscheduled time on our hands.

When I got the call notifying us that the Vice-President was not going to be coming, I informed President Houphouët-Boigny and invited him for a walk in the garden. We filled a long twenty minutes with small talk about Washington, the weather, and so on. It was an uncomfortable few minutes for us both. The problems across the street at the White House had finally penetrated our somewhat cloistered quarters.

Still, for the most part Blair House continued to function in spite of the furor of Watergate. At times, behind our doors, it seemed that we were part of an entirely different world, a retreat from the rigors of the political life that raged outside. One evening Ambassador and Mrs. Smoak gave a small dinner for members of the diplomatic community. The entertainment was provided by Mr. Darling, a harpsichordist, and Miss Rowe, a folk singer, both from Williamsburg, dressed in eighteenth-century costumes. Francie Smoak had brought with her some replicas of seventeenth-century clay pipes, and after dinner, while we served coffee in the drawing room, the butlers passed the pipes around and several of the guests attempted to smoke them. It was a pretty tableau from another time: the costumed entertainers, the men smoking the clay pipes, and the soft light of the candles that stood around the room.

The events of the twentieth century were bound to impinge, however. In October, in the aftermath of the Yom Kippur War, Prime Minister Golda Meir came for a working visit on very short notice. When she arrived I could see that Mrs. Meir was showing the effects of the strain of her country's recent conflict. In fact, she was slightly ill, and a doctor was summoned by the Israeli Embassy. He arrived soon after the Prime Minister had gone to her room and suggested that she go right to bed. He prescribed some medication and we sent up some hot tea. She said she didn't want any dinner.

I was very concerned about the Prime Minister, whom I had never seen look quite so exhausted. But the next morning she seemed to have snapped back. Her eyes were bright and her energy as unflagging as ever.

The day began for Golda Meir with breakfast for eight, including Dr. Kissinger. There followed a busy round of meetings and a private talk with President Nixon. The next day's breakfast companions were a group of senators. Members of Congress came for coffee at eleven. In the evening, Dr. Kissinger, Assistant Secretary of State Joseph Sisco, his deputy Alfred Atherton, and members of the Israeli Embassy were at Blair House for a meeting that lasted officially until the Americans left at one in the morning. But the Israelis remained with Mrs. Meir until some time after two.

I don't know how she managed such a grueling schedule. The next day the whole thing was repeated again, and then it was decided that she would stay an extra day in order to have some more high-level talks with members of our government. It seemed to do her no harm. In fact, when she left she was looking quite well, not nearly as tired as when she had arrived. She seemed to thrive on hard work.

One day not long after this, Dr. Montgomery Blair and Mr. John Halverson, curator of the Portland (Maine) Museum, came to see the Clapp family portraits that Dr. Blair had given to the museum. These pictures of members of the Clapp side of the

Blair family had been on loan to the house ever since it was purchased and we knew that someday they would be returned to the Clapp family's home state of Maine. Several were slated to be copied in oil by the portrait painter Gregory Stapko, who had made copies for the National Gallery, so that we could keep the reproductions at Blair House. Dr. Blair left promising to send us a list of those that were to be reproduced. Several weeks later, I had the list on my desk.

The year ended with a return visit from President and Mrs. Ceauşescu of Romania. Mrs. Ceauşescu brought along an interpreter, Mrs. Nastraşescu, and the President had not only an interpreter but also a waiter and a tailor. Almost no one spoke English in the party, and although they were more relaxed on this visit, they still went about in pairs just as they did on their last stay with us. Mrs. Ceauşescu seemed much more stylish in her dress and was a good deal more open and friendly than she had been. She even smiled quite often.

The Ceauşescus took all their meals in their rooms, served by their personal waiter. The chambermaids had been told that they were not to enter the Head of State's Suite. When they came up the morning of the second day of the visit to change the sheets, they were told that would not be necessary. One chambermaid did manage to get in with a tray one morning. Everyone was intrigued by the atmosphere of mystery that surrounded the room. She reported that the Ceauşescus had brought along their own bed linens, which they had put on the beds right over ours. I gathered that they sent whatever laundry they had over to their embassy, because we never saw any in our laundry rooms.

Chapter Twenty-Five

WE ENTERED the new year with a new Vice-President, Gerald Ford, and an inescapable atmosphere of tension. Soon the Watergate investigations touched us directly. One day we got a call from the Watergate Committee asking for the guest list of a luncheon that had been hosted by Vice-President Agnew in March 1971.

I referred this request to Mr. Smoak, since all such lists were kept on file at the Protocol Office. I assume he gave it to the committee, but it was a shock to be asked for such a list. One of the unbreakable Blair House rules was that we preserved the privacy of our guests and did not give out information about functions. It was hard for me to realize that in the present climate even the tranquillity of Blair House, that traditional refuge from the public eye, could be penetrated by what was happening outside.

But Watergate was far from my mind when, early in 1974, I finally met Mrs. Harry S. Truman. Margaret Truman Daniel had called to ask if she could bring her mother by to show her how Blair House had changed over the years since she had seen it. I was delighted at the prospect of meeting this woman about whom I had heard so much.

The Daniels brought Mrs. Truman to the side door of Blair House so she could have easy access to the elevator. She had bright blue eyes and was very interested and eager to see everything. We walked through many of the rooms and she thought that everything looked a lot snappier. She was delighted with what had been done to her old bedroom and loved Margaret's refurbished suite.

We didn't go up to the fourth floor, but she told us that she had used what was now Room 41 as her office.

I wanted to serve Mrs. Truman tea, but the long tour had tired her and Margaret thought they ought to get back.

It was a real treat for me. I had just about given up hope of meeting the woman who was considered the backbone of her family. I had often talked to Mr. Truman about her. He always referred to her as "the boss."

A few weeks later, I received a handwritten letter:
"Dear Mrs. Wilroy:

I am somewhat embarrassed to have been so long in thanking you for taking your time to show me through Blair House. I enjoyed it so very much, even though it is changed from the time we lived there. The rooms are handsomely done and I am sure the new addition is most convenient. *We* needed that too, but instead, we just had to have *two* teas in an afternoon, instead of one. But in four years, we just got used to it.

Thank you very much for giving me that tour, which meant a great deal to me.

Sincerely,
Bess Truman"

I gave another tour that January. Mrs. Ford had been named honorary chairman of the Blair House Fine Arts Committee, and I was pleased to take her around and could see that she was going to be an enthusiastic addition to the committee. By this time we had made enormous strides in the refurbishing of the Jackson Place side of the house.

On the first floor we now had a grand new dining room. The walls were covered with gold damask and there was a large, beautifully framed mirror hanging over the mantel. The dining room chairs were covered with old-fashioned black horsehair. Mrs. Ford particularly admired the lovely delicate chandelier, a gift from Mrs. Sidi Smith, that hung above the dining room table.

The sitting room, quite Victorian in feeling, featured reproductions of Victorian chairs and tables set on a blue rug. The windows were hung with lace curtains.

The front hall of the Jackson Place House was somewhat smaller than that at Blair House. It had a chandelier and the doors were decorated with panes of etched glass.

But my pride and joy, both for its beauty and for its practicality, was the huge press room, which finally gave us enough room for as many reporters, TV cameramen, and people with microphones as we needed. Two marble mantels, originally in the house, continued to grace the walls between the windows, and over these mantels were two large Blair House mirrors. Two red rugs with Greek key designs covered the enormous floor space. Three tiers of dark wooden shutters covered the windows and permitted us to darken the room for film showings or slide presentations.

At one end of the room there was a Steinway grand, which was used when the room was given over to dancing or when we had a large dinner there. Two beautiful dark red damask sofas from Blair House stood along the side wall and at the other end of the room. A large Chinese chest was placed against a side wall, and there were a few occasional chairs and tables. An imposing chandelier hung from the center of the ceiling. Other lighting was provided by interesting globe lights mounted on pedestals placed at intervals around the room.

It was an impressive room and one that served for any number of purposes. Sometimes there might be a large round table surrounded by chairs for a meeting, or six or eight smaller tables set for lunch or dinner. We could easily accommodate twenty people for a formal meal, a crowd for a buffet, or up to one hundred members of the press.

Pat Mosbacher was responsible for most of the furnishings, all of which were planned with decorator Elisabeth Draper before Ambassador Mosbacher left. Mrs. Draper continued her work with the funds Pat Mosbacher had acquired, and to my delight, Pat stopped by several times when she happened to be in Washington so she was able to see the progress on the job she had begun.

The press was increasingly interested in what was going on at

Blair House. When Mr. Ford took over as Vice-President, he gave three diplomatic receptions at Blair House so that members of the various embassies could meet him and Mrs. Ford. Members of Congress and several reporters were also there. But the press people were not as interested in the diplomats as they were in the new Vice-President, who had been brought in at a time of so much scandal and pressure. At the first reception he was asked at least three times what he thought about the fact that a Democrat had been named to replace him in Congress.

At the next reception much was made of the fact that Mrs. Ford was late. She had in fact suffered a painful accident, in which she scratched her cornea, and had stopped off at the hospital to have it treated. When she came in, the Vice-President, clearly very concerned, broke off what he was doing and held a serious conversation with his wife to make sure that she was all right. They talked earnestly for several minutes. The next day the papers reported that the Fords had had a marital spat in the middle of a diplomatic reception.

But the Washington *Star* at one of the receptions caught Mrs. Ford more accurately. A picture taken by William Streets showed her admiring the party clothes worn by Senator George Aiken of Vermont. The senator, one of Washington's most colorful citizens, was wearing a navy blue tuxedo, a ruffled lavender shirt, a purple velvet bow tie, and red suspenders, which he revealed to Mrs. Ford and to the photographer. In his overcoat, the accompanying story reported, the senator had a bag of unshelled peanuts for the pigeons on Capitol Hill.

At the third reception a well-dressed couple was ushered in. I had never seen them before, but since I didn't know every diplomat by sight, I figured they were new and that if they didn't belong there, someone would let me know.

Later, as I was circulating around the room checking that everything was going well, I kept hearing the other guests speculating about who the mysterious couple were. No one seemed to have a clue to their identity.

After some discussion, I realized that they had not been invited. How they got past the security men I'll never know. The Secret Service was dispatched to ask them politely to leave.

This little event, innocent as it was, also made the papers. It was not the first time I had caught a gate-crasher. Once I stopped a very pleasant lady at the front hall just as she was taking off her coat. When I asked her for her invitation, she said cheerfully, "Oh, I don't have an invitation. I just saw all these people coming in here and I thought there might be something going on, so I thought I'd just come in and see." She was perfectly amiable and understanding when I explained that it was a private party and she simply couldn't stay.

Following the first reception, Vice-President and Mrs. Ford sat down in the drawing room after everyone had left. They had spent the entire time on their feet greeting their guests and chatting with as many people as they could. I don't think either one of them had had anything to eat or drink.

I asked the butler to bring around the trays of hors d'oeuvres that were left over and something to drink. We had what amounted to a light supper together. Mrs. Ford, who was as down-to-earth as my neighbors in Maryland, said she was delighted just to be sitting and even happier to be having something to eat. "Now I don't have to go home and rummage around in the refrigerator to find something for dinner," she said. After that first reception it became the natural thing for us to simply sit down with the party leftovers, saving Mrs. Ford the job of cooking supper.

This was the beginning of my very warm relationship with the Fords. We had many happy times together, but we were all living through a terribly trying period.

One day I got a phone call from a man who identified himself as a member of the President's staff. He said his name was Banks and that he had just come from California. The purpose of his call was to alert us to a package he had sent Blair House. "I'll be coming to pick it up in the next few weeks. I don't know where I'll be staying, so I've sent some of my personal belongings on ahead to Blair House for safekeeping," he said. "When the package comes, please don't send it back to California."

At any other time, I wouldn't have given this request another thought. But we were all extra careful at the time and so I decided to ask around about "Mr. Banks." I made a few discreet inquiries, but no one had ever heard of him. I told the staff not

to accept any strange packages and to let me know if anything
came either for or from a Mr. Banks. In the end, no package arrived and that was the last I ever heard of the whole affair, but
at the time it was rather unsettling.

Mrs. Smoak continued to work energetically for the Blair
House Fine Arts Committee. She rounded up some of the original members and was busy recruiting some new ones. Vice-
President and Mrs. Ford came to one of the several meetings she
called, and they had a chance to see some of the upstairs rooms.
Dr. Blair was at this meeting, too, and he and Mr. Ford had a
long talk about the history of the house. Sadly, this turned out to
be his last visit to his family's home. A few weeks later he had a
heart attack and passed away. I was glad that I had completed
our mutual project of having the Clapp family portraits copied.

In March of 1974 King Hussein once again came for a visit.
The King piloted his own private jet into Andrews Air Force
Base. He had flown on automatic pilot across the ocean, but as
he came in for his landing, the hydraulic fluid began to leak and
smoke and the controls jammed just as the plane made a safe
landing. The King landed about thirty yards short of the red carpet at the other end of which Secretary of State Kissinger was
waiting.

The King stepped from his disabled plane completely unflus-
tered. He said he was "very sorry to have inconvenienced dear
Henry, who had to walk an extra thirty yards to meet me."

King Hussein was in excellent spirits. He came without Queen
Alia, who was expecting their first child, and he was openly
delighted about the prospect of a new baby. As always, his first
request was for a hamburger with all the trimmings. This time
we sent up two. In a short while His Majesty called down to say
they were so good he'd like another.

Later, after Secretary Kissinger called on His Majesty, Prime
Minister Zaid al-Rifai said he'd like a hamburger in his room. He
didn't think that His Majesty would be down for the seated dinner we were preparing to serve, but if he did come, the Prime
Minister would accompany him. Fifteen minutes later, before we
had time to send the hamburger upstairs, the two men came
down. Prime Minister Rifai got his hamburger the next day. And
His Majesty had his favorite food again, just before leaving Blair

House for his annual checkup at Walter Reed Army Medical Center.

Dallas was hardly in evidence during the visit. He had the flu and called in just before the weekend to say that he could come back, but I decided we really didn't need him by that time, since all the planning for the rest of the Jordanian stay had been done. I was getting a little concerned that Dallas was not as reliable as he used to be.

Just at this time Ambassador Smoak announced he would be leaving his post; his resignation came as a complete surprise to me. Like the other chiefs of protocol and their wives, the Smoaks had become my friends. Ambassador Smoak was replaced by Ambassador Henry Catto. Mrs. Catto was the daughter of Oveta Culp Hobby, who had been director of the Women's Army Corps during World War II, and she was an old Washington hand.

And the next blow was that Mary Schenke was leaving us to move to Atlanta with her husband. To replace her, we had found a former high school language teacher who was fluent in French and Spanish and was something of a gourmet cook. These attributes sounded like just what was needed at Blair House. Her name was Mary Schneck, a name that was so close to Mary Schenke's that it seemed almost eerie.

I interviewed the new Mary and found her charming, very eager to take the job, and eminently suited to it. She was soon at the house, learning from her predecessor about the fine points of her new position. As she began to learn the ropes, I found myself wishing I could have both Marys there all the time.

Secretary of State Kissinger's new bride, Nancy, was an official State Department hostess for the first time during the visit of Algeria's President Houari Boumedienne. Mrs. Kissinger was obviously quite at home as a hostess and I was secretly pleased that we would no longer have to deal with the bachelor Secretary of State, a man who clearly was used to getting his own way, yet, like many men, not at all aware of what was involved in setting up a state dinner. More than once he had given us less than a day's notice for an event that required much more careful planning. After talking with Mrs. Kissinger, I felt reassured that she would be able to explain to her husband that we needed a little more notice. The day before she was hostess at her first luncheon, she went to the trouble of coming over to see how we ran such an event. We went through the entire routine and she made several good suggestions. One of her best ideas was to serve champagne instead of mixed drinks at lunches where the guests were all women. This became a regular practice at her luncheons and was enthusiastically received.

President and Mrs. Boumedienne arrived with a small party for an informal overnight visit. But a large welcoming contingent came with them to Blair House, including Ambassador and Mrs. Catto and Dr. and Mrs. Kissinger. Because it was the first visit for both couples, the first half hour or so was a little chaotic. No one seemed to know quite what to expect. They stood around and chatted for several minutes, which stretched into nearly a half hour. Gradually, however, our officials moved out and the Boumediennes were shown to their rooms, and everything fell into place, as it usually did.

Later in the month, Mrs. Nixon hosted a tea for one hundred fifty wives of the heads of the Pacific Basin Economic Group. These women came from Japan, Canada, Indonesia, Australia, and New Zealand, among other countries. Because of the large numbers involved and because Mrs. Nixon was not able to give the whole afternoon to this function, we had to plan everything to the last detail. The guests were to arrive in buses and would be ushered into the house through the front entrance. They were to go immediately to the Jackson Place dining room, sitting room, and press room, where our staff would serve them tea. A half hour later, Mrs. Nixon was to arrive and she would greet her guests in the rear Blair drawing room as they returned down the hall on their way to the entrance of the house or for a tour of the house.

Luckily we had the assistance of six military aides from the White House. They were marvelous. They followed instructions to the letter and they somehow managed tactfully to steer the guests to the tea tables and then to meet Mrs. Nixon without making it seem as if we were herding them around.

Everything went like clockwork. Mrs. Nixon had not had a chance to see the Jackson Place rooms, and so after the guests left, we walked over to the new addition. We were not alone, however, since a contingent from the press followed her wherever she went in those days, and they were close on her heels even during this short walk to Jackson Place.

Then she walked back to the White House accompanied by her social secretary, Lucy Winchester, a military aide, and the cluster of newspaper people. She looked lovely and, in her shy way, expressed her appreciation for our help. She said that there had simply been too many functions scheduled at the White House that day and she was pleased that we were able to accommodate her guests for tea.

In June we had a visit from His Royal Highness Prince Fahd Ibn Abd al-Aziz, Deputy Premier of Saudi Arabia (now Crown Prince). This was a working visit, all male, all business. Secretary Kissinger and the Prince signed an agreement between our two countries at a ceremony in the Jackson Place press room. When the busy visit was over, the Prince said he'd be seeing me again. I got the distinct feeling that there was a lot of unfinished business between us and the Saudis.

That Saturday I suddenly felt very tried, but I didn't think it was anything but the aftermath of an unusually busy week. I went home and spent the weekend quietly; but when I got back to Blair House on Monday morning, I still felt exhausted. I hadn't had a physical for some time, so I arranged to have a thorough checkup later that week. Then I went out to do a few errands.

When I got back, I began to have chest pains, which I attributed to my old reliable ulcer, but I didn't object when Dallas called the medical division at the department and Dr. Nydell ordered me to go immediately to Sibley Memorial Hospital.

I didn't want to believe it, but I was having a heart attack.

I spent the next three weeks at the hospital, with orders not to return to work for at least three months.

I will always be grateful for Mary Schneck, who had taken over from Mary Schenke at the end of the month. She just came in and took control of the house. Fortunately, we had no visits scheduled until August, but she managed the busy schedule of functions and handled all the day-to-day problems and crises.

I was allowed no visitors at the hospital, but I was able to get Dr. Mishtowt, my internist, to let Mary come over once so that I could sign a check to cover the next few weeks' expenses. "Make it a big check," he said. "I'm not letting her back here again."

I was told not to worry or even think about Blair House. But Mary and I did talk on the phone every day. I suspect that she kept any problems she was having to herself because in every conversation she told me how well everything was going.

The doctor also insisted that from then on I have enough full-time help at the house so that I could take some time off. It was clear that I could never go back to my past schedule, so Mary was assigned to stay on at the house full-time even after I returned.

When I got home from the hospital, I felt quite well. I didn't realize that I must have been good and sick until I tried to take a ten-minute walk. I was immediately exhausted. But with the help of my daughter Ann and a dear neighbor, Ayesha Smith, who came every day, and my loyal, once-a-week maid, Irene Dye, who took on my full-time care, I was soon feeling almost as good as new.

It was the first time I had been ordered to do nothing and I took advantage of it, reading books I'd put off for years and relaxing as much as possible.

While I was home recuperating, President Nixon resigned and President Ford took over the office of President. It all seemed very far away, I thought, as I watched it on television in my house in Takoma Park. But of course, I was in touch with Mary every day, either by phone or when she came to visit.

She told me that, as far as she knew, the impending visit of King Hussein and Queen Alia was coming off as scheduled on August 15. The White House had been under a certain amount of pressure, since they had to plan a state dinner in the unusually short space of a week. It had not been clear who was going to be President during the King's visit. The resignation of Mr. Nixon, though rumored for some time, happened only a week and a day from the arrival day. As it happened, the Fords were not yet in residence at the White House, but the dinner—their first state visit, of course—went off splendidly.

The papers were full of pictures of the new President dancing with the gloriously beautiful young Queen. She sent me a clipping that showed her on the dance floor with President Ford.

She was dressed in a lovely diaphanous dark gown, and her long, dark hair was worn loose. Across the bottom of the photograph she had written a get-well message to me.

In 1977 Queen Alia was killed in a helicopter crash. She was on her way to inspect a hospital in southern Jordan when a sudden rainstorm caused the crash.

King Hussein still often comes to Blair House. I see his picture in the Washington papers. In fact, he holds the record for the most visits to Blair House. I will always recall his visits to us, his voracious appetite for hamburgers, but most of all, that happy visit when he first brought Queen Alia to Blair House. I felt pleased for him a few years ago when he remarried. For the first time since Queen Alia's death, he looked like the King Hussein I had gotten to know so well.

Chapter Twenty-Six

❧ THE DAY AFTER Labor Day I was back at work in time to welcome Israeli Prime Minister Yitzhak Rabin and Mrs. Rabin, old friends from the days when the Prime Minister had been Israel's ambassador to this country. As usual, the Israelis put in long hours, beginning with official breakfast meetings, followed by coffees, and so on. I think I must have set up that press room for meetings at least ten different times as Mr. Rabin met with reporters, senators, congressmen, and a large group of Jewish businessmen. When they were not involved with official functions, the Rabins visited with the many friends they had in Washington.

The following Monday Mrs. Ford came over to look at a display of possible gifts set up by ten different manufacturers or purveyors of glass, silver, and other objects that might make suitable presents from our government to the visiting heads of state.

Mrs. Ford wanted the gifts presented during her husband's administration to be typically American. Another consideration was the cost. With prices rising every day, it had become very hard to keep within the budget for gifts and still present something of value.

We had similar exhibits of gifts periodically for all the First Ladies. On this occasion I worked closely with Mr. Thurston of Steuben Glass and with Mr. Hall from Galt's jewelers.

We set up long tables in the press room. They were covered with silver desk sets, Steuben glass bowls and vases, silver picture frames (often used to frame a copy of a treaty or a photograph of the President), pencil and pen sets in stands made of silver or semiprecious stones, silver letter openers, and other items.

The Gorham Silver Company sent over some of their decorative metal trees from which sprouted enamel flowers in many colors. These had been a special favorite of Mrs. Nixon, who had presented them several times to the wives of heads of state.

The marvelous porcelain figures fashioned by Cybis and by Edward Boehm were often given as gifts. Sometimes a clock or a copy of an early American wall barometer was selected. If the visitor was known to smoke, the gift might be a silver cigarette case or a humidor of wood or leather.

If he had a special hobby he might receive a set of golf clubs, an antique pistol, an album of rare stamps, a book on his subject of interest, or something to add to his collection of porcelain or glass.

Occasionally the gift would be very specially crafted. For instance, a visitor from Brazil received a cigarette box on which was engraved a map of North and South America, with both capitals highlighted in semiprecious stones. Another visitor received a large desk with a silver plaque engraved with the date of his visit.

Mrs. Ford suggested that we might try to get some pieces of American handicrafts, such as quilts or Indian pottery, for future gift giving.

She made a list of the things that interested her and gave them to Patrick Daly, the protocol officer in charge of gifts. The gift selection was part of the initial planning for every visit. When a visit was announced, Patrick would consult Mrs. Ford's list, discuss a selection with her secretary, and see that the gift was ordered and ready for the official presentation.

Since this had been one of my jobs at the State Department, I knew how time-consuming and complicated it could be to get the gift ordered in time, get it engraved if need be, and, often, send it overseas to the home or palace of the visitor. The cost of the gift came out of State Department visit funds. The most elaborate gift I ever had to order was a reproduction of a marvelous file table invented by Thomas Jefferson. It featured a rotating top and a series of little drawers marked with the letters of the alphabet. The table was one of a number of gifts taken by President Eisenhower on a trip around the world.

Usually the gifts were not that exotic and the selection process began with these exhibits, most of the time being a smooth operation, just another part of the visit routine.

Now the visits were coming in a rush. Our next guests were President and Mrs. Giovanni Leone of Italy, who brought along their three sons, Dr. Mauro Leone, Paolo Leone, and Giancarlo Leone. Mrs. Leone, a few inches taller than her handsome husband, was a strikingly beautiful woman with thick black hair and a wonderful tan, which was shown off to great advantage by the sleeveless white crepe Valentino gown she wore to the White House state dinner. Also in their party were Foreign Minister Aldo Moro and Ambassador and Mrs. Ortona, along with several others. They were all beautifully dressed and were a lively and voluble group. Whenever they left the house it seemed terribly quiet.

The dinner was a great deal of fun for everyone. Those members of the party who had not been invited for the official meal went over afterward for the entertainment. And Susan Ford had asked several of her young women friends to fill the seats at a table reserved for the younger members of the Ford family and the Leone sons. This was one of the happiest groups we had in the house.

By contrast, our next guest, Prime Minister Sheikh Mujibur Rahman of Bangladesh, came for a brief working visit with a serious agenda. Once again Bangladesh was suffering from a severe drought and its people were starving, so Sheikh Mujib came to discuss American aid to his country. There were no arrival ceremonies, no state dinners, just business meetings and working luncheons, breakfasts, and teas.

The First Secretary of the Polish United Workers' Party, Edward Gierek and his wife, arrived during the second week of October, bringing with them a large, outgoing group of very friendly people. Unfortunately only one or two of them spoke English, and although they brought interpreters, it was difficult to have the kind of joking conversations they wanted to engage in. I learned once again that a joke in translation is simply not funny.

While her husband was away on official business, Mrs. Gierek investigated American life. She visited the National Institutes of Health, a suburban town house development, a shopping mall, and other sights around the city.

The Giereks left early on the day of the arrival of the President of the Supreme Revolutionary Council of the Somali Democratic Republic, Major General Mohammed Siad Barre, and his party. We barely had time to change the linens on twenty-two beds and clean the same number of baths and bedrooms.

The Somalis had planned to stay only overnight; they were paying their first official call on the President of the United States. But they decided to extend the visit by two days. One of the events scheduled was a visit from Somali students. We had often had such visitors, but Somali Ambassador Addou, who was very concerned about this, his first such visit, decided that Blair House contained too many beautiful things. He was afraid the students might damage some of the furniture. "You know how young people are," he said, and transferred the reception over to the Somali Embassy. Perhaps it was just as well, since many of the visitors did not get back to Blair House until three in the morning after the student reception.

The Somalis had had a difficult time in New York, their first stop in this country. Perhaps they had expected a larger welcome than they received or better, more personal, service at the hotel. Perhaps they were simply overwhelmed by New York. At any rate, they arrived in Washington quite wary and suspicious. But when they left, their chief of protocol, Mr. Wassane, thanked every member of the staff and then thanked me for the courteous and friendly manner with which we had welcomed them. "Frankly, we hadn't expected that," he said. "We will remember the United States as it was at Blair House, where we were treated as friends." I was pleased that we had achieved our goal for every visit: to help our guests see America in a favorable light.

The President of Portugal, Francisco da Costa Gomes, came on very short notice, causing a bit of a scramble to get everything ready in just a matter of days. This was a very informal visit, marked by the usual round of social events. I took a few minutes one day to show Mrs. Costa Gomes some of the Portuguese handwork in the house, notably the rugs and hangings in several of the bedrooms. They had worn very well, even though they had been put into the house ten years before by Robin Duke. It was hard for me to realize that ten years had passed. Because we had had so little time to prepare for this visit, it seemed to fly by and the Portuguese were gone like a whirlwind.

We then had a few weeks' breathing space before we were to welcome President William Tolbert of Liberia. He came for an informal overnight visit.

During the next visit, that of Dr. Bruno Kreisky, Chancellor of Austria, I found Cora, one of our chambermaids, in the dining room, sitting on a chair and obviously not feeling well. I insisted that she go to the doctor immediately, and it was discovered that she was suffering from a severe heart condition. Cora said she'd been too busy with our crowded schedule to get medical help, although she'd been feeling ill for some time. She said she wanted to come back just as soon as the doctor would let her, but I knew that in any case she wouldn't be able to resume her old duties. She had worked so hard and so loyally for Blair House I realized I'd have trouble replacing her.

Helmut Schmidt had been elected Chancellor of West Germany during the year just past, and he was our last visitor for 1974. He was no stranger to Blair House, having often visited us when he was a high-ranking minister in other West German administrations.

Ambassador Catto asked us not to have a formal greeting for President Ford when he came over to the house to meet with Chancellor Schmidt, since that would only cause a big rush at the door from the press. I suggested that at least one butler be there to take coats as it was a very cold day. Ambassador Catto laughed and admitted that, in the urgency of being efficient, he had just forgotten the amenities. When the President came that afternoon he was accompanied by the White House physician, Dr. William Lukash and several other officials, and the butler quietly took their coats.

Chancellor Schmidt had a tight schedule, but he managed to slip out for several brisk walks every day while he stayed with us.

Our first guest in the new year was the young Sultan of Oman,

Qabus bin Sa'id. One of his official functions while with us was to present $100,000 each to Georgetown University, the University of Pennsylvania, and Johns Hopkins, to promote Arabic and Islamic studies. Representatives of the three schools came to a large, posh reception for business people and government officials that the Sultan held at Blair House, and the next day the formal presentations were made at the house.

The Sultan was a guest of honor at a dinner given by Mr. David Rockefeller at Decatur House the day of the reception, and he held meetings with a great many of our political leaders.

The Sultan was a handsome young man, educated in England, who had led a very sheltered life while his conservative father was on the throne. He had been instructed in what was expected of him when he took over the rule of his country, but had not had much in the way of a social life, I was told. When I expressed surprise that such an eligible bachelor was still unmarried, he said with a smile, "I'll see what I can do about that before my next visit."

But I knew that by the time he came back I would be retired. I had decided to leave Blair House by the end of July of that year. Each visit was now providing me with a certain amount of sadness, especially when the guests were old friends whom I had come to know over the years. I knew that I wouldn't be seeing these friends again unless I took them up on their repeated invitations to come visit them in their countries.

But I put these feelings aside and went on with the business of Blair House. Ambassador and Mrs. Catto had shown an immediate interest in the continuing renovation of Blair House. Mrs. Catto had even earmarked several projects for quick action. She thought, for instance, that several chairs and sofas in the Blair-Lee drawing room were beginning to look a bit shabby after eleven years. And she remarked that two bedrooms on the Blair-Lee third floor had never been completed. After several meetings with Camilla Payne, Mrs. Catto selected an off-white damask for the sofas and chairs. We had not received a donation to do this work, but Mrs. Catto hoped to get help from friends in her home state of Texas for some of these projects.

In fact she was successful, because later in the year the third-floor rooms were done. A generous check from the Catto Foundation paid for the reupholstery downstairs. And there were meetings with the Kohler Company about renovating two bathrooms in Blair House that were beginning to need attention again. Under Mrs. Catto's enthusiastic supervision, the Blair House Fine Arts Committee was continuing to flourish.

Late in January we had a pleasant visit from Prime Minister and Mrs. Harold Wilson and a large group of officials. The Prime Minister, relaxed and cheerful and almost never without his pipe, was busy with the usual variety of speeches, interviews, and meetings. Mrs. Wilson was one of the friendliest women I ever met and one of the least pretentious. I could imagine her serving tea at 10 Downing Street, having first gone into the kitchen to make it.

The day before the British group left, Sir Joseph Stone, the Prime Minister's physician, called me aside. He was very apologetic when he told me that some British bank notes seemed to be missing from a jacket that had just come back from the cleaners. He said sheepishly that he must have left the money in his pocket. Usually our butlers check the pockets of anything going out to be cleaned, but this time there was an oversight.

I called our cleaner and he kept me waiting on the phone for just a moment. Then he came back to say that the bank notes were right on the table where his presser had put them. He had thought they were play money. They were sent over at once, and Sir Joseph was very pleased and probably a little surprised at how easily they were returned. In all my years at Blair House, no visitor ever lost any valuables to my knowledge.

One morning Ambassador Catto came over with Mr. Mafato Kodama, deputy superintendent of the Emperor's palace in Japan. They brought with them Mr. Donowaki, embassy counsellor of the Japanese Embassy, to see the house. Mr. Kodama was traveling around the world visiting guest houses and was particularly interested in Blair House because the Emperor would be coming for his first visit to our country that fall. They took a two-hour tour of the house, checking on everything from the top floor to the kitchen, from the beauty parlor to the press room, and asked very probing questions about how we managed the house during a visit.

After a busy two-day visit from Israeli President Ephraim Katzir and his wife, I checked into the hospital for some minor surgery that had been scheduled for some time, so I missed the visit of the President of the Federal Executive Council of Yugoslavia, Džemal Bijedić. I was able to work on the plans for the visit, but I turned it over to Mary on the day of their arrival. By all accounts, the visit went marvelously.

President Kenneth Kaunda of Zambia and his wife and a very large party came before I was able to return to Blair House. This was a weekend visit, something we rarely had, since the staff was never pleased to be working on a weekend. But a visit from Harry Belafonte, who called on President Kaunda at the house, may have added a little something extra to their weekend. Mary reported that everyone came to take a look at him in person.

When I came back, King Hussein arrived for a working visit, which was like old home week for us. As usual, the King made himself right at home in Blair House.

The Jordanians were followed immediately by the Prime Minister of Tunisia, Hédi Nouira, and Mrs. Nouira. Mary was able to put her impeccable French to good use during this visit, since none of our guests spoke English. It was a great help not having to call on an interpreter for every conversation.

On the other hand, Dallas was once again not able to be at work. For the past several months he had been calling in sick at the last minute, or finding it necessary to leave in the middle of a visit. It was getting to be a real problem. At least this time I knew in advance and I was able to get a cook to come in for the duration of the visit. But I had to do the food orders, which meant that I was constantly checking to make sure that we had enough supplies on hand, a job that Dallas had always done. He always knew what we had in the freezer, and what perishables were needed, and he planned the menus with me with all of that in mind. Now I had to fill in for him, and it was hard to manage that in addition to all my other duties. It looked as if the days when Dallas had been my mainstay in the kitchen were drawing to a close. I didn't really know what was wrong, but something was not right.

The pressures of the job seemed to be getting too much for Dallas. When I retired he was still in charge of the kitchen, but two months later he left to serve as the luncheon chef at the Women's Democratic Club, a five-day-a-week job with, I'm certain, none of the sudden emergencies and last-minute arrangements that were a part of his routine at Blair House. Recently Dallas retired after a long career.

When the Shah of Iran and the Empress came for their visit in May, I thought the Shah didn't look at all well. He didn't complain but he seemed to look drawn and thin. Outside on the street Iranian students greeted him with catcalls and boos whenever he entered or left the house. Once in a while a smaller group applauded him. He seemed to take it all in stride, and in fact he was almost oblivious to the hecklers. But I thought he was quieter than usual, even for a man who didn't engage much in small talk and was often withdrawn; he seemed depressed.

He had a tough schedule for this full-scale visit. Every minute was filled. The Empress was also booked from morning until late afternoon. She taped the "Today" show at Blair House while we tiptoed around to make sure that no one rang the doorbell, dropped a tray, or made any noise that would disrupt the interview. She also went to do a live broadcast of "Meet the Press" at NBC's Washington studios and met with Robin Duke at Blair House to discuss their mutual interest in UNICEF, of which Robin was now the chairman.

The Shah's visit came only a day or two after the *Mayagüez* incident, in which one of our ships had been seized by the Cambodians. President Ford had been constantly busy with this, and he was still very involved in matters in Vietnam. I thought he must have been exhausted the night the Shah and the Empress came to the White House for their first state dinner with our new President, but he and Mrs. Ford looked happy and welcoming as always.

The Shah hosted the first meeting of the joint Iran/United States Business Council at Blair House during this visit. He went to Andrews Air Force Base to look at some new American fighter planes, and he met with a great many of our officials on their mutual interests in oil and arms.

When I said my good-byes to these good friends of whom I had become so very fond, none of us had any idea of the fate that awaited them.

We then welcomed President Léopold Sédar Senghor of Senegal and his wife, who had also often stayed with us.

In between visits and functions I was trying to wind up the unfinished business of Blair House in preparation for my leaving in July. Ambassador Catto had tried to convince me to stay on until the end of the year, but I had decided to stick with my plans. Mary Schneck was going to take over when I retired, and I felt very pleased to be leaving the house in such capable hands. Mrs. Will Murray was to be hired as her assistant; I hoped that she would come to work before I left.

We spent many hours trying to anticipate any problems that would arise in the next few months. One thing I tried hard to pass on to Mary was some idea of the lines of communication between the house, the Department of State, GSA, and other agencies. It was a very complex setup, and knowing who was in charge of what, and who to call and when, was a big part of the battle.

I was also getting the last of the Blair portraits copied and the originals sent off to the Portland Museum, as I had promised my very dear friend Dr. Montgomery Blair.

There was as well a certain amount of paper work to finish regarding my retirement and several meetings at the department to get all the formalities settled. Every day I took home some of the personal effects that I had collected over my fifteen years in the house. It was a bit of a wrench to begin to dismantle my life there.

My last official visit was in June, when the President of West Germany, Walter Scheel, and his wife, came for a two-day stay. Several members of the party had been with us previously. One of these was Mr. Weber, the interpreter. His first visit to the United States had been as a prisoner of war, but he didn't seem to hold that against us. Mr. Weber had been in the Foreign Office since 1951 and had come to this country often with other Presidents or high-ranking officials of his country.

Mrs. Scheel, a radiologist who had met her husband when he

was hospitalized with a kidney infection, was particularly interested professionally in the kind of radiation therapy we were using in this country to treat cancer. She visited several Washington area hospitals while she was here. She also visited the National Cancer Institute. On their trip around the country after they left Washington, she visited other cancer research facilities.

Ambassador and Mrs. Berndt von Staden were extremely helpful on this, the first visit of President Scheel to the United States. Wendi von Staden and I had become great friends over the years and had often relaxed over a cup of tea or coffee together. We both realized that this was my final visit, and if I had not been so busy winding up the affairs of Blair House, I would have been even sadder than I was.

Among the things I had to do was a sort of house cleaning, sorting out in the storage areas those things that were still useful and discarding those that were no longer needed. I was amazed to find bits of upholstery material and rolls of wallpaper at least a decade old. They had been stashed away in case repairs were needed on chairs and walls that had long ago been done over in altogether different materials.

The number of loose ends that had to be tied up was endless, but there were also some more pleasant activities. I found myself in a veritable merry-go-round of farewell parties. The most exciting was given by the First Lady. Mrs. Ford asked me to a tea at the White House. She had invited the wives of all the chiefs of protocol under whom I had served at Blair House or at the department. Only Mrs. Wiley Buchanan was missing because she had gone to Austria, where her husband was posted as ambassador.

I had a moment or two to chat with Mrs. Ford before we went in to meet the other guests, and as always Betty Ford was sweet and gracious, and very informal. She was not one to stand on ceremony.

My two daughters and a daughter-in-law were invited, as were several of the people with whom I had worked at Blair House. I was also happy to see Nancy Kissinger.

Mrs. Ford presented me with an autographed picture of herself and the President. Then I was given a gold medallion with a replica of the Presidential Seal. It was attached to a lovely fleur-de-lis pin. Robin Duke handed me an enormous light blue box with the single word "Tiffany" on the cover. Inside I found a spectacular silver bowl inscribed with the names of my chiefs of protocol and their wives.

There were several speeches, which were flattering. At the same time they made me feel very fussed over. Altogether it was quite an afternoon. I had often been to the White House, but to be there as the guest of honor was perhaps the most extraordinary moment in a very exciting career.

The Cattos hosted a lovely party a few days later at their home to bid farewell not only to me but also to Louise Nichols, who was leaving the Protocol Office, where she had served as a ceremonial officer. It was a large reception and gave me a chance to see all the people with whom I had worked at the Protocol Office.

Then the Blair House staff gave a party, and that was very special indeed, since these were the people who make the house run. I could have accomplished nothing without their help, their loyalty, and their real affection for me and for the people they served so well. The General Services people who had been assigned to the house were also invited.

When I thought all the partying was done, I was bowled over by Bill Barton, one of the Secret Service agents I had worked with often during visits, who called to say that the Secret Service would like to present me with the Director's Honor Award. I was invited to a coffee in the entertainment area of the Secret Service headquarters. Some of my family were there, and many of the agents with whom I had worked were also present. The plaque was presented by Director H. Stuart Knight. I was very proud to have been so honored and thrilled to think that this group of men, for whom I have the very highest respect, considered my work to have been of help to them.

On July 19 I put in my last official day at Blair House. It was hard for me to believe that I was really retired. I came back to the house several days to finish clearing out my belongings and to talk to Mary about some unfinished business. And then I left to start my packing at home in preparation for my move to St. Petersburg, Florida, where I had bought a home for my retirement.

The visit of the Japanese Emperor was coming up in the fall. I would be watching it with interest just like the other citizens of this country who had not been privileged to spend fifteen years behind the doors of that remarkable house on Pennsylvania Avenue.

Appendices

Appendix A

COMPLETE LIST OF VISITORS TO BLAIR HOUSE
DURING MRS. WILROY'S TENURE AS HOSTESS

On the next few pages readers will find a complete list of the visitors to Blair House during my tenure there as manager. Many of these visits have been covered in detail in this book, but it would have been impossible to have included every single visit. There are hundreds of anecdotes that I was forced to omit, many delightful guests about whom I have been able to say only very little or nothing at all. These omissions should not be taken to mean that the visit or the visitor was less important than the ones chronicled here. Space was the only consideration, and even now as I read over this list of distinguished visitors I can remember vividly their stays with us at Blair House. I hope that those who are not mentioned in this book will understand.

KENNEDY ADMINISTRATION

ANGIER BIDDLE DUKE, CHIEF OF PROTOCOL

1961

Prime Minister of Greece	Constantine Karamanlis
President of Tunisia	Habib Bourguiba
President of Congo (Brazzaville)	Fulbert Youlou
Prime Minister of Japan	Hayato Ikeda
President of Pakistan	Mohammad Ayub Khan
President of Nigeria	Sir Abubakar Tafawa Balewa
Prime Minister of Nationalist China	Chen Cheng

President of Peru   Don Manuel Prado y Ugarteche
Prime Minister of Sudan   Ibrahim Abboud
President of Liberia   William V. S. Tubman
President of Senegal   Léopold Sédar Senghor
Prime Minister of India   Jawaharlal Nehru
President of Finland   Urho Kaleva Kekkonen

1962

Prime Minister of Congo   Cyrille Adoula
   (Léopoldville)
King of Saudi Arabia   Ibn Abd al-Aziz al-Saud
President of Cameroon   Ahmadou Ahidjo
President of Togo   Sylvanus Olympio
President of Brazil   João Goulart
Shah of Iran   Mohammad Reza Shah Pahlavi
Prime Minister of Great Britain   Harold Macmillan
Prime Minister of Norway   Einar Gerhardsen
President of Ivory Coast   Félix Houphouët-Boigny
President of Cyprus   Archbishop Makarios
President of Panama   Roberto F. Chiari
Prime Minister of Australia   Robert Menzies
President of Ecuador   Carlos Julio Arosemena Monroy
President of Rwanda   Grégoire Kayibanda
President of Guinea   Sékou Touré
Prime Minister of Algeria   Ahmed Ben Bella
Crown Prince of Libya   Hasan al-Rida al-Sanusi
Prime Minister of Uganda   Milton Obote
Maharaja and Maharani of
   Jaipur
Chancellor of West Germany   Konrad Adenauer
Prime Minister of Somalia   Abdirashid Ali Shermarke
President of Honduras   Ramón Villeda Morales
President of Chile   Jorge Alessandri Rodríguez

1963

Prime Minister of Italy   Amintore Fanfani
President of Venezuela   Rómulo Betancourt
King of Laos   Sri Savang Vatthana
King of Morocco   Hassan II
Grand Duchess of Luxembourg   H.R.H. Charlotte
President of India   Dr. Sarvepalli Radhakrishnan

President of Tanganyika	Julius K. Nyerere
King of Afghanistan	Mohammed Zahir Shah
Emperor of Ethiopia	Haile Selassie
Prime Minister of Ireland	Sean F. Lemass
President of Bolivia	Victor Paz Estenssoro
President Harry S. Truman	(Funeral of President Kennedy)

JOHNSON ADMINISTRATION

1964

President of Italy	Antonio Segni
Prime Minister of Canada	Lester Pearson
King of Jordan	Hussein I
President Harry S. Truman (visited twice in two months)	
King of Burundi	Mwambutsa IV
President of Ireland	Eamon de Valera
Prime Minister of Israel	Levi Eshkol
Prime Minister of Turkey	İsmet İnönü
Prime Minister of Greece	George Papandreou
President of Costa Rica	Francisco José Orlich Bolmarcich
Prime Minister of Malaysia	Tunku Abdul Rahman
President of Malagasy Republic	Philibert Tsiranana
Secretary General of UN	U Thant
President of Philippines	Diosdado Macapagal
President of Zambia	Dr. Kenneth David Kaunda
Prime Minister of Malawi	Dr. H. Kamuzu Banda

LLOYD N. HAND, CHIEF OF PROTOCOL

1965

Prime Minister of Japan	Eisaku Sato
Inaugural guests of President and Mrs. Lyndon Johnson	
President of Upper Volta	Maurice Yameogo
Prime Minister of Italy	Aldo Moro
President of South Korea	Park Chung Hee
President of Pakistan	Mohammad Ayub Khan
Chancellor of West Germany	Ludwig Erhard

JAMES SYMINGTON, CHIEF OF PROTOCOL

1966

Prime Minister of India	Indira Gandhi
President of Nicaragua	René Schick Gutiérrez
King of Saudi Arabia	Faisal Ibn Abd al-Aziz al-Saud
Prime Minister of Australia	Harold E. Holt (two visits)
Prime Minister of Guyana	Forbes Burnham
Prime Minister of Great Britain	Harold Wilson
President of Israel	Zalman Shazar
Luci Johnson's wedding party	
Premier of Burma	Ne Win
President of Philippines	Ferdinand E. Marcos
Chancellor of West Germany	Ludwig Erhard
President of Senegal	Léopold Sédar Senghor
Prime Minister of Laos	Prince Souvanna Phouma

1967

President-elect of Brazil	Artur da Costa e Silva
King of Morocco	Hassan II
Emperor of Ethiopia	Haile Selassie
Prime Minister of Korea	Chung Il Kwon
Prime Minister of Afghanistan	Mohammed Hashim Maiwandwal
President of Turkey	Cevdet Sunay
Prime Minister of Nationalist China	Yen Chia-kan
Prime Minister of Australia	Harold E. Holt
President of Malawi	Dr. H. Kamuzu Banda
King of Thailand	Bhumibol Adulyadej
President of Iceland	Ásgeir Ásgeirsson
Chancellor of West Germany	Kurt Georg Kiesinger
President of Ivory Coast	Félix Houphouët-Boigny
Shah of Iran	Mohammad Reza Shah Pahlavi
President of Italy	Guiseppe Saragat
Prime Minister of Lesotho	Chief Leabua Jonathan
President of Niger	Hamani Diori
Prime Minister of Malta	Giorgio Borg Olivier
Chairman of National Liberation Council of Ghana	Joseph A. Ankrah
Prime Minister of Jamaica	Hugh Lawson Shearer

Prime Minister of Singapore Lee Kuan Yew
Prime Minister of Laos Prince Souvanna Phouma
President of Cameroon El Hadj Ahmadou Ahidjo
President of Mexico Gustavo Díaz Ordaz
King of Nepal Mahendra Bir Bikram Shah Deva
Crown Prince of Laos Van Savang
Prime Minister of Japan Eisaku Sato
Mr. and Mrs. Charles Robb

1968

President of Commission of the Jean Rey
 European Communities
Prime Minister of Somalia Mohamed Ibrahim Egal
President of Paraguay General Alfredo Stroessner
President of Liberia William V. S. Tubman

ANGIER BIDDLE DUKE, CHIEF OF PROTOCOL

Chancellor of Austria Dr. Josef Klaus
King of Norway Olav V
Prime Minister of Thailand Thanom Kittikachorn
President of Tunisia Habib Bourguiba
Prime Minister of Australia John Grey Gorton
President of Costa Rica José Joaquín Trejos Fernández
Shah of Iran Mohammad Reza Shah Pahlavi
Prime Minister of Barbados Errol W. Barrow

TYLER ABELL, CHIEF OF PROTOCOL

President of Chad François Tombalbaye
Prime Minister of New Zealand Keith J. Holyoake
Prime Minister of Iran Amir Abbas Hoveyda
Emir of Kuwait Sheikh Sabah al-Salim al-Sabah

NIXON ADMINISTRATION

EMIL MOSBACHER, JR., CHIEF OF PROTOCOL

1969

Prime Minister of Canada Pierre Elliott Trudeau
King of Jordan Hussein I
Prime Minister of Australia John Grey Gorton

King of Belgium	Baudouin I
Prime Minister of Netherlands	Petrus J. S. de Jong
President of Colombia	Carlos Lleras Restrepo
Emperor of Ethiopia	Haile Selassie
Chancellor of West Germany	Kurt Georg Kiesinger
Prime Minister of New Zealand	Keith J. Holyoake
Prime Minister of Israel	Golda Meir
Prime Minister of Laos	Prince Souvanna Phouma
Deputy Premier of Saudi Arabia	Prince Fahd Ibn Abd al-Aziz
Shah of Iran	Mohammad Reza Shah Pahlavi
Prime Minister of Japan	Eisaku Sato

1970

President of France	Georges Pompidou
Duke and Duchess of Windsor	
Chancellor of West Germany	Willy Brandt
Prime Minister of Denmark	Hilmar Baunsgaard
Deputy Prime Minister of Nationalist China	Chiang Chin-kuo
President of Indonesia	Gen. Suharto
President of Venezuela	Dr. Rafael Caldera
Secretary General of UN	U Thant
President of Finland	Urho Kaleva Kekkonen
President of Congo	Lt. Gen. Joseph-Désiré Mobutu
President of Romania	Nicolae Ceauşescu
King of Jordan	Hussein I
Prime Minister of Great Britain	Edward Heath

1971

Prince of Spain	Juan Carlos de Borbón y Borbón
Prime Minister of Italy	Emilio Colombo
Prime Minister of Ireland	John M. Lynch
President of Commission of the European Communities	Franco M. Malfatti
President of Nicaragua	Gen. Anastasio Somoza Debayle
Chancellor of West Germany	Willy Brandt
President of Senegal	Léopold Sédar Senghor
Deputy Prime Minister of Cambodia	Lt. Gen. Sisowath Sirik Matak
Prince of Japan	Hitachi
President of Mauritania	Moktar Ould Daddah
President of Yugoslavia	Josip Broz Tito

Prime Minister of Australia	William McMahon
Prime Minister of India	Indira Gandhi
President and Mrs. Lyndon B. Johnson	
President of Brazil	Emílio Garrastazú Médici

1972

Secretary General of UN	Kurt Waldheim
Prime Minister of Turkey	Nihat Erim
President of Mexico	Luis Echeverría Álvarez

MARION SMOAK, ACTING CHIEF OF PROTOCOL

1973

Inauguration ceremonies

Mrs. Lyndon Johnson and family	(Funeral of President Johnson)
King of Jordan	Hussein I
President of South Vietnam	Nguyen Van Thieu
Prime Minister of Italy	Giulio Andreotti
Prime Minister of Israel	Golda Meir (private visit)
Chancellor of West Germany	Willy Brandt
Emperor of Ethiopia	Haile Selassie
President of Liberia	William R. Tolbert
General Secretary of USSR	Leonid Ilyich Brezhnev
Shah of Iran	Mohammad Reza Shah Pahlavi
Prime Minister of Japan	Kakuei Tanaka
Prime Minister of Pakistan	Zulfikar Ali Bhutto
Chancellor of West Germany	Willy Brandt
President of European Economic Community	François-Xavier Ortoli
President of Ivory Coast	Félix Houphouët-Boigny
President of Upper Volta	Lt. Col. Sangoulé Lamizana
President of Romania	Nicolae Ceauşescu
Prime Minister of Israel	Golda Meir (private visit)

1974

King of Jordan	Hussein I
President of Algeria	Houari Boumedienne
Deputy Premier of Saudi Arabia	Prince Fahd Ibn Abd al-Aziz

FORD ADMINISTRATION

HENRY CATTO, CHIEF OF PROTOCOL

King of Jordan	Hussein I
Prime Minister of Israel	Yitzhak Rabin
President of Italy	Giovanni Leone
Prime Minister of Bangladesh	Sheikh Mujibur Rahman
First Secretary of Central Committee of Polish United Workers' Party	Edward Gierek
President of Somalia	Maj. Gen. Mohammed Siad Barre
President of Portugal	Francisco da Costa Gomes
President of Liberia	William R. Tolbert
Chancellor of Austria	Dr. Bruno Kreisky
Chancellor of West Germany	Helmut Schmidt

1975

Sultan of Oman	Qabus bin Sa'id
Prime Minister of Great Britain	Harold Wilson
Prime Minister of Pakistan	Zulfikar Ali Bhutto
President of Israel	Ephraim Katzir
President of Federal Executive Council of Yugoslavia	Džemal Bijedić
President of Zambia	Dr. Kenneth David Kaunda
King of Jordan	Hussein I
Prime Minister of Tunisia	Hédi Nouira
Shah of Iran	Mohammad Reza Shah Pahlavi
President of Senegal	Léopold Sédar Senghor
President of West Germany	Walter Scheel

Appendix B

A TYPICAL STATE DEPARTMENT FACT SHEET
SENT TO BLAIR HOUSE BEFORE EACH VISIT

THE CHIEF OF PROTOCOL
DEPARTMENT OF STATE
WASHINGTON

MISCELLANEOUS INFORMATION FOR USE DURING THE STATE VISIT TO THE
UNITED STATES OF HIS IMPERIAL MAJESTY MOHAMMAD REZA SHAH PAHLAVI,
SHAHANSHAH OF IRAN, AND THE EMPRESS FARAH.

This information is prepared for the use of host organizations.

<u>Name and Title</u>:	His Imperial Majesty Mohammad Reza Shah Pahlavi Shahanshah of Iran
	The Empress Farah
<u>Form of Address in Conversation</u>:	Your Imperial Majesty or Your Majesty (Singular) Your Imperial Majesties or Your Majesties (Plural)
<u>Correspondence Salutation</u>:	Your Imperial Majesty: (Singular) Your Imperial Majesties: (Plural)
<u>Correspondence Complimentary Close</u>:	Very respectfully,
<u>Envelope Address</u>:	His Majesty: His Imperial Majesty the Shahanshah of Iran, Local address.

Her Majesty:
The Empress Farah, Local address.

Both:
Their Imperial Majesties the Shahanshah of
Iran and the Empress Farah, Local address.

"In honor of" line   In honor of Their Imperial Majesties the
on invitations: Shahanshah of Iran and the Empress Farah

Place Cards: His Majesty: His Imperial Majesty the
Shahanshah of Iran

Her Majesty: Her Imperial Majesty the
Empress Farah

-2-

Name of Country: Iran (also known as Persia)
A native of Iran is known as an "Iranian."
Adjective form is "Iranian."

Language: His Imperial Majesty speaks English, French,
and Persian (Farsi). The Empress speaks
French, Persian (Farsi), and some English.

Pronunciation: Mohammad: Moe   háh   mad
Reza: Ray   sáh
Pahlavi: Páh   lah   vee

Farah: Fár   rah

Religion: Their Majesties and all members of their party
are of the Moslem faith.

Beverages: Alcoholic beverages may be served whenever
desired by the host organization. It is
suggested that fruit juice and soft drinks
be served in addition to the customary
alcoholic beverages.

Smoking: His Imperial Majesty smokes.

Shaking Hands: On introduction, His Imperial Majesty and the
Empress will shake hands.

Toasts: The first toast should be made by the host to
"His Imperial Majesty the Shahanshah of Iran";
or, if the Empress is also present, to "Their
Imperial Majesties the Shahanshah of Iran and
the Empress Farah."

Response will be made in a toast to "The President of the United States." (Subsequent toasts, if any may be made to other persons in declining order of precedence.)

National Anthem: Except at outdoor functions where there may be honors, troops and military bands, it is NOT recommended that the national anthem of the United States and the anthem of Iran be played unless the sponsoring organization

-3-

is confident that the orchestra is able to play the anthems very well. It is not necessary to play the anthems at strictly social functions or at formal luncheons and dinners, as frequently awkward situations and inconveniences are created. It is not the custom in Washington to play national anthems at State dinners. When the anthems are played, it is customary to play the anthem of the visitor's country first and the anthem of the United States second.

Flags: When the flags of the United States and Iran are used, consider the area where the flags are to be placed as a stage or focal point, then place the flag of the United States on the left as viewed from the audience, and the flag of Iran on the right.

The Iranian flag consists of three equal stripes of green, white and red.

Protocol
March 31, 1962

Index